THEY FINISHED THEIR COURSE
IN THE 90s

THEY FINISHED THEIR COURSE IN THE 90S

Compiled by
Robert Plant

JOHN RITCHIE LTD
CHRISTIAN PUBLICATIONS

40 Beansburn, Kilmarnock, Scotland

ISBN 0 946351 97 X

Copyright © 2000 by John Ritchie Ltd.
40 Beansburn, Kilmarnock, Scotland

Typeset by John Ritchie Ltd., Kilmarnock
Printed by Bell & Bain Ltd., Glasgow

Contents

Publishers' Preface

At the beginning of a new century and a new millenium we look back into the closing decade of the last. We believe that it is appropriate to recall some of the servants of God whose lives ended in those years, and put on record something of the manner in which their lives touched many others, and how these contacts brought much blessing to individuals, homes, and assemblies throughout the UK and beyond. It never could be our role to assess or scrutinise these lives - there is only One who is uniquely qualified to do this - but we can and should appreciate the service given by so many in their own day and generation. "The day will declare it" in its fullness. But we are here attempting to record what we can, trusting that we all as present day servants of God may be encouraged to continue His work in our generation likewise, and to "finish our course with joy" (Acts 20.24).

It is indeed our desire that this volume, recording something of the lives of thirty three servants of the Lord who finished their course in the nineties, will inspire and encourage its readers to "press on" also for the prize which beckons all who seek it (Phil 3.14). This was the objective of the two companion volumes which have preceded this, and we pray that God will bless this one in a similar way.

We also express our sincere thanks to the many who have contributed much time and effort to make the production of this volume possible. This includes those who provided information and recollections, those who sifted and sorted, who wrote and typed, who arranged and proof-read. We are especially indebted to Mr Robert Plant who undertook the onerous task of collating and putting in order this present volume, and to Dr Bert Cargill for his considerable input in editing.

John Ritchie Ltd
November 2000

vii

"Whose faith follow"

These words are most applicable to this volume of "They finished their course", indeed they appear on several occasions throughout these records of some of the dear servants of God who were called to higher service during the 1990s. Looking back through the two previous volumes compiled by Jim Anderson, one could conclude that in the last thirty years of the last century the Lord has taken to Himself some of the most able and most respected Bible teachers and evangelists associated with the assemblies of the Lord's people. We cannot help but acknowledge that the assemblies are much the poorer for their passing. *"Whose faith follow."*

In compiling this volume, I have tried to keep younger believers very much in mind. It is my prayer that, as they read this account of the lives and deeds of some of these servants of God, they too might be greatly inspired to take up the torch of assembly testimony and run the race set before them for the glory of the Lord. As a young man, shortly after my salvation, I read the first of these books dealing with servants of the Lord who had all been called home before I was saved. I remember reading over one weekend the accounts of their lives and service for the Lord. That book spurred me on greatly. I still have notes that I wrote in my Bible over that weekend while reading of those who had finished their course in the 70s. *"Whose faith follow."*

Now I have had the pleasure and privilege of compiling the volume for the 90s, which consists of records of those who mostly were known to me. Often I still call to remembrance some of these men who ministered the Word of God to me as a young man and gave me greater desires for service of the Lord. Many were and are household names amongst the Lord's people. Some left the homelands to serve the Lord on the mission field abroad. Others had a more limited service in their own locality. All served faithfully! *"Whose faith follow."*

With any publication of this nature there will always be one and another who have been omitted. Of these, some of their families were reticent about their loved ones being included, being happy to know that their record is "on high". The book is nevertheless the poorer for their omission. Others, perhaps worthy of a place, had to be left out due to limitations of space, and perhaps others were unintentionally overlooked in the preparation stages. We do trust, however, that the lives of those who have been included will be an encouragement to all who read the accounts to live their lives to the full for God. *"Whose faith follow."*

It must never be forgotten either that behind the majority of these men was a wife or family who frequently made sacrifices so that husbands and fathers could go about the Lord's work. These dear sisters and families too should be openly acknowledged, and thus time and again throughout the pages of this book we read of their devotion and sacrifice for the work of the Lord. *"Whose faith follow."*

The reader will notice some differences in this publication from those so well and faithfully compiled by Jim Anderson. The main one is the sections entitled "Other Recollections". This gave others who knew the brethren the opportunity to give some memories of them, and we trust thereby a more full picture has emerged. Many such accounts were submitted, but space and repetition prevented the inclusion of them all.

Lastly, this publication could not have been possible without the willing and diligent work of many contributors researching and compiling the various accounts. My grateful thanks must go to them all, and also to Sarah Ramsey from Helions Bumpstead who did an excellent job of typing many hand-written submissions, sometimes having to decipher rather interesting handwriting!

Read, remember and reflect upon those who gave so much in the service of Christ and His people. *"Whose faith follow."*

Robert Plant
September 2000

"Whose faith follow"

James L. Aitken

1925 - 1992

"For out of the abundance of the heart the mouth speaketh."
(Matthew 12.34)

James Aitken was born on 13th April 1925 in the mining village of Haywood. It is now a derelict waste in the Upperwood of Lanarkshire. Of the house where we lived there is now a stunted tree, growing where there once was a collier's fire. Jim, as he became known, was third in a family of four; two sons and two daughters. Jean was the oldest, then myself, followed by Jim and the youngest, Jenny. There was five years between each of us.

Our parents, Matthew and Jenny Law, were not Haywood folk. Mother had come from Coalburn where she had spent her life until marriage. Father was from Lesmahagow, but had moved widely all over Scotland with his family. They were both of mining stock.

Jim was a 'braw wee laddie' with curly auburn hair of which he was proud. He soon showed something of his mother's disposition. She was a quiet, unassuming, warm person, the one who listened to and helped others in the community. He inherited his love of the study of God's word and prayer from his father. From his teenage years Jim spent considerable time reading the Bible, learning from the Saviour, and communing with Him in prayer.

The family home was used by many preachers and this influenced us as children. A Mr. McPate was holding meetings in Wilsontown in January 1934 and it was then that the nine-year-old Jim made his personal decision to trust and follow the Lord Jesus Christ. That choice was to become the focus of his life and witness. A few years later he followed up this initial step of faith and was baptised.

He never excelled at school except, perhaps, on the football pitch. On leaving school at the age of fourteen he was more fortunate than most. He did not go straight to work down the pit but was given a job with Lipton, the grocer in the village of Forth. Shortly afterwards he was moved to their branch in Falkirk where he was promoted to assistant manager, but left just as rationing was introduced because he did not agree with the unfair distribution of food by the manager. He found a post as a cleaner at Carstairs railway junction and was then promoted to the footplate as fireman. Often he travelled on the milk train from Carstairs to Peebles and he said on one occasion it was a joy to have work that carried him through one of the loveliest parts of the land. However, his employment there was short lived as it involved working on Sundays, and so he found himself working in the pits. It was during this time that he gave service to the assembly at Forth, teaching in the Sunday School and taking other responsibilities. He had a good singing voice and even took singing lessons. On occasions he would sing at special meetings and socials. The following is the first verse and chorus of one of his favourites:

> By and by when I look on His face,
> Beautiful face, thorn-shadowed face,
> By and by when I look on His face,
> I'll wish I had given Him more.
> More so much more,
> More of my life than I e'er gave before.
> By and by when I look on His face,
> I'll wish I had given Him more.

Another favourite, which was sung at his funeral, was 'My Redeemer'. He also wrote a little including poetry and hymns.

While living in Forth he was especially close to his sister Jenny and her husband Jimmy Stephen from Lanark, and remained so throughout life, perhaps because they were the younger two of the family. As a brother to his siblings he was a good listener, a great confidant, and a wise counsellor. As a sensitive, caring individual he had the ability to empathise with people.

In 1947 he married the girl next door, Cathie Stewart. As they had no family of their own, his siblings' families were very dear to him and he took a genuine and prayerful interest in them.

The saints at Forth assembly were happy to commend him to full-time service in 1964. The range of his ministry was diverse. He was an able conference speaker. He was engaged in gospel campaigns and consecutive Bible teaching which took him all over Scotland and N. Ireland. He conducted marriage services. Young people benefited from his teaching at Bible class weekends. He was involved in the Edinburgh Bible School, a team of which visited the town of Penicuik from Edinburgh under his leadership. Doors were knocked, contacts made, and tracts distributed. But he was essentially a one to one man, and had a God-given ability to engage a person in conversation and direct the talk to his Lord and Saviour. He bore an attitude of courtesy and kindness in his approach to people, whether in a crowded hall, open air or on a one to one basis. During his lifetime he sent out thousands of letters to contacts he had made over the years.

Jim was a man of his time, one of a number of personal workers. He proved his worth and Forth's commendation by serving the Lord locally with the Lanarkshire tent, before concentrating on the field of service in S. W. Scotland. 'Bonnie Galloway' became his parish. The years that followed were to prove that this choice was the Lord's doing.

In this corner of the country he spent hours, days, and years travelling, knocking doors, and speaking to individuals as well as small companies. Before setting off each day he equipped himself with God's Word and spent time in prayer seeking His leading and blessing. Many local people supported him, names that spring to mind are Willie Scott of Machermore; Jim and Martha McDonald from Dumfries; Willie and Nellie McCullock of Sandhead; Tommy and Ann Lochhead of Kirkcudbright; Mr and Mrs Robert McCall of Leadhills, and many more. They all opened their homes to welcome this humble evangelist.

In 1985, after a period of illness, Cathie passed away. Jim curtailed his public ministry to nurse and care for her during that time, but never stinted on his time alone with his Master, often rising early or retiring late.

1986 saw him remarried to a lady by the name of Eva Killner, and together they were to prove God's hand of blessing on their lives. He moved to Glasgow and met with the Lord's people in Anniesland. He settled there very quickly and soon became an asset to the assembly, teaching and ministering. Shortly after this marriage Jim was diagnosed with cancer. This greatly restricted his travel and ministry, but together he and Eva continued to write letters of encouragement and help to others. When he was no longer able to get out he and Eva shared with each other their love for the Saviour and the Scriptures. She unstintingly and lovingly nursed him through his last eighteen months before he was called home on 18th March 1992 to be forever with the Lord.

As a person Jim had few interests apart from those directly involved with evangelism, although he did have a love of trains born, perhaps, from his short time of employment at Carstairs. In many ways he was a solitary figure and could be found enjoying a picnic beside a stream or on a hillside drinking in the beauty of creation and his Creator.

In this life he sought neither recognition nor riches – these were transient things. He sought only to do what the Lord willed – 'go and preach the gospel'. The seed was sown and in that great day the harvest will be gathered in.

For Jim Aitken, his life work is ended. He lived for the Book, and his life echoed the lessons he learned there.

> *When in heaven I see Thy glory*
> *When before Thy throne I bow*
> *Perfected I shall be like Thee*
> *Fully Thy redemption know*
> *My Redeemer*
> *Then shall hear me shout His praise.*

Robert Aitken, Edinburgh

Other Recollections

On 3rd June 1956, I was invited to the home of Alex and Jean Campbell, a lovely couple who had a great concern for souls. After lunch, they invited me to Strathclyde Park where an open-air service was conducted by the assembly of Roman

Road Gospel Hall, Motherwell, where Alex and Jean attended. The invited speaker for that day was James Aitken. After the service, in the Park Ranger's shed, James Aitken pointed me to the Lord and I was gloriously saved.

A few years afterwards James revealed to me that, before he had come to the park that day, he had asked the Lord to give him two souls and (like Gideon putting out the fleece) it would be an indication to him that the Lord wanted him to go out in full-time service. About six months after, a young lady came before the elders asking for baptism and fellowship. The elders asked for her testimony and she said, "I was saved on 3rd June 1956, the day that Billy McKellar was saved. That day I went home and gave my life to Christ." That young lady was Sheena Campbell; the daughter of Alex and Jean. The Lord had given James Aitken the two souls he had prayed for.

Billy McKellar, Motherwell

When travelling from Glasgow to Aberdeen by train some years ago, a young man, who obviously had been drinking, sat beside me. Soon after the train left Glasgow, he dosed off, and ended up leaning against my shoulder. Finding this uncomfortable, I felt like pushing him off, but thought it might spoil the opportunity of giving him a tract.

When we arrived in Aberdeen, early in the morning, he was very annoyed to discover he had slept passed his destination. He asked if I could give him the price of his fare back to Dundee. I gave him the money, and a gospel tract, and asked him to promise he would read it. He said he would, and would also send me the money I gave him. To my surprise he sent me the money a few weeks later, but with no address.

That same day I attended Lossiemouth conference, where James Aitken was one of the speakers. You can imagine my astonishment when, during his address, he said, "What do you do, when travelling on public transport, a drunk man leans against you? Do you push him away or do you speak to him about the Saviour?"

Bobby Cameron, Coatbridge

James Aitken started full-time work for the Lord in the Newton Stewart/Stranraer area. His route to the south of Scotland brought him through our village, Leadhills, and he frequently dropped in unannounced to the assembly, where his help to our very small company was much appreciated.

Also at that time we were in charge of the South of Scotland Youth Camp, and had one camp in the Kirkcudbright area. James used to join us in the evenings to give Bible teaching to the young folks, and did this for the next few years. At least four young people professed faith in Christ under his preaching, and time has proved these professions were real.

The first two of our young campers to get married asked James to officiate at their wedding.

Robert McCall, Biggar

His zeal in the gospel was displayed at an early age. I remember an occasion when he spoke to me regarding the salvation of my soul. I would have been about nine years of age at the time, and he would have been ten.

I think he invented what I would call 'car evangelism.' He would pick up hitch-hikers and to a captive audience he would present the gospel until they got out of the car. One such raised the question of the resurrection of Christ. Jim said, "I could argue about it logically, but the greatest proof to me is *that He lives within my heart*," and the passenger said, "If I was going to believe it, that is the kind of evidence I would accept."

His humility was proverbial. He never counted heads, but he did say on one occasion that if all his converts were gathered together, they would fill an average Gospel Hall.

In the summer he was often responsible on a Saturday to minister the Word at Lanarkshire Gospel Work gatherings. The ministry he gave would be what he had gleaned that morning in his daily reading.

James Aitken, Newmains

Here was a Christian gentleman who fulfilled the scripture which says, "pure religion and undefiled before God and the Father is this, to visit the fatherless and widows in their affliction and to keep himself unspotted from the world" (James 1.27).

My father was killed in a railway accident when I was nine years old. My mother was left with a family of three. My oldest sister was 16 years of age and had just started work, a younger sister was seven years old. Four months later my youngest sister was born. These were difficult days for the family.

James Aitken and his wife Cathie practised the above Scripture, as far as our family was concerned. For many years almost every Friday night they visited our home. This involved getting a bus from Forth where they lived, to a point where they had to walk two miles to our home in Carstairs village. We had many happy times with them. James had a good sense of humour, and brought comfort and cheer to our family, while they enjoyed my mother's homebaking. Their two hour visit passed very quickly; then they had to walk the two miles back to catch the bus to Forth.

Hugh Reid, Motherwell

They finished their course in the 90s

James Anderson

1925 - 1992

"and I will very gladly spend and be spent for you"
(2 Corinthians 12.5)

Jim Anderson was a small man physically but of great stature in the kingdom of God. Affectionately known as "wee Jim", he was a bundle of energy. Even his speech, both in conversation and preaching, had a certain breathlessness about it. Jim was nothing if not an enthusiast. He willingly devoted himself, his time, talents and almost boundless energy to the service of the Lord and His people in many and varied ways. He served in his home assembly, the surrounding area and much further afield. Jim was a Bible teacher, writer, door to door evangelist, Sunday School superintendent – a real all-rounder. Not long before his home call, he quoted the above text in the company of friends and expressed that it contained his own aspirations. To a very large degree, by God's grace, they were fulfilled.

Jim was born in the Ayrshire mining village of Annbank. He spent his whole life there. Indeed to many Christians in assemblies in Scotland and beyond, he and Annbank were almost synonymous. Jim was reared in a godly home. His parents were in fellowship in the assembly in their community. He came to personal trust in Christ when he was twelve in an evangelistic campaign conducted by John MacAlpine. Later he joined the assembly at Annbank Gospel Hall.

After his Secondary education at Ayr Academy, he proceeded to Glasgow University to do an arts degree. However, he was able to complete only one academic year there before wartime call-up intervened. Jim became a Bevin Boy (a conscripted mine-worker) for the rest of the war. He used his spare time to tremendous effect, continuing his studies in history by reading for an external London University degree. He was able to

9

complete this course by self study and correspondence in almost the same time that he would have taken to finish the Glasgow full-time course. What a tribute to our brother's self-discipline and diligence. Those who knew him best all comment that throughout his life Jim never wasted time but sought to redeem it.

Jim then qualified as a secondary teacher and taught in several schools in his native county including his own old school, Ayr Academy. Later he transferred to the field of Further Education and worked at Ayr College until he retired from professional life in 1985. Jim once wrote, "It cannot be over stressed that one can serve the Lord well without committing himself to full-time service." He was an outstanding example of this himself, combining his teaching career with a wide variety of spiritual activities. Jim felt that having a working life enhanced his service for the Lord as it kept his feet on the ground and himself in touch with the realities of life. Jim's deep interest in young people was a common strand between his school and college work and his assembly service. Also his keen sense of history was very much carried over into many aspects of his ministry. Jim had a deep appreciation of his spiritual forebears and what he owed to them. In particular, he was deeply conscious of the heritage of the assemblies and of similar movements that sought to bring the church back to New Testament simplicity in corporate testimony and personal discipleship.

From his early Christian life, Jim had a deep interest in the things of God. He was nurtured in the Annbank assembly and even as a teenager he engaged in open-air meetings and other out-reach in surrounding villages. In many of these ventures his partner was George Waugh who married Jim's sister Mary and is himself a respected Bible teacher. The Ayr Bible readings took place for the first time during the Second World War and Jim has recorded the tremendous impression made on him by Harold St. John and his ministry especially in Mr St. John's visit to these meetings in 1945. That influence deepened in subsequent visits and Mr St. John became one of Jim's spiritual heroes. In 1989, he was able to collect and edit Harold St. John's writings for re-publication. W.F. Naismith was another teacher whom Jim quoted often in his own ministry, describing him as someone who had given him part of his theological education. Years later, Jim also fondly recalled impressions left by the preaching and teaching of Tom Richardson in a gospel campaign in Annbank in 1946.

Another formative influence in Jim's early days was Willie Scott of Machermore. With other young men, our brother spent summers with Mr Scott in his evangelism in Galloway. Some of the Machermore boys went on to the mission field or to full-time work at home. Jim never did, however he developed a passionate interest in evangelism and world mission which marked him for life. He also spent a summer with the Cumberland and Westmoreland Gospel van and another one, after his marriage, with Charlie McEwen of Exeter in Devon village work.

Our brother soon developed into a capable Bible teacher with a wide ministry. He even ministered at a conference at Camelon, near Falkirk, on his honeymoon in 1950! For some years he travelled in a grey bubble car, serving many assemblies throughout Scotland. Later his ministry also took him to England, Wales, Northern Ireland and to Canada. Jim spoke at many conferences over the years, spending most of his Saturdays in this service. He was also one of the speakers on several occasions at the Bible Reading weeks at Ayr, Aberdeen and Kilravock. Jim had a comprehensive grasp of the broad sweep of Scripture. What he delighted to do was to bring out the up to date, practical relevance of a passage and to exhort his hearers to greater commitment. Jim ranged over many parts of God's Word in his preaching and teaching. The Acts and the pastoral epistles were favourite books which gave him ample scope for the leading themes of his ministry which were mission and evangelism and the living out of New Testament Church life in the 20th century.

Not surprisingly, these were also the themes emphasised in our brother's written ministry. Jim wrote the volume on Acts in the "What the Bible teaches" series published by John Ritchie. Although on a much smaller scale, Jim's best and perhaps most characteristic publication was his pamphlet "Our Heritage" produced in the early 1970s from a series of articles written earlier. Jim's aim was to give younger Christians in assemblies an appreciation of their history and to re-emphasise positively assembly distinctives in days when they were being discarded or ignored in some quarters. He wrote with great zeal seeking to re-kindle the devotion of earlier generations in his readers. He emphasised the value of the truths recovered by the early brethren and practised in the assemblies over the years. Jim's tone was always constructive as he wanted to see these truths continue but held along with a spirit of aggressive evangelism and spiritual commitment in every-day life. Indeed, as Jim rightly argued, assembly principles and practices can only flourish in such an atmosphere. Jim greatly desired to see the preservation of all that was best in the heritage of the assemblies, but in a way that was Biblical, balanced and relevant and not merely traditional. These issues greatly occupied his editorials during his service as one of the editors of the Believer's Magazine. Towards the end of his ministry Jim was sorrowful at the growing polarisation of assemblies. He always sought to preserve and promote unity among the Lord's people as he served in a very wide circle of assemblies.

Jim's deep interest in the history of the assemblies and his wide knowledge of so many of the Lord's servants bore fruit in his biographical sketches: "They finished their course" and "They finished their course in the 80s". These are valuable records of a wide range of brethren who together made a significant contribution to the life and witness of the British assemblies in the 20th century.

What our brother preached he practised. His commitment to New Testament Church principles was seen in his local assembly life and his exhortations to evangelism were reflected in his own involvement in gospel work. Jim served tirelessly in every activity of the Annbank assembly. Above all, he was a great encourager especially of young men and women, any sign of spiritual interest was cherished and fanned into flame. This was true locally and in a wider sphere in particular his involvement in ministry to teenagers at camps in different parts of the UK. He was a 20th century Barnabas who had a tremendous interest in people and a real desire to see them go on for the Lord. Jim was devoted to door to door work in his own village, being welcomed in nearly every home. He was deeply respected by his fellow villagers, often conducting funeral services for people with little or no connection to the assembly. Few brethren have had had so great a testimony and influence not only in their own assembly but also in their own community as Jim, yet this was combined with a wide-spread itinerant ministry and full-time secular work.

Jim's evangelistic endeavours extended beyond his home village. As well as engaging in regular gospel preaching, he was actively involved in the Ayrshire Gospel Tent, now the Ayrshire Gospel Outreach. He arranged many of the campaigns and even helped with the erection of the tent. He constantly sought to muster support for the meetings, not only in the assembly but also among the villagers. Jim also edited the monthly Gospel leaflet, "The Messenger". Finding it difficult to get regular contributors, he, like many editors, had to write many of the articles himself.

The foreign field was not forgotten. Our brother possessed a detailed knowledge of missionary work throughout the world. He had also a deep personal concern and interest for the well-being of many of the missionaries. Many of the Lord's servants abroad were close personal friends. Jim's missionary interest expressed itself in the arranging of report meetings, his involvement as a trustee of the Lord's Work Trust and the building of the Annbank Missionary Home (for which Jim and Helen donated the ground).

Jim was blessed with a happy home life. In 1950 he married Helen Brown from Lanarkshire who was always fully supportive of his varied service. Indeed his activities could not have been sustained without her steadfast help to say nothing of their gracious and generous hospitality. Their two children, Andrea, a housewife and teacher in Teesside, and Gordon, an Ayrshire solicitor, continue their father's commitment to the work of the Lord.

Our brother Jim was very human and approachable. He had a warm sense of humour and no trace of pomposity or sanctimoniousness. Jim was very down to earth and concerned about living out New Testament faith in the 20th century. He was very sincere with a great capacity for friendship.

Helen has emphasised to me that Jim was deeply concerned that many Christians of his own generation had lost their spiritual edge as they got older. This was certainly not true of Jim himself. He continued in harness to the end, maintaining most of his activities until a few days before his home-call in December 1992. Indeed, in his short final stay in hospital, he witnessed earnestly to his fellow patients. His gravestone reads "A man who believed in Christ, lived for Christ and died in Christ." That sums up Jim's life. We desperately need many like him today.

Alan Gamble, Glasgow

Other Recollections

I first met Jim Anderson when, as young men, we were helping the evangelist Willie Scott (Machermore) in gospel work in the south of Scotland, during our holidays. Soon afterwards, we left to serve the Lord in Brazil. Our brother Jim spoke at almost all our farewell and welcome home meetings.

On our first furlough he drove me to a meeting in Dalmellington in a peculiar little car. He was proud of the fact that he was "independent", not requiring to rely on public transport.

On our second last furlough we were living in the missionary home at Annbank, next door to Jim and Helen. Closer contact with him showed his vast understanding of missionary affairs and it would have been difficult to mention a missionary he did not know personally. Because of this knowledge, I myself am indebted to the counsel he was able to give.

James Crawford, Brazil

The summer season was when the work of the Ayrshire Gospel Tent was set in motion. Months of earlier planning and correspondence had now been completed mainly as a result of the tireless workload of Jim in his capacity as secretary to the Ayrshire Tent Committee.

The main task was now the transport and erection of the wooden sided, canvas topped tent. Jim's role became that of site manager. "Pull to the right," he would call as the main poles were fixed in place. "Tie it down," he would cry again as the canvas would fill with a sudden gust of wind almost lifting him off his feet, but soon everything was in place ready for yet another gospel mission.

On one occasion at Tarbolton due to heavy rain the tent was sinking in the soft ground, but not for long. Jim had organised a delivery of 'red blaes' to solve the problem and avert disaster.

To use alternative accommodation might have been easier, but to this generation of men to remove the "ancient landmark" was not an option and so the tent work continued until 1976, when finally the tent was destroyed by fire at Mossblown.

To all who knew him, the Ayrshire Tent symbolised for us a man who was totally separated unto the "gospel of Christ" and for this many are eternally grateful.

Ian Wallace, Kilbirnie

For ten years the writer and Jim Anderson were senior managers in the same college. For most of that time their offices were next door to one another. At very close quarters the writer was able to scrutinise a godly man in the workplace, to see how he dealt with a difficult boss or a troublesome member of staff or a rudderless student.

The same tireless energy the saints saw as brother Jim rushed from meeting to meeting was brought to the daily routine of work. Jim saw that honouring the Lord Christ as a servant of an earthly master was as important as praising Him publicly by lip among the saints. All knew of Jim's Christian confession and would have been all too ready to criticise, had he be found wanting.

Jim's keen interest in people was evident. The heart of the evangelist ever beating in Jim's breast yearned after people from his beloved village and county and those with whom he worked. None who shared his workplace would ever question that sincere interest in others and their spiritual good.

Tom Wilson, Springburn

There were few nights of unbroken sleep for Jim, but rather than lie awake and count sheep he would get up, throw on his robe, and make his way through to the lounge and pray for the Lord's sheep. Our names featured on his prayer list and we lost a faithful prayer partner when he passed into the Lord's presence.

Brothers and elders from a wide area sought his godly and wise counsel. On one of our visits to Scotland, I offered to drive him to a Bible Study. Afterwards he excused himself and was locked in conversation with two brothers, and when he arrived back in the car I sensed his tiredness. He virtually collapsed into the seat, closed his eyes and was silent for a long time. When he did open them I saw tears there, and the only words he said were, "They just can't treat the Lord's people like that!" Although he shouldered much care, he was always approachable and willing to listen to our concerns and share from a wealth of experience. He did not always tell us what we wanted to hear, but rather what we needed to hear.

Walter Alexander, Portugal

To my father-in-law, Jim Anderson was "the wee maister", a term he used with great affection of a man on whom the little assembly in Muirkirk, Ayrshire depended year in and year out. "The wee maister" was primarily a reference to Jim's daily occupation as a teacher. But there was more than a hint of something else in the term: there was respect for one who was due the kind of respect among God's people as once-upon-a time a schoolmaster would have commanded in his community.

Small in number they may have been, but still the little assemblies like Muirkirk knew that "the wee maister" would give them a series of ministry over a winter month. And if the Lord called away one of their number he would disrupt his schedule to lay that loved one to rest. Many an assembly felt keenly when that same "wee maister" was laid to rest.

Tom Wilson, Springburn

He was concerned for individuals, even those who did not look promising spiritually and who appeared unlikely to give much back in return. My first meeting with him was on the door step of a house in Quarrier's Homes, Bridge of Weir, as he returned one of the boys in whom he and his wife took an interest. Their home was open to him for long afterwards. This lad is one of the many who would agree that Jim believed in "doing good to all men". I last met him in John Ritchie's shortly before he departed to be with the Lord. Even although ill, he spoke of the future of the gospel, his plans and hopes. His gospel vigour was as strong as ever.

John Grant, Bridge of Weir

Jim Brown

1929 - 1992
"A faithful minister of Christ"
(Colossians 1.7)

Jim Brown was the only son of Mr. and Mrs. Frank Brown of Cookstown, a godly couple who contributed much to the local assembly there. He was born on 22nd August 1929, and had a very careful and sheltered upbringing as a boy. Jim was saved on 14th February 1944, while attending gospel meetings in the Cookstown Gospel Hall, conducted by the late Alexander Cooke, thus bringing great joy to his parents, and to many others in the assembly.

After his baptism and reception to the local assembly, he soon gave evidence of spiritual growth, with a developing interest in spiritual things. In secular employment he served his apprenticeship to the drapery trade in his family's business. Later he took up business on his own account quite successfully, being popular with the large clientele he served.

Jim married Miss Ethel Crawford in June 1963, and the Lord blessed them later with a girl and boy who are presently in assembly fellowship. As time passed, his mind and heart turned increasingly from the secular world to things divine and eternal. This was seen in his involvement in Sunday School, and open air work. He shared too in more than one series of meetings with full-time workers. An important turning point came in his life when with two young brethren (Norris Stewart and the writer who were later, with himself, to be commended to full-time service) he had a portable hall made by a local joiner. They conducted gospel meetings in the outlying village of Curran for some weeks, where blessing was experienced. This led to further series of meetings in various places, with others being saved.

19

In 1966 Jim left his employment, being commended heartily to full-time service, by his home assembly at Cookstown, with other local assemblies extending to him the right hand of fellowship. He soon proved to all who knew him, his devotedness to the Lord, and the work to which he had been called. Jim was a most honourable and honest man in all his dealings with other people, and he maintained these moral qualities through his life as a Christian and servant of the Lord. His reverence for God, and his love for the truth never diminished, while his care and sympathy for the sick, the sorrowing, the elderly, and widows was recognized and appreciated throughout the province.

In his early full-time labours in the gospel, he accompanied Mr. Alexander Lyttle, and together they had fruitful meetings in a number of places, with quite a few being saved and added to various assemblies. He also shared in his labours with the late Mr. Thomas McKelvey, the late Mr. Robert Beattie, and also with some gifted local brethren. In January 1971, the writer was commended to the grace of God and to full time service, and later in that year became Jim's fellow worker. This partnership continued harmoniously for the last 21 years of Jim's life. Their labours together took them as far as Skibbereen in the south of Ireland, and to the Isle of Bute in Scotland. Their first series together was in a portable hall on the outskirts of Kilkeel, Co. Down, where the hall was filled to capacity with a rich sense of God's presence enjoyed each night, resulting in some blessing.

Because of his serious view of spiritual things and his fidelity to the Lord, Jim was never idle. This series of meetings with his new fellow labourer was followed by meetings in Gospel Halls, portable halls, and in tents, year after year. He was very faithful in visitation and tract distribution, wherever he went for an extended spell of meetings. If it was a town, it had to be fully covered in visitation. If it happened to be a rural area the whole district had to be visited and all the people invited to the meetings. In August 1979 he and his wife were exercised to move house from Cookstown to Randalstown, Co. Antrim, where they were very happy to be with the assembly at Clonkeen where they continued until his homecall.

As it would not be possible to go into every detail of Jim's labours, it might be of interest to highlight some of the places he brought the gospel to. He had an interest in the small market town called Kilrea, known for its opposition and hardness. Even during the 1859 revival in the province, it seemed to have missed out in the blessing and refreshment of those fruitful times. Not so many people came from the town itself, but quite a number came from the local surroundings and some blessing was experienced there. He loved working in country areas, helping to encourage smaller assemblies, many of which were built up and increased in numbers. To name but a few of these, there was Newtownstewart, Kilmore, Fintona, Zion Mills, Cookstown, Kingsmills, Aughavey, Tullylagan and Drumreagh, all of which profited by his faithful and patient labours. He was not neglectful of the larger towns such as Bangor, Newtownards, Ballymena, Coleraine, and Limavady, where he with his fellow worker had much joy in reaping after much sowing. Quite a number remain in assembly fellowship until this present time.

The city of Belfast came into the sphere of his exercise and labours. It was during the height of the troubles in Northern Ireland that he and I were invited to have a series in the gospel in fellowship with the Bloomfield assembly. Some nights it proved difficult to get to the hall in Bloomfield Avenue because of barricades, burning vehicles and protest gatherings on the streets. However in spite of these adverse conditions the meetings were well attended every night. There was great joy among the believers when the late Mr. John Hawthorne's son Stephen got saved, completing the family in Christ. There were others too in the families of the believers who were reached at that time, bringing further joy after times of barrenness. Fruitful meetings were also held in Cregagh Street with some conversions in the Christians' families. Other assemblies in the suburbs of Belfast were helped by his gospel efforts, such as, Newtownbreda, Dunmurry, and Derriaghy, to mention but a few.

Co. Armagh was not forgotten in his movements in the work. He had fruitful meetings in Lurgan, Portadown and Armagh city, where evidence of his labours remain until this present time. He also laboured much in Co. Antrim at Ballymena,

Broughshane, Ballinaloob, Clough, Ahoghill, Ballywatermoy, Rasharkin, and in his home assembly at Clonkeen where much profit from his evangelistic efforts was granted. Jim never went anywhere for meetings without being invited by the local brethren, and he always worked in fellowship and mutual understanding with them. He was careful in his approach to the unsaved and never interfered in that which he felt was the Lord's own prerogative, and by so doing he was largely preserved from leaving behind him a lot of false professions.

Jim had physical problems, which he did not divulge to many. From boyhood days he suffered quite frequently from severe migraine headaches, and had often to revert to medication to obtain relief from his distressing condition. He was not a complainer, and although far from well at times, he put the Lord and His gospel at the forefront of his thinking.

As well as his interests in the furtherance of the gospel, he was quite often asked to take ministry meetings, especially on Saturday nights, and sometimes after a spell in the gospel, where souls had been newly brought to Christ. His ministry was usually of a devotional, practical or exhortational nature, and was mostly warm, weighty and forceful. Being a sympathetic person, he also officiated at many funeral services during his life, in support of those who were in sorrow and bereavement.

At one time I took ill with a viral infection and was for some months restricted in my movements. Jim then joined Mr. Robert Eadie in a series at Harryville in Ballymena, and this was followed by a further spell at Antrim. Latterly Jim was having some problems with periods of weakness and some pain in his left arm and in the muscles of his chest. He visited his local GP who attributed it to stress resulting in these muscular spasms. However he kept going and rejoined the writer for his last series in the gospel at a place called The Birches, near Portadown. These meetings commenced on 26th April 1992 and continued until 28th June 1992.

A sad day came on 4th August 1992 when he was taken to hospital having suffered a mild heart attack. While hospitalized he developed complications which incurred damage to his heart. However after some days he was discharged from hospital feeling quite weak. On 25th September he took quite a severe stroke, and was rushed to hospital a second time. His condition deteriorated, and suddenly and quietly he passed into the presence of his Lord and Master at 4.40pm on 29th September 1992, bringing to a close a life of usefulness on earth. He was a fine singer and on that day joined the Song of Redemption in glory. His funeral was one of the largest seen in his hometown for many years. The service was shared by Mr. Thomas Matthews of Brazil and Mr. Albert McShane. His remains were laid to rest in Ballee New Cemetery, Ballymena.

".... for so He giveth His beloved sleep" (Psalm 127.2).

Jack Lennox, Magherafelt

Other Recollections

Thinking of our brother Jim Brown, the words of John 1.47 came to mind, "Behold an Israelite indeed in whom is no guile."

His links with the work of the Lord in this part of Donegal go back to 1961 when he first came to preach the gospel on a Lord's Day evening. From then until the Lord called him home he maintained a prayerful and practical interest in the work here.

On occasions he stayed in our home leaving many happy memories of fellowship shared. He was a plain man, content with what God had given. Often when in conversation about the great men of this world and their possessions he would say, "Sure they can have it all."

Tommy McClay, Laghey

I remember the first time I heard our brother preach the gospel and although it is more than forty years ago I can still vividly recall the message he delivered that night.

In 1968, sharing a meeting with him in Laghy, Co Donegal, he told me of his exercise to preach the gospel in his portable hall in a country district near Newtownstewart, Co Tyrone. He asked me to share with him in the preaching of the gospel.

I recall the earnestness with which he preached. Also his burden for souls and his consciousness of the need for divine help were very real as we prayed together in our home and in the prayer meetings with our brethren from the Newtownstewart assembly. Our brother used to say that he believed the purpose of gospel meetings was threefold - the glory of God, the training of His servants and the salvation of sinners.

Rutherford Armstrong, Newtonards

Encouragement, is the one word that springs to mind as I recall my dear brother Jim Brown.

It was with much joy that we welcomed Jim and his wife Ethel to the local assembly at Clonkeen when they moved as a family from Cookstown to Randalstown.

One night, after the mid-week Bible Reading, brother Jim invited me and a number of other young brethren over to his car. There we were to find a choice selection of good, sound, easy to read commentaries and Bible helps. On selecting a particular volume (which I still find very beneficial) we were informed that he wanted us to have these absolutely free of charge! This is just one example of how he sought to help and encourage.

Prior to him coming to live in our area, he with his preaching partner, Mr Jack Lennox, joined with the brethren and sisters of the Clonkeen assembly for four weeks' open-air meetings in Randalstown and district. Those were most memorable evenings spent together in the spread of the gospel. Our brother ever sought to encourage us even though there was open opposition at that time.

What we remember, in addition to his encouraging words, was his prayerful interest for us and also for the assembly, which has sustained a very big loss as a result of his home-call.

Carson McDowell, Clonkeen

My recollections of Jim Brown are both manifold and fragrant. Jim had quite a profound effect upon my early Christian life (1964-68), particularly in regard to gospel testimony. At that time we both lived in Cookstown, County Tyrone, and he often took me with him to preach on Lord's Days. I quickly learned from Jim that such spiritual exercises required the utmost dependence upon God, and must be accompanied by godliness of life, along with a deep compassion for the souls of men.

I recall one incident of profound sadness, which served to highlight Jim's deep compassion for those in distress. On one particular Saturday as I was preparing to leave for the open-air gospel meeting at which brother Jim Brown was a regular attender, he arrived at our home stricken with grief, openly weeping. He carried the news of the sudden death, in a road accident, of the only child of one of our fellow open-air workers. Jim's capacity to feel keenly for others in pain was well known, and certainly gave great expression to the meaning of 1 Cor. 12.26, 'And whether one member suffer all the members suffer with it...' Neither was he lacking in practising the latter part of this verse of Scripture.

Robin I. McKeown, Ballymoney

Often in ministry he spoke about the widows of Scripture and showed care and concern for present day widows in many ways. He took his work very seriously, at times unable to sleep as he thought of perishing people around. He was not given to jesting, gossip, tale bearing, or criticism. He would choose his comments and words with care. As he moved around his presence and conversation adorned the doctrine. All felt he was in touch with God and had His glory in mind. He had a nice singing voice. As many of the assemblies in Ireland operate without musical instruments, we found him very useful. He was not given to asserting himself, and nothing of pride or self-importance marked him. He was happy to take a quiet place and give what help he could.

James G. Hutchinson, Newtonards

Jim was a helpful man, an excellent organiser. When I purchased a pharmacy Jim was quick to offer to help me move stock from one shop to another nearby. Avoiding working on Sunday, we had only a few hours available. I was surprised at how well he had goods classified on the shelves, largely unsupervised, for his training was in drapery.

The same organising trait came to light at my wedding, when Jim was best man. He had everything arranged to perfection. I was also best man at his wedding and Jim had everything arranged to perfection! Some young folks had done-up Jim's car for his going off after the wedding. Now, Jim was so unworldly that this was totally out-of-character to those who knew him. The vehicle was quickly restored! He returned the favour, when my new wife and I were sitting awaiting take-off in our Jersey-bound plane. It was Jim who saw to it that a mislaid jacket was rushed on board.

If one word must be used to describe Jim Brown, it would have to be 'fatherly'. Even as a young man it was spiritually healthy to be in conversation with Jim. In those days he used to take me with him on a Lord's Day to tell how I was saved.

Raymond Stewart, Magherafelt

I knew about Jim Brown for many years, but did not have any personal contact with him until March 1990 when I got to know our brother very well during twelve weeks' meetings with brother Lindsay Carswell in Clonkeen. They were happy days, and it was a great joy to him to see his son, Crawford, saved at that time.

The following year I had the privilege of joining brother Jim in the gospel in Harryville, Ballymena. I still remember the untiring work of our brother as we went together from door-to-door meeting the people. After these meetings we spent another eight weeks in Antrim Gospel Hall. We never thought that a short time later he would be with the Lord. He was a most considerate man in every way. I had health difficulties at that time, and he was more worried about me than himself. He spent time visiting the sick and lonely saints and I am still meeting individuals whom Jim faithfully visited and sympathised with in their difficulties.

Robert Eadie, Belfast

Jim Brown

Frederick F. Bruce

1910 - 1990
"If the Son therefore shall make you free,
ye shall be free indeed."
(John 8.36)

Think of what you were when you were called: "Not many wise men after the flesh". Paul's words (1 Cor 1.26) allow for the church to include some wise by human standards and among such in 20th century Britain, the name of F. F. Bruce is distinguished. Yet while he accepted the recognition he received from many quarters, he made no capital out of it, preferring, like the apostle, to be simply a servant of his Lord, His Word and His church.

Frederick Fyvie Bruce was born on 12th October, 1910, in Elgin, north-east Scotland, the eldest son of Peter Fyvie Bruce and Mary, née MacLennan. His father (1874-1955) was an itinerant evangelist, based at the assembly in Elgin and there F.F.B. grew up, being baptised shortly before his eighteenth birthday. From 1928-1932 he studied Classics at Aberdeen University, graduating with a First Class degree. There he met Annie Bertha (Betty) Davidson, a fellow-student, whom he married in 1936. Meanwhile he had won a scholarship to read Classics at Cambridge (1932-34, again graduating First Class). He then moved to Vienna intending to study for a doctorate on the subject of Roman slave-names. However, from October 1935 he was appointed to a three-year lectureship in Greek at Edinburgh University, so never completed the doctoral thesis. His benefit from Austria was fluency in German. In 1938 he was selected for a lectureship in Greek at Leeds University and, when the University of Sheffield established a Department of Biblical History and Literature in 1947, he was chosen to head it, being created Professor in 1955. Four years later he was invited to fill the vacant Chair of Biblical Criticism and Exegesis at Manchester, the position he held until his retirement in 1978.

Brought up among the assemblies, F.F.B. never felt any need to seek a different style of church fellowship and wherever he lived, he worshipped with the assemblies. From Elgin he went to Hebron Hall, Aberdeen, then to Cambridge where he became a member and an Elder at Panton Hall. In Vienna and in Edinburgh (Bellevue Chapel) he found the same congenial spiritual homes. Resident in Leeds, the Bruces met with Christians at Fenton Street Gospel Hall; in Sheffield they were members of Cemetery Road meeting Hall (later Lansdowne Chapel) and there he served as joint-secretary. His gifts were recognized in each church he joined and for many of the last thirty years of his life he was an elder and teacher in Stockport at Crescent Road Hall (which became Brinnington Evangelical Church in 1973). Typically, he commented, "Perhaps the church recognized that I was not likely to be much good at anything other than teaching". In fact, he could be involved in many other aspects of church life, greeting people at the door and handing them hymn books, giving thanks for a new baby, conducting marriage and funeral services, using his musical ear to act as presenter. For many years he and Betty were house-parents at the North Midlands Young Peoples' Holiday Conference and interested themselves in other activities for young people, "A class for which," he wrote, "I have a special concern."

It was truly for his gifts as a teacher that he was most widely esteemed. Whether giving the Presidential Address to the international Society for New Testament Studies, presenting regular lectures to his students, or speaking in a small Gospel Hall, his speech, with Scottish accent, was clear, his sentences straightforward, his message readily intelligible. Always aware of the weaker brother, he could choose to express his own opinions in such a way as to avoid offence. He was well-known for seeking the good in others and refraining from criticism, even of those most Christians would condemn. When he disagreed, he would say so with courtesy and give his reasons. His father taught him never to accept anything offered in the way of Christian faith or practice unless he saw it clearly for himself in the Scriptures. He maintained that attitude, always examining the facts before making any statement.

A voracious reader, as a schoolboy he preferred books to football. He roamed widely; his extensive library held dictionaries of numerous languages, ancient and modern, and works ranging from *Das Kapital* to the thirty-four volumes of JN Darby's *Collected Writings* and the *Documents of Vatican II*. Possessed of a retentive, photographic memory, he was able to write fluently, bringing to mind the information he needed, or the routes to finding it. That gift fitted him for answering questions orally in the lecture room and at conferences - sometimes with a simple, but firm, No! - and for twenty years in the Answers to Questions pages of *The Harvester*. (A selection from them was published in 1972 as *Answers to Questions* by Paternoster Press.)

The clarity and factual basis of his thought endows his books with lasting value. *Are the New Testament Documents Reliable?* (Inter-Varsity Press, 1943) was his first title, *The Acts of the Apostles: The Greek Text with Introduction and Commentary* (Tyndale Press, 1951) his first major commentary. Altogether he wrote some fifty books; the total number of his articles, essays and book reviews is many hundreds. Unlike many scholars who try to gain a reputation by propounding some novel or contentious idea, F.F.B. aimed to explain Scripture through careful exegesis of the original texts (he had taken the opportunity to learn Hebrew during his tenure at Leeds), bringing archaeological discoveries to bear where appropriate, assessing current theories and setting out his views, often a few sentences revealing to the alert that he had read, analysed and accepted or rejected the burden of a large academic volume. Whether he drew from such a source or quoted an old hymn to make a point, he always added the bibliographical reference so that anyone could find it. This ability is masterfully displayed in *This is That. The New Testament Development of Some Old Testament Themes* (Paternoster Press, 1968). That was part of the integrity which coloured every part of his life and brought his scholarship its high reputation.

Although he began as a classical scholar, his interests turned more and more to biblical studies while he was at Leeds

University, leading to his Sheffield appointment. Nevertheless, the skills he had learnt in studying Greek and Latin authors informed his approach to the Bible. He saw nothing odd in his Manchester title, Professor of Biblical Criticism, demonstrating in his work, that, despite the bad reputation biblical criticism had gained through its use by liberal scholars to undermine Scriptures' authority, criticism could be brought to bear in a positive way on the sacred text. Elucidating the historical circumstances in which Paul wrote his letters, for example, the local situations to which he alludes, brings greater accuracy to their understanding for today's church. Scrutiny of language and literary style may show the hands of different writers; discrepancies may help to a better appreciation of the progress of revelation or of the distinctive outlooks of individual writers [*In Retrospect* 312]. Using this tool presented no difficulty to him and the calibre of his scholarship led to an honorary Doctorate of Divinity from Aberdeen University (1957), the presidency of the Society for Old Testament Study (1965) and of the Society for New Testament Studies (1975), Fellowship of the British Academy (1973) and its Burkitt Medal for Biblical Studies (1979).

Invitations to attend conferences and to lecture abroad became frequent and, from 1954 onwards, he accepted many, the lectures frequently forming the basis for new books. He enjoyed the travel especially when the maturing of their children permitted Betty to accompany him. In later years their son Iain settled in Newfoundland and their daughter Sheila in Australia, they and their families providing other enjoyable reasons for travel, sometimes in alternate years. His fondness for young people was renewed as his grandchildren arrived and he would play uninhibitedly with them, as with the children of other friends and students, crawling across the floor and hiding behind the furniture. Yet work was never far away; he set out his priorities, firstly I do what I am paid to do; then I do what I have to do; and then I do what I would like to do. He would sit with visitors conversing around him while he was seemingly immersed in correcting the proofs of a book, interjecting germane comments into the conversation. Happily, a few weeks before his death, he told the writer he had finished all he wanted to do.

Fred Bruce's impact on Christians has been immeasurable. He showed that a positive approach to the Bible can make sense of it; there is no need for Christians to shy away from the academic study of God's Word, while allowing it its authority. The result has been an enormous growth in evangelical biblical scholarship, notably through the Tyndale Fellowship for Biblical Research and Tyndale House, Cambridge, in both of which F.F.B. played a founding role and sustained an active concern to the end of his life.

For thirty years he edited *The Evangelical Quarterly*, a journal that was for long the principal outlet for scholarly evangelical studies, thus stimulating others to write and, by his judicious but kindly reviews, encouraging new authors. A close friend for many years was Cecil Howley, editor of *The Witness* for whom he wrote in serial form a commentary on John's Gospel and his autobiography, *In Retrospect. Remembrance of Things Past* (published as books by Pickering & Inglis in 1983 and 1980). His Bible teaching gave guidance to many in realising that the relevance of the ancient texts to modern life was to be discovered in their plain meaning rather than types and fantasies. He played a key part in the (young men's) Bible Teaching Conferences from the 1950s through to the 1970s, which aimed to instruct in the basic truths of Scripture and teach how to preach sound expository biblical addresses.

Here is his summary of four themes of Paul's teaching which he deemed needed continued emphasis.

(a) True religion is not a matter of rules and regulations. God does not deal with people like an accountant, but accepts them freely when they respond to His love, and implants the Spirit of Christ in their hearts so that they may show to others the love they have received from Him.

(b) In Christ, men and women have come of age, as the new humanity brought into being through His death and resurrection-life. God does not keep His children on leading-strings but calls them to live as responsible adult sons and daughters.

(c) People matter more than things, more than principles,

more than causes. The highest of principles and the best of causes exist for the sake of people; to sacrifice people to them is a perversion of the true order.

d) Unfair discrimination on the grounds of race, religion, class or sex is an offence against God and humanity alike. [*Paul. Apostle of the Free Spirit* (Paternoster Press, 1977) 463]

Frederick Fyvie Bruce, honoured by his academic peers, admired by Christians world-wide, loved by his friends and family, was a shy, modest and frugal man, generous in supporting deserving individuals and Christian causes. Little of his home life and his emotions are revealed in his autobiography. They were private matters. The constant occurrence of the pronoun "I" in it was unavoidable, but somewhat distasteful to contemplate. What was important to him was the service of his Saviour to whom he wholeheartedly devoted his remarkable talents.

Alan Milard, Liverpool

Frederick F. Bruce

Geoffrey T. Bull

1921 - 1999
*"Called me by his grace, to reveal his Son in me,
that I might preach him among the heathen."*
(Galatians 1.15)

I am looking at an old black and white photograph in my study of a young man in his twenties with a broad smile, smartly dressed in a suit and tie, with round rimmed spectacles and a head of dark hair. It is my father, or dad, as I would refer to him. To others he is Geoff or Geoffrey T. Bull (but in this article I will refer to him as Geoff as he was affectionately known by his friends). As I look at this picture there is a freshness and eagerness in his very being. I look back at the picture and I can imagine the photographer has made him laugh, and in that moment of my dad's life, the photographer draws out that inner joy of a young man who knew and wanted to serve the Lord Jesus Christ. It was what instinctively drew me to this picture in the first place. There was something in that picture that I yearned for, for myself.

What made this man? What was he like as a child? How did he come to faith? What is more, how did he finish the course? Why ask all these questions and indeed why write again what Geoff himself wrote? It is because of the challenge, that in his century he followed his Saviour to the very end and through the course of his life advanced the kingdom of God in sharing the good news of Jesus Christ. By looking at what he did in the last century may it be a stimulus in our walk with God to enter this century and indeed a new millennium with the same vision and faith to serve our Lord and Master.

I look back at the photograph again and know that this young man could not possibly have realised the high cost to be involved in serving His Lord. This healthy young man, would at the end of his time of imprisonment in China, be a shell of his former self, the smile would be removed from his face and all he would have materially would be the clothes he wore. However, when those iron gates would eventually yield, out would come a richer man than before, for he had discovered at the deepest and lowest points in his life, that a merciful God was with him.

Geoffrey Taylor Bull was born into this world on 24th June 1921 in Eltham, London. He and his sister Gwyn grew up in an exciting time for his family, as his parents were one of twelve founding couples of Woodcroft Hall, Edgware. He was part of a Sunday School that grew to 1000 children.

His commitment to Christ took a step forward when he professed his faith, and was baptised, in 1937 at the age of 15. At the age of 17, in the young peoples' group he began to preach in the open air, and, during World War II he played the piano in the Sunday services, only on the proviso of the elders that he did not jazz up the hymns!! Significantly, in a letter drafted for the 70th Anniversary of Woodcroft Hall, Geoff remarked, "Under God, I am indebted to the united, wise and supportive leadership of the elders of those early days and the way I was encouraged and given opportunity to develop in the service for the Lord."

It was during these early years that he felt the call to the mission field, and an early indication of his future came when the initial words from Galatians 1.15 struck him, "Called by his grace, to reveal his Son in me". On returning to the passage again he read, "that I might preach him among the heathen". This seed of Scripture embedded in his very being and began to grow, even during the interjection of World War II where he served in the non-combatant Corp in the quarries. The calling did not diminish in his mind and God's will continued to work within him. This was confirmed by the elders of Woodcroft Hall who commended him in 1947.

Much has been said of Geoff's advances into Tibet in 1950 and also, when he was in fear of losing his life during his time of imprisonment. However, there was an incident that I consider singled him out as a man who was able to stay the course when his life-long purpose was being wrenched from him. It is recounted in his book *When Iron Gates Yield* when he was taken as captive out of Tibet. Geoff wrote, "As we came to the summit my eyes ranged back over the plain. There lay the little city, the fort and the lamasery in the far distance. My heart was nearly breaking. Away on the great skyline I could pick out the ranges and grasslands to the north. I could see the pass in the hills leading on to the Chamdo trail. I had hoped so highly to be treading that road further into Tibet and onto Lhasa. Now I was leaving this immense country and this stricken people, leaving as a prisoner led on into an unknown and unthinkable future. As I gazed out to that lost horizon, I could only cry out in agony of soul: "Lord, Thou knowest all things, Thou knowest all things." For me it was the greatest disappointment I had ever known...To me it was a stark tragedy. Broken, baffled and amazed, I turned in my saddle and looked down a new valley." Even in his thoughts he seemed to be entering a new spiritual valley when he went on to say, "Into my saddened spirit the Lord in His own special way poured in His peace and calm. He will not allow his children to be swallowed up with over much sorrow. In His grace He breathed into me the sense of His will transcending all that had transpired and as we descended so great did this reassurance become that I found myself saying almost without thinking, 'It is the will of God, it is the will of God that events should befall us so.' "

These events involved solitary confinement, physical and mental torture, losing his possessions, the removal of his Bible, severe interrogation and the threat of execution. This took place over a prolonged period of three years and within that time he was sustained by the discipline of daily prayer, memorising Scripture, meditation, singing hymns and choruses and composing poems. Thankfully, in December 1953 events moved quickly and resulted in Geoff's release. He tasted freedom once again and found himself walking across the border to Hong Kong, being met by a Roman Catholic Priest saying the words, "Welcome to freedom." Believers all around the world were giving thanks to answered prayer.

With freedom came responsibility to forge out God's will in a new way. His frail body supported by a walking stick, and his fragile mind, needed healing and that came initially from solitude, enjoying the simple delights of touching the grass, paddling in the sea (one of his first childhood memories), sitting at a piano, to sharing with the affirmation of the multitudes that came to hear his story when he returned to the UK. One such place was in St.Andrew's Halls, Glasgow where 1800 reserved seats were taken, along with overflow meetings in two lesser halls. For many that is what Geoffrey T. Bull will be remembered for. But freedom also broadened his horizons and the discovery of love and being loved became very real when he met Nan Templeton. A romance then blossomed into marriage in 1955. He also found a new spiritual home in Allander Evangelical Church, Milngavie, Glasgow, who commended him in 1957 for a world wide ministry as an itinerant preacher and writer which started in Australia and Borneo. He would through the years minister in Scandinavia, Germany, Africa, USA, Canada, New Zealand, the Far East, Australia and the United Kingdom. It was a major adjustment and a ministry he would have for the rest of his life, preaching, teaching, plus writing a trilogy of his prison experiences, writing devotional and children's books and speaking on radio broadcasts. How was he able to sustain the course? He did not forget the benefits of solitude. I still recall walking into the study at home and finding my dad on his knees, praying with an intensity, and then looking to his desk to see his copious notes written so small I wondered who else could ever read them, but they were the fruits of hours of personal meditation.

Coupled with this widening ministry was his increasing responsibility as a husband and father. Ross was born in Australia in 1955 and Peter 18 months later, back in Scotland. I was born a few years later in 1964. The mountain ranges of Tibet were now replaced by the Campsie Fells and the Trossachs. By now my father was an itinerant preacher and writer and was often away from home for long periods of time. He was able to sustain this with the team support of Nan, his wife, who ensured that the family remained close and faithful to the Lord. He could not have ministered as he did if it were not for the confidence he had in his wife and in her role. This gave him the peace of mind to focus clearly on advancing God's kingdom through his gifts of teaching, to touch souls for Christ and to build up the church. He deeply loved his sons, and as they grew up, their families. He had a tender spot for all his grandchildren.

The pace of ministry was curtailed when in 1989 he suffered a series of major heart attacks that ripped a hole in his heart. Major surgery was required and he was given a 10% chance to pull through. He had been operated on by a Chinese doctor in the morning and by lunch time we had received a phonecall that he had been returned to the operating theatre because of a leaking heart. We knelt in the lounge of missionary friends and prayed again for the Lord to give him a new lease of life. A few hours later our prayers were answered. The Chinese surgeon estimated that he would have another 10 years. Little did we realise how close his estimate would prove to be. In the meantime, he recovered a good quality of life, managed a last overseas visit to Singapore and had the added blessing of seeing the remainder of his grandchildren born, eight in all. On Sunday 10th April 1999 he was worshipping with his fellow believers at Brisbane Evangelical church in Largs. One of the elders, Dr. Willie Naismith, recounted what happened, "It was most fitting that this godly man's service on earth was to extol his Lord and Saviour at the Sunday morning Remembrance Service . . His last words were, 'He is worthy,' and before he sat down, he was called to heaven." He rested in the arms of Nan and their eyes met, knowing this was their last good bye. He was gone.

As I look back in the quietness of my study at the photograph of my dad, it now speaks volumes to me. This young man, even at that stage of life, had much to give thanks for, and indeed in the years to come would have much more for which to give thanks. The combination of that inner drive to fulfil God's calling on his heart, a supportive and encouraging fellowship, the prayers of many believers through his time of imprisonment, an obedience to continue his calling in new ways, the goodness of God found in the security of a loving wife and family and the sustaining power of God's Holy Spirit to minister to the very last moment of his life, is testament to a godly man who was a brother in Christ, a pioneering missionary, a devoted husband and father. This is how I choose to remember him, both as a 26 year old, and as a 76 year old, at the watershed years of his life and at the finishing line of one who had run the race well. If we could have the same impact upon the world as this one saint of the previous century, then this new century holds much promise. The challenge is there from those who have gone before us. It comes to our generation to take up God's call to reveal His Son.

Alister W. Bull, Kilbarchan

Other Recollections

On a Saturday afternoon in December 1953, two of us were working and talking at the Gospel Hall, Hong Kong. The other brother asked, "Do you think we'll ever see Geoff Bull again, or do you think he is already dead?" There was, of course, no answer to that question, although in faith many of us had prayed earnestly for his release from prison.

On arrival home in North Point, Hong Kong, my wife, Barbara, met me at the door and said, "Geoff's in the bathroom." The story of Geoff's release, his arrival in Hong Kong and his being brought to our house has been told elsewhere. Barbara had never met Geoff, and he had no idea that I was in Hong Kong and had married. The subsequent weeks spent together in our home and a brief visit to an isolated hut on Laan Tau island were outstanding. Geoff shared his experiences in Tibet and China; also some of his glorious meditations in the communist prison. For our part, we only needed to supply food, shelter, and clothing, and an open ear to hear all that he had to share.

Raymond Guyatt, Queensland, Australia

In April 1960, my co-worker and I made a flight from the Philippines to North Borneo, to survey the field for possible expansion of our mission work. Our contact in Jesselton was a member of the Tanjong Aru Assembly who invited us to the meeting on the Lord's Day.

Here we met brother Geoffrey Bull and his wife who were labouring there. We had read much about him and his prison experience while a missionary in Tibet. We enjoyed his ministry of the Word. After the meeting he and Nan invited us to have lunch with them. This was a wonderful time of fellowship as we had many questions to ask concerning his time in prison. His response was God-honouring as he explained how God through His faithfulness, mercy, and grace, sustained him through all the hardships he suffered.

After some time of fellowship brother Geoffrey said, "Brethren, we gather this evening to break bread, so you are welcome to gather with us to remember the Lord." This was our first time to gather with an assembly to remember the Lord. It was a wonderful meeting where the Lord was truly honoured. How thankful I am for this time of fellowship and spiritual influence of brother Geoff.

Harold Preston, Harrodsburg, USA

It was not without reason that one British newspaper described the Non-Combatant Corps (NCC) as "Europe's Strangest Army". A number of soldiers who served in the Corps during World War II became missionaries after the war, amongst them Geoff and myself. We had been brought up together as teenagers at the Woodcroft Hall, Burnt Oak Assembly. Although we served in different Companies of the NCC, we were able to meet from time to time during our war service. Both of us had received a call to missionary work in the Far East and had much to share during such precious times of fellowship. Geoff was a year older than me and, even at that time, had spiritual insights beyond my own. His inspiration and encouragement did much to stir me on in the call that was upon my life. He eventually reached Tibet and I spent many years in Hong Kong.

Raymond Guyatt, Queensland, Australia

How wonderfully inspiring to see the moral features of "The Altogether Lovely One", developed in Geoffrey Bull. "Of the abundance of the heart the mouth speaketh", hence the ignition, fervency and continuous power of Geoffrey's motivation became conspicuous.

His majestic Lord's revelation of His omnipotent power, love and perfections, so moved the personal mountain of Geoffrey Bull's heart, giving such pleasure to his Lord, that God chose, called, took up and used him to a great furthering of God's people in their knowledge and understanding of the present and eternal

43

purposes which God purposed in Christ Jesus our Lord. Geoffrey Bull is therefore catalogued with those who, "yet speaketh".

More than 40 years have passed since I saw him, however his characteristic fervency of spirit with his ministry through tapes and writings still draws the hearts and affections of God's people in meditation, in awe of, and to His Beloved Son.

Alan Brimblecombe, Warkworth, New Zealand

Geoffrey Bull was a man with a warm heart which reflected on a radiant countenance when he preached from a platform, prayed from a pew, or when you met with him socially. You warmed to him immediately.

J. Barclay, Largs

Geoffrey will be remembered by the fellowship at Allander Evangelical Church, Milngavie where he associated for some 40 years, for his unique contributions at the "Morning Meeting" in both thanksgiving and in ministry on the person of Christ.

He was especially gifted in being able to lead on from some feeble contribution made, and take and expand the thought with rich devoted language which would take us all to the very gate of heaven. Geoffrey was able to do this because he himself had a radiant passion for Christ, a remarkable understanding of the Scriptures, and a deep, deep love for the Lord Jesus Christ. He saw Christ in all the Scriptures. He was a powerful example of a man who grew in grace and in the knowledge of the Lord Jesus Christ.

His three years of imprisonment in Tibet was the seedbed not for bitterness and resentment, but as he recalled the Bible passages he had memorised as a young man he developed a fresh, rich, poetic loving vocabulary about his Saviour. Geoffrey could speak with rapture on the glories of Christ and with deepest feeling about the sufferings of Christ which moved everyone that listened.

Like Moses it could be said of Geoffrey Bull that he "knew the Lord face to face".

Jim Hopewell, George Russell, Glasgow

Geoffrey T. Bull

Donald W. Coulson

1926 - 1991

*"The path of the just is as the shining light,
that shineth more and more unto the perfect day"*
(Proverbs 4.18)

It was into poor circumstances in Rochester, Kent, that Donald William Coulson was born on 9th September 1926. The eldest of four children, he described his mother as a kind-hearted woman of stern countenance who had the reverence for divine things that was common to most of her generation. His father, however, was a rogue who, as a Royal Marine, was often away from home on duty, but also rarely to be seen when ashore at his home base of Chatham. A fighter and a drunkard, the father kept his young family and poor wife destitute. Indeed, so total was the father's neglect of his family that the two boys were taken into the Dr Barnardo's Home at Stepney from where, after a few months, they were put out to foster homes.

Donald (his mother would not tolerate the shortening of any of the children's names) was fostered out to a farm in Little Horwood, Buckinghamshire, when he was nine years old, and to the day he died he bore the scars around his legs where the tops of his wellington boots chafed and cut in the icy winters. As a foster boy he had neither socks nor long trousers and, besides the scars on his legs, his toes and knuckles were permanently affected by the chilblains of his childhood. His one hot drink of the day came in his foster-father's shaving mug, so tea and bristles were the standard breakfast! Every 'Sabbath' Donald was taken to the Church of England service in the morning and the local Baptist Chapel service in the evening. He also attended the Chapel's Sunday School where a Mr Russell was his teacher, and it was there that he first heard the gospel of God's grace.

At the age of fourteen, Donald Coulson was a miserable specimen of a youth. Thin, pale and with a shock of red hair, he was delivered by Dr Barnardo's into the care of Watts Nautical Training School at HMS Ganges, near Ipswich, to be schooled, drilled and prepared for service in His Majesty's Royal Navy, because Britain was once again at war. Life at Ganges has been thoroughly documented elsewhere, and by any account it must have been a harrowing experience for the young boys who endured its regime. Barefoot runs on a cinder track before daybreak, often with a heavy .303 rifle held above the head, were not as dreadful as having to climb the infamous 'Ganges Mast' in wet, slippery and windy conditions with a bullying Petty Officer beating the legs of the slowest with a rope's end. Notwithstanding the brutality, Donald found life at Ganges better than he had previously known, and it was there that he was first able to apply himself to academic studies, exercising a mind that proved to be sharp and analytical. That sharp mind was also applied to card games, and it wasn't long before an addiction to gambling was added to the other vices that flourished in such a brutal establishment. Earlier knowledge of the gospel, imparted by Mr Russell, was quickly stifled and it was a brash, aggressive and utterly godless young man who was drafted from Ganges to a landing craft that was being prepared for the great D-Day invasion of Europe.

The thoughts that passed through the mind of a bitter, loveless, young sailor just seventeen years old as he headed for Normandy on 6th June 1944 can only be imagined. One of the crew of a landing craft carrying Canadian troops to the invasion beaches, Donald never spoke of the horrors of that day. No sooner had the craft made it to the beach than it was hit by shellfire, sending scores of young men into eternity. Donald awoke on a hospital ship and spent the next three months in a Leeds hospital. Out on leave one evening he was invited into a mission hall and, again, he heard the gospel preached, but by this time he was fit for active duty so was drafted to Portsmouth for further training.

God was certainly dealing in grace with this young man, however, for he was no sooner in Portsmouth and out on the streets looking for fun or trouble, whichever came first, than he was 'fished in' by young Christians to the home of a newly-converted train driver called Harold Young. This man and his wife opened their home to young servicemen and women, and gladly shared their war rations with them. It was in this warm home, the first he had ever really known, that young Donald Coulson was convicted of his sin and, crying out to God for mercy, was soundly saved on the night of 22nd October 1944.

From the outset he had a thirst for the Scriptures and, given a Bible by the Youngs, he began to read. In later years Don (as he was always known amongst the Lord's people) would recount how the Adversary would swiftly strike to knock a young believer off a true course. He had sat down in the Young's home to write to his family, telling them of God's dealings with him. There was a swift response from his younger sister Eunice who, pleased that something had delivered her brother from a sinful life, had enclosed for his encouragement "a religious book for him to read". Don was delighted with this and hurried to the Young's to display his new prize. Now Mr Young, newly saved himself, didn't know much about books but he did know the dangers of Watchtower Publications, of which Don's new book was one! Said he, "My dear brother Don, I'm afraid that this book will do you no good at all because it comes from people called Russellites (Jehovah's Witnesses) who deny the deity of Christ." "What should I do with it then?" enquired Don, turning his sister's gift over in his hands. "To be quite truthful, dear brother, the best place for that book is in the fire," replied Mr Young, and without hesitation Don said, "Fair enough," and threw the book into the flames. His awareness of the Devil's deception through false doctrine was awakened by that incident so early in his Christian life, and alerted him to the need for purity of doctrine, based on the Scriptures alone, that became the cornerstone of his ministry.

Don was soon baptised in the Baptist Chapel that Harold Young and his wife attended, and as he looked back on those days, he would recall that the meetings were warm and friendly, the gospel was faithfully preached and baptism taught, but beyond that there was nothing to feed his soul.

His electrical training finished, he was drafted to Devonport and went back to sea until a few months after the end of the war. Coming back ashore he was demobbed and got a job as a bus conductor in Plymouth but, because he refused to join a trade union, he was promptly sacked. The Lord provided another job, this time with the Post Office but, a year later, the same thing happened and he was sacked again for refusing to join a union. The one place where the union problem would not arise was the Royal Navy, and in 1949 Don rejoined as an electrician. In the meantime, when ashore, he attended St Budeaux Baptist where, again, the gospel was preached well and folk were saved and baptised, but still there was something lacking. "Activity in the things of the Lord" was the way to find spiritual fulfilment, Don decided, and with characteristic vigour he became the local secretary for Youth for Christ, a preacher on every local circuit there was, and had a deepening desire to study for the Baptist ministry. One Saturday morning at an open-air gospel meeting he saw a young sister whose baptism he had witnessed some weeks earlier. That young nurse, Daphne Glanville, was to become his wife, but not before God had further dealings in the direction of Don's life.

On Lord's Day mornings, when duties had allowed Don to be ashore for the Baptist Chapel morning service and he was returning to his ship, he would regularly meet a brother from the Wolseley Road assembly, Wilf Lakeman, as he was returning home from their morning meeting. Wilf was a blacksmith in the RN and a cheerful, gracious brother. The regular conversation would be: "Morning brother Don!" "Morning Mr Lakeman." "Have you had a good time this morning, Don?" "Yes, thank you Mr Lakeman." "Not as good a time as we've just had, brother!" Don put up with this exchange for a few weeks until his red hair got the better of him one morning. He asked what Wilf had been patiently waiting for him to ask: "What makes you think that you've had a better time than I have, Mr Lakeman? I might have had just as good a time as you have had yourself!" "You can't have, dear brother," replied Wilf kindly, "you see, you're in the wrong place." Over the weeks Wilf Lakeman chipped away at Don, often inviting him to the meetings at the Gospel Hall. "I can't possibly come," Don would say, "I simply don't have a free minute."

One Lord's Day morning Wilf said, after the usual exchange,

"Don, why don't you come to one of our special ministry meetings this week? We have a man J M Davies of India taking a series on the Feasts of the Lord." The usual protestations were made until Wilf said, taking Don by the sleeve in his earnestness, "Look dear brother, just come for one of the nights and I promise I'll never pester you again!" Thinking that this was a reasonable bargain, Don agreed that he would attend the meeting the following night. He would often say later in life as he remembered hearing the Word of God expounded that evening "that it was like taking a starving man into a banquet". He cancelled all his evening engagements for the rest of the week and came along to soak up the good Word of God. Realising that it was such teaching that his soul had longed for since he had been saved, Don severed all his denominational links and threw everything into the local assembly of the Lord's people. His courtship with Daphne flourished, and they married and came into assembly fellowship at Wolseley Road in 1950. Knowing with assurance that this was where God would have him to be, Don took up his pen to write to Mr Russell, his former Sunday School teacher. Mr Russell, despondent that so many years had apparently been fruitless, was about to tender his resignation to the minister when, on the very day, Don's letter arrived. Resignation turned to rejoicing at the grace of God!

Early years in the assembly were spent in Plymouth and Malta before demob for the second time in 1959. For the next thirty years Don moved amongst the assemblies in the UK, teaching the Scriptures with the conviction of a man who knew why he was where he was. He gave short shrift to those men who sought to dilute the clear teaching of the Word, and would not depart from the forthright statement of truth for the sake of popularity. He liked nothing more than discussing the Scriptures, and many are the saints who have been grounded in the truth by the unswerving, faithful teaching of this man who was wholly devoted to the wellbeing of the Lord's people. His death at the age of 64 was brought about by mesothelioma caused by asbestos dust in his Navy days, and as he grew increasingly ill he was most faithfully nursed by his wife whose constant support had enabled him to give so much to the saints for so many years. He blessed the Lord that he had seen his four sons and only daughter saved, baptised and brought into the fellowship of local assemblies, and it was his four sons who bore his body to the burial when his work for the Master was done.

Philip Coulson, Forres

Other Recollections

As a young bell-bottom sailor in Plymouth, Don was introduced to brother Avery Wood from the Wolseley Road Gospel Hall assembly, who asked him two questions. Firstly "Are you saved?" and being assured he was, the second question followed, "Have you read Romans yet?" This second question started Don on a life-time study of that Epistle. It also commenced a life-long friendship with this older brother and his family; and it was Don who was asked to conduct brother Wood's funeral service.

During his early years in assembly fellowship in Plymouth, Don would spend as many Saturdays as possible travelling to 'open-platform' Fellowship Meetings in assemblies throughout Devon, where he became a recognised and appreciated contributor. He always had one seat vacant in his van and invariably took another young convert, Michael Browne, then serving in the Royal Marines, with him. This laid the foundation for both their teaching ministries in the following years.

Don was an instinctive Bible teacher. During the final months of his life when he was lying so desperately ill, a young brother from Poland, Jacek Pruszynski, was brought to visit him. A conversation on assembly principles ensued for over an hour, which left a deep and continuing impression upon the Polish brother. Jacek still recalls that memorable time with "brother Coulson" and the truths he learned on that single visit.

Michael Browne, Bath

During my last student year in England I lived with the Coulson family in High Wycombe, by kind invitation of Don and Daphne. That invitation was typical of their largesse, generosity and hospitality, bearing in mind that they had a family of five children. I come from a large family, so it was rather like a "home from home" experience. One factor I must single out was his unflagging interest in the Holy Scriptures. From him I learned the importance of the systematic reading and study of the Word of God. Often after the family had gone to bed, Don sat at one end of a table reading his Bible, while I set at the other end reading mine. From him I learned much about the interpretation and meaning of scripture.

An example of Don's magnanimous spirit was an occasion when he received a telephone call after midnight asking him to drive to Heathrow Airport to collect a brother in Christ (whom he had never met and did not know) and give him accommodation for the night. Don regarded it as a great honour before the Lord to respond to such a request.

Robin McKeown, Ballymoney

When I first left Southampton to study in Manchester, I was invited to stay with the Coulson family in Stretford. I fear no contradiction when I say that Don was never noted for being shy and retiring. Among my fondest recollections were the hours spent with him in the open air at the Underground Car Park in Manchester, and later at Speaker's Corner in London. He was masterly at dispossessing would-be orators off their soap box, so that he could occupy it himself to preach the gospel. No mean heckler himself, he had a way of silencing members of the audience who dared to barrack him when he was preaching. Often Daphne and I would cringe in the crowd as Don took on all comers. In one such incident, a hot head who was probably a little the worse for drink was being a nuisance. Don silenced him most effectively with, "If you had as much brains as you've got mouth you'd be Prime Minister!"

Mark Smith, Bridge of Weir

One Sunday evening on Liverpool pierhead, having so distracted and exasperated a speaker that he gave up his soapbox, Don immediately engaged the crowd by asking if anyone had a question about the Bible. A man called out "Where did Cain get his wife?" and, thanking the man for his question, Don repeated it loudly to the swelling crowd. "Did you hear that, friends? A man here wants to know where Cain got his wife."

To the man he said, "I'll gladly tell you where Cain got his wife if you tell me where I got mine." "Is that a fair exchange, friends?" he shouted and, of course, the crowd roared "Yes!" The man, uneasily, called back "How do you expect me to know? I've never even seen you before!" "That," cried Don, "is what a fine Christian man (Sir Robert Anderson) once called 'the irrationalism of infidelity'. Here is a man standing near me, in my day and generation. He can't tell me where I got my wife, but he expects me to tell him where a man who lived 5000 miles away and 6000 years ago, got his!" Having interested the people, Don then answered the question before preaching about 'the way of Cain'.

Philip Coulson, Forres

Don was always a firm upholder of fundamental New Testament doctrine. This was reinforced to me many years ago on visiting an assembly of which Don was a member. On entering the foyer I noticed a statement attached to the wall. It read something like this: 'It is required that all sisters wear a head covering at all gatherings of this assembly'. On making some enquiries I found that Don was the influence behind this notice being displayed. It was very necessary at that time for such a stand to be taken, and it was true to Don's character.

Jim Sinclair, Hamilton

Donald W. Coulson

They finished their course in the 90s

William E. Craig
1924 - 1991
"The memory of the just is blessed"
(Proverbs 10.7)

Bill Craig was a well known figure amongst the saints for many years as a teacher of the Word of God in assemblies gathered to the Name of our Lord Jesus Christ throughout the United Kingdom and elsewhere. He was born in 1924, and born again at the age of 15 under the preaching of Mr Edward Rankine from Ireland in Wellmeadow Gospel Hall, Paisley, Scotland. Shortly afterwards he was baptised and received into the fellowship of the above assembly where he continued for 42 years. His last ten years were spent in happy fellowship in the assembly which meets at the Gospel Hall in Barrhead near Glasgow.

He was conscripted to Military Service in 1942 and became a physical training instructor in the Army. In 1944 he was so badly wounded in Normandy that he was left to die. The late Alastair Robertson of the Abernethy assembly, who was in the Medical Corps, saw him and took him to the field hospital where after treatment he began to recover. Later he was brought to a hospital in Cardiff for convalescence. While standing there with the help of two crutches, he first met Mr William Trew, who was a regular visitor at the hospital. Bill was preaching the gospel to a ward of wounded soldiers at this first encounter!

In early times after the war, Bill formed a close friendship with the Leckie family and often visited their home in Airdrie. On such occasions Bill and Albert would sit with Mr Leckie (senior) and discuss the Scriptures. Those evenings often ended with Bill catching the last bus back to Glasgow! They were formative times for both young men in laying a basis of knowledge and understanding of the sacred text. The fruit of such study was seen in the subsequent teaching ministry of both of them. Bill Craig's friendship with Albert Leckie lasted throughout the remainder of his life and culminated in him speaking at brother Albert's funeral in 1988.

As the years progressed it was clear that our brother had become not only an interested reader of the Word of God but also a careful student of its truth. He loved ministry of the Word and Bible Readings and was never happier than sitting in some house discussing a passage of Scripture. He was always courteous to people but this did not in any way prevent him from taking a different view in looking at the meaning of a passage. On occasion he would throw some controversial issue into the conversation then sit back and listen to the various responses! In his own ministry he obviously enjoyed the Gospels dealing with such sections as the upper room ministry of the Lord Jesus in John 13 - 17, or some aspect of Ephesian truth as well as that of the epistle to the Hebrews. He would also take up aspects of the Levitical Offerings as they portray the person and work of Christ, and the ministry on such matters was presented in a heart-warming way and was always well expressed. He was a speaker easy to listen to. Our brother was not a prolific writer although a little appeared from his pen in the Believer's Magazine.

Bill Craig always made a substantial and helpful contribution to the local assembly where he was in permanent fellowship. Apart from being away for preaching commitments he would be present at all the assembly gatherings. His ministry was with a view to strengthening the truth of the local assembly in the minds and hearts of the saints, and this was done not only by his teaching of these subjects but also by his example. On the conference day at Barrhead assembly he would be seen welcoming the saints and later helping with the distribution of the food. He was a brother who liked to be involved in all that was taking place. Our brother had a shepherd heart for the saints of his own assembly and was loved by them. In his obituary in the Believer's Magazine it was stated "In the assembly he was a faithful shepherd, ever mindful of the needs of the Lord's people from the very elderly to the very young." An index of the help our brother gave locally is seen in the present progress of some of the younger men who had contact with him in their earlier years.

Brother Craig's shepherd care was not restricted to those in his own assembly. He was in general an excellent visitor of the sick with a word of comfort and cheer to all. The present writer remembers back in 1985 being admitted to hospital suddenly with a suspected serious illness. Apart from family, the first visitor who came to the hospital very quickly was Bill. This was quite characteristic of him. He appeared to have a genuine care for those who had a need. On occasion he had older brethren from a distance, staying in his home for a time of fellowship and holiday. Such a heart lends character to a man's ministry.

Our brother never married and seemed content to use his greater freedom from domestic responsibilities to engage in undisrupted service for the Lord. He lived with his parents until both were taken to be with the Lord and was very kind and helpful to them until the end. For many years he enjoyed a close friendship with Isaac Cherry of Stevenston, having previously served in the army with him. Bill accompanied Isaac and his family for their annual vacation for number of years. After brother Cherry was taken to be with the Lord in 1967 our brother, in conjunction with Mr W Nelson of Stevenston, Ayrshire began to arrange a group holiday abroad for believers in assembly fellowship. This ran successfully for over twenty years and seemed to meet a need for many. Various countries in Europe were visited and were always arranged to places where a local assembly could be attended and encouraged, and travelling was never on the Lord's Day. Bill's friendly and gracious disposition was a big factor in the whole project as such an undertaking carried many problems at times.

Bill Craig was one of a number of gifted brethren in Scotland who were well known in local assemblies throughout the British Isles as ministering brethren, yet they maintained normal employment throughout life. He was for many years the Managing Director of the Company he worked for, yet despite such responsibility, he travelled throughout the UK at weekends, teaching and preaching the Word of God. Our brother was always immaculate and dignified, and his charm and generous personality endeared him to his many friends. He was as content at the smallest rural assembly, as being at the large Belfast Easter Conference. The present writer travelled many miles, and shared with him in many different places. He was always a pleasant brother to work with.

The ministry of such men has helped to confirm and consolidate assembly testimony in many parts of the country. Many of these men had themselves faced the ongoing problems of assembly life and therefore ministered on such matters from experience. It was at the end of such a period of ministry in the assembly at Wallingford, Oxfordshire, that our brother was taken home to be with the Lord. He had finished the particular series of meetings and retired to his bedroom on the night of 2nd October 1991. It seems that before he had undressed he had suffered a heart attack. The next morning it was discovered that the Lord had taken His servant, he was "with Christ which is far better".

Jim Baker, Hamilton

Other Recollections

Bill Craig was a true teacher and genuine shepherd of whom there seems to be fewer in the days in which we live. All he cared about was the assembly, the well-being of the saints of God and their spiritual growth.

I first met Bill when I was saved at the age of 33. On that occasion in 1964 he had heard that I had been at the Sunday morning meeting having turned up at the door wanting fellowship with those of like mind. I say he "heard" because he was himself away most weekends taking meetings elsewhere. Little did those at the door know that I did not know that there were four Gospels in the Bible, let alone how we should gather. At that time, I was in employment in an engineering firm in Glasgow that Bill frequented. The very next week he looked me up, opened the Scriptures and showed me from Acts 2 that the right order of things was salvation, baptism and fellowship. This was my first introduction to sitting at his feet to hear the Word of God. I was baptised a few days later. It was my blessing and privilege to be continually instructed by him thereafter. Most of what I learned was while standing on the street, in all kinds of weather, after the prayer and ministry mid-week meeting, the hall being shut, and a few of us picking his brains for a "nugget" of scripture.

F. B. Gibson, Barrhead

One of my chief memories is of a Lord's Day afternoon meeting when he issued a most searching challenge to us. Did we want to know how much progress we were making in divine things? Did we want a gauge by which to measure that progress? Then, said he, get alone with God, find out for how long you can converse with the Father about His Son. Speak of nothing else and of no one else, just talk to God about Christ. How long? This will be the measure of your intimacy with divine persons and the measure of your progress in spiritual things.

It was a great privilege and pleasure, in later years, to get to know him better and to share conference meetings with him, both in Scotland and in Northern Ireland. I valued his fellowship and advice, his help and his encouragement, and with so many others I thank God that I was ever allowed to know him. Very especially, his appreciation of Christ made a deep and lasting impression upon me.

Jim Flanigan, Belfast

To the assembly at Swinton, Bill became a much loved and respected brother having ministered God's Word many times at our annual conference. His first visit was shortly after recovering from a complete nervous breakdown. He arrived, as always, looking immaculate wearing a bowler hat (which at the time was his trademark), but more to the point his ministry thrilled the soul. To this day brethren and sisters alike speak of his ministry on subjects such as the 'Garments of the Priests', and the 'Upper Room' ministry of the Lord.

Bill and I were involved together in various business projects in the UK, Denmark, and the Middle East. I recall on one occasion having travelled for many hours from Manchester to Denmark in a four-seater aeroplane to attend a sales conference. On landing, Bill's first question was, where is the nearest assembly, and will there be a meeting tonight? This truly sums up where our brother's real interests lay.

The assembly was precious to Bill as we know it is to the Lord. Although on occasions Bill's interpretation of Scripture varied from the accepted line of thinking, he was utterly fearless in his presentation of the Scriptures backing up his views with chapter and verse. Several times over the years he told me his desire was to be a servant of the Lord and not a pleaser of men.

My memories of Bill are a brother beloved, a man of total integrity, and a tireless worker and servant of the Lord. He was an example to us all and surely Hebrews 13.7 is so apt - 'whose faith follow'.

Geoff Payne, Swinton

One humorous incident occurred when travelling back to Scotland after taking weekend meetings. His car ran out of water having broken a fan belt on the journey. The very next car to pass stopped to see if assistance was required, and it transpired the gentleman not only produced water he was carrying in his boot, but he had a spare fan belt too! He was bemused no doubt to hear he had been sent by God, and the stranger heard the gospel that night before he went on his way.

F. B. Gibson, Barrhead

Bill Craig had a very sharp mind and loved to engage in the cut and thrust of debate over the Scriptures. Not only could he hold his ground irrespective of the number who held opposing views but he had an incredible ability to wind up those who disagreed with him into a state of frenzy whilst he remained totally unruffled and oozing self control.

Much could be written about the Spirit-endowed ability that so clearly manifested itself when he handled the Word of God – whether publicly or in private. However one feature that made a deep impression on me was not just the way he ministered the Word of God, but the very way he read publicly. Even if he was sharing a conference and hadn't as much time as usual it mattered not to Bill. Whether he was reading a few verses or a whole chapter he never treated it as merely a precursor to his message but read with dignity, clarity and reverence. His very style of reading made you conscious that you were listening to the Word of God and it focussed the mind on the Scriptures.

Now Bill has gone, he has passed into the presence of the Living Word, but his reading of the Scriptures was not in vain. As opportunities come my way to teach the Scriptures I seek to read the Word of God in a similar manner as was demonstrated to a far greater degree by Bill. "He being dead yet speaketh."

Richard Collings, Caerphilly

I was privileged to spend the last few days of his earthly service with him. He knew the time of his departure was near. He spoke of it often – he was waiting for the moment; it would be at the end of his ministry meetings and at the end of the day. Thus it was. His four days of meetings in Wallingford over, he retired to his room and within minutes he was "at home".

Of Enoch, Bill once said, "One day, as was his habit, he was walking with God. God said to him, 'Enoch, you've spent so much time with me recently, you might as well just come and live with me, and we can fellowship without a break.' Enoch was delighted and so he went." By faith Enoch was translated...so it was with Bill.

John Davies, Reading

John M. Davies
1895 - 1990
"In journeyings often...in perils by the heathen"
(2 Corinthians 11.26)

John Mathias Davies was born in south Wales in 1895 into a Christian home, the second son of a family of nine children. His father was a farmer who attended the local Baptist church and it was there that J.M., as he was known in the family, received Christ as his Saviour at the age of fifteen. After leaving school he worked in a government office as a land surveyor. This experience stood him in good stead in India.

In 1914 he emigrated to Missoula, Montana, USA to join his brother. While working on the local farms he met a godly preacher, a graduate of the Moody Bible Institute (MBI), who encouraged J.M. to study the Scriptures, and in 1915 he enrolled for the two-year course at MBI in Chicago. While there, he met a missionary from India who was with a faith mission, and at the time he felt the Lord would have him go to that country. Later he attended special meetings at Austin Gospel Hall (now Oak Park assembly), to hear Mr Alfred Mace. J.M. was greatly taken with this ministry. It was his introduction to the assemblies, and from then he continued to have fellowship among them. After some further studies at Wheaton College, he was commended to the Lord's work by Austin Gospel Hall, initially for a short time in tent work in Iowa and Nebraska, and then in India.

In 1919 he married Miss Barbara Gilmour, and in 1920 they left for India via Britain where he particularly wanted to bear testimony to his family and the townsfolk of his call to India. He was especially happy that one of his brothers was saved at that time, who later served the Lord in north India until he had to return to Wales due to ill health.

Arriving in Bangalore he began language study and later moved to Trichur, Cochin State (now Kerala). He became very fluent in the language (Malayalam) and was able to preach and teach to many who attended the meetings and large conventions, without an interpreter. Unlike other parts of India, there is a large nominal Christian community in Kerala, and it was among these folk and also the Hindu and Muslim people that assemblies were planted.

While at MBI J.M. had asked the Lord to give him the privilege of ministering to His people. This request seems to have been granted in that he had an extensive teaching ministry, not only in India, but also in the United States, Canada, and Britain, and in over 40 years he also visited Australia, New Zealand, and at the invitation of the Indian brethren from Kerala, the Persian Gulf. He travelled to Yugoslavia and also spent four winters in the Faroe Islands. In the fifties he was able to visit several countries in southern Africa, and also went to Turkey and Israel.

He authored sixteen books from small booklets to larger ones, including *The Christian's Statue of Liberty*, an exposition of Romans; *The Lord and the Churches*, Revelation 1-3; 1 and 2 Corinthians, besides many articles and essays for Christian magazines and symposia. Many will remember him for his remarkable memory, not only of the Scriptures which was incredible, but also for names and places, and for the ease with which he spoke with people of all ages.

Mr Davies trusted the Lord in everything, and the Lord was truly faithful in this also. When questioned by his father in 1920 as to how he would support himself, he replied, "He (God) doth not send forth soldiers on their own charges... He will supply bread to the eater and seed to the sower." In later years his father had to acknowledge this to be so.

Much of his travelling was done after his wife, Barbara, who for 48 years had been a true helpmeet, went to be with the Lord in 1967. He eventually decided to make his home in Canada, first with his daughter and son-in-law, and subsequently in Vancouver, where in 1981 he married his second wife, Sarah, who lovingly cared for him in his declining years.

Of his seven children (all of whom know the Lord), one son,

Cedric, predeceased him in 1987. Another son Dr. Gilmour Davies and his wife served the Lord in India at the mission hospital in Tiruvella, Kerala, where Gilmour often had the opportunity to share the platform with his father (Gilmour went to be with the Lord in 1992). Other members of the family live in Britain, Canada and Australia.

Mr Davies' complete trust in the faithfulness of God, his total commitment to the Scriptures, and the importance of prayer for life's decisions are an inspiration to all of us.

Handley Davies, Australia & Fred Greer, Canada

Other Recollections

We moved here to Victoria in 1949, and we had the pleasure of entertaining our brother Davies in May 1950. We had a few in the house and before leaving we passed the guest book around for signatures and comments: this is what our brother wrote; 'India, J.M. Davies, 'The barbarous people showed us no little kindness' Acts 28.2, and the real 'butter'! Altogether a most happy evening that will be long remembered.'

There were other occasions but we forgot to get a signature. One of the last times at Victoria Chapel we remember is when he almost lost his teeth! However, we can assure you that we always enjoyed his ministry.

Joe Gilmour, Canada

J.M. Davies always seemed to be completely absorbed by his calling. When he decided to come to Vancouver to reside, he requested a temporary suite in Blenheim Lodge. That was when I saw this able teacher in a new light. He, as a resident, fitted into life in the Lodge very admirably and quickly made close friends in the dining room.

My observation of brother Davies as he mixed with the residents showed me that despite his vast knowledge of the Scriptures, he very capably and humbly became to one and all just 'one of the crowd'.

Few of the residents in the Lodge knew him as a profound Bible scholar, but his deep knowledge of the Scriptures shaped his thinking and attitude toward those around him.

W.J. Livingston, Canada

Sydney Emery

1909 – 1995

"Eye hath not seen, nor ear heard,
neither have entered into the heart of man, the things
which God hath prepared for them that love Him."
(1 Corinthians 2.9)

Workington, Cumbria is the town where Sydney Emery lived all his life, and the Gospel Hall, Corporation Road was the only assembly of the Lord's people in which he had fellowship from being born again until he finished his course in May of 1995.

While at junior school he won a scholarship to Workington Technical College where at sixteen he completed his secular education. He then went on to work in the offices of the United Steel Company and was eventually trained as an accountant. He continued in the same department until his retirement at the age of sixty-five. However that did not mean the end of work, for the work that was most important to him "the Lord's work", was to increase.

Sydney was born on 17th April 1909 into a Christian home. He was the fifth member of the family, having one brother and three sisters. All the family were in fellowship at the Gospel Hall. This assembly originated with meetings in his grandparents' home until the Gospel Hall was built on Corporation Road, Workington, in 1891, eighteen years before Sydney was born. Sydney started Sunday School practically as soon as he started to walk, and was brought up under the sound of the gospel. From an early age he was made aware of his sinful condition and knew that the only way of salvation was through the Lord Jesus Christ and the sacrifice He made. Sydney trusted the Lord as his Saviour before he reached his teens. (This same Sunday School is the one in which he taught for many years from his teens until the Lord's work took up so much of his time that most weekends were spent in other assemblies away from home.)

Having become a Christian and listening to those who preached the Word of God at the meetings that he attended regularly in the Gospel Hall, he became very interested in the Scriptures. He set aside one evening a week to the study the Bible. This gave him the knowledge to preach the Gospel and minister the Word of God to others, very acceptably. He began to receive invitations to preach from assemblies nearby, these invitations eventually spreading to assemblies further afield, and to all parts of the British Isles.

In earlier days many of these engagements took place at weekends and bank holidays. At this time all his travelling was done by train. Workington was not on the main line, so this meant that the journeys had to start on Friday evenings and the return journeys did not arrive back in Workington until 7.15am on Monday morning. This was only made possible by faithful Christian brethren and sisters at Carlisle making arrangements for Sydney to enter their homes in the early hours on Monday morning so that he could catch two or three hours of sleep while waiting for the first train to Workington. Although many of the invitations that our brother accepted were to conferences, Bible Readings, and ministry meetings, at very large assemblies or combined gatherings with many in attendance, this was not always the case. In the late sixties-early seventies he was responsible for the ministry in the winter months at the Todhill assembly which was a little Gospel Hall on the side of the main road between Carlisle and Gretna, alas no longer in existence. (This hall will be remembered by many because of the large double sided text that was in its grounds, that would light up with the headlights of passing vehicles.) These meetings went on for six or seven years under the title of "Todhills Bible School". Each person attending was provided with a complete copy of the notes for that session, with space provided to append their own notes if they so desired. This proved to be a great help to many. He also assisted in ministry in many other small assemblies, small numbers being of no consequence.

The study of the Scriptures that started early in his Christian experience was a continuous exercise throughout his life, and this caused him to amass a large number of books, and it was obvious that the books in his library were well used. Upon examination of them it was found that only a very few had no underlining or comments amongst the text.

The knowledge that he aquired was also used in the written word. From the late 1940s his articles started to appear in different Christian magazines that were circulating amongst the assemblies, such as 'The Witness', 'The Harvester', 'The Believer's Magazine. He also worked in co-operation with other brethren contributing to publications such as Precious Seed 'Day by Day through the New Testament', 'Day by Day through the Old Testament', and 'Day by Day in the Psalms'.

Retirement really opened up the opportunity to go full time into the Lord's work more than ever before, taking series of ministry meetings all over the country for periods of one or two weeks at a time. His ability in the ministry of God's Word and being available and becoming known in wider circles caused his diary to be loaded quite heavily. By this time he had a car, so train times didn't bother him. However after a good number of years in full-time service, in the early 1990s his wife's health began to deteriorate after she fell and broke her wrist. Then, due to illness, she spent a number of periods in hospital which made it difficult for Sydney to accept engagements and some of his appointments had to be cancelled at short notice. However also during this time Sydney himself took ill, with periods in hospital, and then his work for the Lord down here finished altogether. He passed into the presence of the Lord on 13th May 1995, and before his wife.

The Lord used Sydney Emery's gift of ministry for the purpose of encouraging and teaching saints all over this country and across the seas. The writer has heard from the lips of many of the saints in many parts, an appreciation of the written ministry of our brother, two extracts of which follow.

The Place and Importance of Doctrine

(1 Tim 3.15) "Does the behaviour matter in the assembly? To this end 1 Timothy was written. The assembly is the house of God, not a place where licence may be labelled liberty, and activity is regulated by the God of the house. Bethel must ever be viewed in the light of El-Bethel. Laxity and carelessness in assembly life to-day is largely due to insufficient teaching and conviction about New Testament doctrine relative to the subject and the epistle which calls for assembly behaviour directs us to give heed to this teaching. Nothing but a correct understanding of the great principles regarding the presence of God, the Christian ministry, the authority of elders and so on will effect becoming decorum amongst the people of God."

"The Harvester", January 1950

Christian Baptism

(Matt 28.19-20) "As we carefully re-read these wisely chosen words of One who taught as never man taught, and bear in mind the many implications they present, what an important and essential thing we discover baptism to be...the owning of a new mastery, the beginning of a new relationship, the entering into a new association, and the commencement of a new life. Has the reader been baptised yet? Then shall we more diligently live, day by day, in the light of our baptism..."

"The Harvester" May 1951
John Fox, Manchester

Other Recollections

As Sydney left Workington to attend his first conference at the assembly meeting in the Werneth district of Oldham on that first Saturday in May 1946, little did he realise that on that day two long term relationships would have their beginnings.

The first of these occurred on his arrival at the conference, when he was introduced to the other invited speaker. On subsequent visits he would often refer to that moment when, he found himself looking at a somewhat plump, lame and dishevelled man who peered out from behind a pair of thickset spectacles. This was not the usual type of speaker he associated with assembly conferences, and he wondered just what type of conference he had come to. That was until he heard that brother speak, for the man he was listening to was Harry Bell from Jarrow, and from that time a firm and longlasting friendship was formed.

The second relationship was with the assembly itself, for such was the appreciation of Sydney's ministry that for the next 38 years he made on average one visit each year. This was no mean feat especially in those early post war years. Travelling by train would involve arriving back in Carlisle in the early hours of Monday morning, having to sit and wait for several hours on a cold and dimly lit station platform until the first train to Workington arrived, before doing a full day's work. This however was typical of his sacrificial service for his Lord.

Over the many years of close fellowship with Sydney, we saw at first hand the cost of maintaining a full-time job by day, studying his Bible in the evenings and ministering God's Word at the weekends. He also suffered from progressive loss of control of his right hand, and had the additional stress of retraining his left hand to take over. Lesser men would have heeded their doctor's advice and rested, but our dear brother knew where his priorities lay. He was a faithful and much used servant for his Lord.

Alan Ramsbottom, Oldham

Sydney Emery came to Brierfield in the early years of the formation of the assembly, and his ministry was a tremendous help to the believers. He was often one of the speakers at our annual conference, for he loved ministering the Word of God and preaching the gospel. Regularly he spoke at one of our Saturday night ministry meetings and would stay over for the Lord's Day. After preaching the gospel he would visit the home of Mrs Doris Fryer, and with other believers from the assembly talk about the Scriptures.

Our brother Walter Miller had a fish and chip shop which involved him working very late, so for him it was usual to go to bed in the early hours of the next day. Walter would stay late at Mrs Fryer's when the rest had gone home, and as he was the only brother in the assembly with a car he would transport Sydney to Preston to catch his train home to Workington. Sydney arrived home early next morning with just enough time for a wash, something to eat, and then go straight to work, foregoing a night's sleep so he could help young believers grow in the things of God.

Fred Parr, Brierfield

It was while serving in the army (Non Combatant Corps) and stationed for three years at Carlisle that I first met Sydney. It was our practice to travel to Workington to the Saturday evening rallies in the Gospel Hall when off duty, where, of course, we met Sydney. Although he registered as a Conscientious Objector like ourselves, his work in the local steelworks meant that he was not called to serve in the forces. He said to me on one occasion when he had met the number of believers in our company (50-60 or more) and saw the fellowship among us, that he half wished that he had not been exempted.

It was after the war that I had the privilege of sharing with him at numerous conferences. He was a gracious man, easy to work with, and a great encouragement to me. I appreciated the quality of his ministry; he was a Bible student. His written ministry will continue to be a blessing to the Lord's people.

Jack Kirkham, Bromborough

After Sydney's call to be with Christ I was allowed to take custody of his notebooks. From his large book collection my special choice was a well-marked, extensively used Bible exposition with much underlining, comments of approval, corrections, and some question marks. He was a real student of the Word, expounding and teaching the truth with a sincerity for which he will be greatly missed. Many young ones regarded him as a father-figure, and experienced a special friendship as I did. My most poignant and endearing memories of him were his unashamed emotion and tears when my wife and I left his assembly to support the much smaller assembly in Moss Bay, and my final visit to his bedside a few hours before he died as he waited patiently for his call to glory. Being asked to take the thanksgiving service prior to his burial, was an honour and a unexpected privilege.

Geoff Scott, Carlisle

Sydney Emery

Stan Ford

1920 - 1991

*"This is a faithful saying, and worthy of all acceptation,
that Christ Jesus came into the world
to save sinners; of whom I am chief."*
(1 Timothy 1.15)

My contact with this "man of God" began in 1945. During that year the late HP Barker of the West Indies told me that a young missionary from the West Indies named Bill Paterson from Tillicoultry, was home on furlough and was being wonderfully blessed of God, souls being saved every time he preached the gospel. At that time, I was the secretary of the assembly at Ebenezer Gospel Hall, Gorse Road, Swansea and brother Paterson was invited to give a report on the Lord's work in Jamaica. The elders were so impressed and felt he was blessed with the gift of an evangelist that they invited him to come to Swansea for a week of gospel meetings. God used Bill Paterson in a remarkable way for in seven to eight days forty seven precious souls were saved, many of them scholars from our Sunday School. Bill Paterson and I became close friends and I kept in contact with him while he was on furlough.

One day he phoned and said he was coming to see me in Swansea and stay the night. He came with a real burden for souls in the city and asked me if I would be prepared to have a gospel campaign and take over a large church for two to three weeks. This I was very happy to do and we had the use of the largest Baptist Church in Swansea for three weeks in March 1946. Bill Paterson had also heard about Stan Ford, a converted boxer whom God was using.

In December 1945 Stan Ford was taking meetings over the Christmas holidays in a little assembly in the mining village of Pengroen near Ammanford in South Wales. I arranged to take a coach party from our assembly to hear this young preacher. When we arrived the little hall was packed. Some benches were placed down the aisle to accommodate some of our party, others stood and I managed to get onto the steps of the platform. There stood this young heavy-weight boxer (18 stones and over 6ft tall) and alongside a little 5ft 6ins man about 12 stones. What a comparison! The hall was overflowing and crowds were outside hoping to hear the young preacher. Suddenly a voice from the back shouted, "Would you like to hold the meeting in our church?" So all moved along to the other building. That night Stan Ford gave a moving testimony of how he came to know the Lord and I was thrilled. I invited him to come and speak at a New Year's Eve service in Swansea and he came, giving a tremendous gospel message on John 3.16.

Arrangements were now well in hand for a three weeks' gospel campaign in Mount Pleasant Chapel, Swansea in March 1946. Bill Paterson asked me to invite Stan Ford to join with him. He was actually booked for a gospel campaign at Thornhill outside Cardiff but the brethren there agreed to allow him to serve in the Swansea effort. At the first meeting eleven souls were saved. News came that Bill Paterson had to return to the West Indies, leaving Stan Ford to carry on with the rest of the meetings on his own. Night after night the building was packed and during the three weeks more than one hundred made professions of faith.

Following these meetings Stan Ford had a burden for Swansea and asked if I would be prepared to organise another effort in a tent. We obtained permission for a month in June 1946. Here again God took up Mr Ford and these meetings were well attended. On the last night of the campaign the Mayor and Mayoress and the town councillors were invited to the tent. The title of the campaign was "Christ for Victory", a slogan that was advertised all over the city. Visits were made to prisons and many canteens were available for us to go at lunch times and preach to the workers. Whilst we knew of hundreds being saved in the meetings, over the years that followed, we have met many whom we didn't know about who were thrilled to tell us they were saved at the "Christ for Victory" meetings.

His own story leading to his conversion is very interesting. He tells of an incident, prior to his conversion, when he was in a public house in Bournemouth. A young lass from the Salvation Army came in selling the "War Cry". With bravado he offered to buy all the magazines she had if she would stand up and sing. Well she agreed, he lifted her up on the counter, "chaired" the meeting, and asked all the men to keep quiet while she sang. I believe it was "The old rugged cross". That may have been the beginning of things. Some time later, a young lady stopped him on the street and invited him to a gospel service being held nearby and conducted by Mr Victor Cirel of Cardiff, a fine, stately gentleman with a message from God. One evening Stan Ford and a few other young men decided to attend a meeting in the tent, with the intention of causing a lot of trouble. But God's servant was able to preach the message unhindered. At the end of the meeting Mr Ford went to have a chat with the preacher, asking him, "You didn't believe that rubbish that you were speaking about did you?" Mr Cirel invited him to sit down and fire his questions, and after answering them Mr Cirel said, "Now young man, you have asked me many questions, I will ask you one." "What have you got against Jesus Christ?" For an hour or two Mr Cirel explained the gospel and eventually led him to Christ. It was very late and he felt he had better take Stan home and explain to his mother why he was so late. He said to Stan's mother, "I will come and see him in the morning". Next morning, he called and he was told Stan was in the garden. To his amazement he saw his convert training in a boxing ring rigged up in his garden. Mr Cirel just wondered however this young man would grow as a Christian mixed up in boxing. But surely God had his eye on Stan Ford for a special service. I should mention that the young lady who invited him to the tent meetings later became his wife.

There are several incidents Stan Ford told me that happened after his conversion. He was in Greyfriars for a boxing match, sitting in his dressing room reading the Bible, while waiting to be examined by the doctor. The doctor came along and saw him reading. "What book are you reading?" asked the doctor, "It's the Bible, doctor," said Stan. "Well I didn't know that boxers and the Bible go together." "It makes them go, Sir," replied Stan. One morning sitting on a seat in a park in Bournemouth, he was reading in 1 Timothy 3.2-3 that, "a bishop then must be...no striker". That was another arrow into his heart. After he gave up boxing he was unemployed and seated in his usual park he asked the Lord to find him employment. An old friend passed by, saw him and asked him if he was looking for work. With eagerness, Stan was up, and "Yes I am! Where is it?" His friend took him to a field to dig potatoes – but it was a job. He was beginning to prove the faithfulness of the God, under whose wings he had come to trust.

After his conversion he joined Mr Cirel in a boys' camp to assist a chaplain to the camp. He had not finished with boxing at this time and was due to go to London for a match on the Tuesday. On the Monday evening his friend reminded him, "You are going to London tomorrow, Stan, so come into my tent to see me before you go." This he did. Mr Cirel said, "Let us just have a word of prayer." So our dear brother began to pray, saying something like this, "Lord, dear Stan is going up to London to a boxing match. Give him a safe journey, Lord, and when he gets into the boxing ring, give him power in his hand." Stan opened his eyes in amazement and looked through his fingers as Mr Cirel prayed for Stan to knock his man out. When he finished praying, Stan asked, "Is it right for you to pray to God like that for me?" "Stan if you are doing anything you can't pray about – give it up," was the reply. That I think was what finally brought his boxing career to a close. Someone said to me that he gave up £30,000 a year, but he gave it all up for Christ and rested on the word, "For to me to live is Christ".

There is no doubt God raised up Stan Ford as a man with the "message" for the day. For years he conducted children's meetings on the sand at Hoylake. His contact with his friend, the late Mr Dick Wright of Liverpool, led him to tent campaigns and other meetings in this area. His name is a household name in south west Wales and particularly in Swansea. Not only was he a great evangelist, but he was also accepted as a good teacher and minister of the Word of God benefitting by help from Dr David Gooding.

There are many in heaven today through the faithful preaching of our beloved brother and still more on earth who are waiting for the home call. They put their faith in the sacrificial death of the Lord Jesus Christ on Calvary's cross, having listened to the simple, sincere, clear message of the gospel preached by an ex heavy-weight boxer, redeemed by the precious blood of Christ. Stan Ford travelled the world preaching the grand old story of the Saviour. He visited over 30 countries. He was a regular visitor to Cambridge University where the Lord blessed his ministry. A brother once asked me however could Stan Ford get in to preach to the students in Cambridge? I said it is the Lord's doing and it is marvellous in our eyes.

A wonderful friendship began in December 1945 which lasted for 46 years, until the Lord called him home suddenly on 9th March 1991 at 8.30pm at 71 years of age. My friendship with his dear wife Mary, his children, Stephen, Janet and the grandchildren continues. I thank God for the privilege of knowing them all. It was my privilege with Colin Payne and John Lennox (who was saved under Stan in Cambridge) to share in his funeral service at Charminster Gospel Hall in Bournemouth.

I have lost a faithful friend and brother in Christ and thank God for the privilege of knowing him.

Wilfred Beale, Swansea

Other Recollections

During the 1960s, when Stan was conducting some special services at Roseford Chapel, Cambridge, he was invited to come and address some lunchtime meetings of the Christian Union in Trinity College. I was a first year theology undergraduate at the time, and can still remember clearly the enormous impact that the integrity of his preaching had on us all. From those beginnings, there developed a close relationship with a number of the students, and in the summer vacations we used to go and help him in the tent missions which he was then pioneering in West Cornwall. I think it is fair to say that he and I were surprised to find an especially close affinity, and so it was that having graduated I asked, and he agreed, that I should work with him for the next year or so. We travelled the country extensively during 1969-70, and he introduced me to some of the techniques of his preaching style, both to adults and (unforgettably) to children, which have stayed with me to this day.

Hugh Williamson, Southwold

In 1964 our brother Stan arrived at our farm near Truro, Cornwall, and announced that the Lord had laid it on his heart to come to Truro and hold a tent campaign for 3 weeks. He put his tent in the Truro Football Club field, and we had fellowship with him in this work. The nearest assembly at that time, was at Market Hall, Newquay.

The meetings in the tent were well attended and God blessed. The following year our brother Stan returned for another 3 weeks with some undergraduates from Cambridge, and they camped on our land. The fellowship was great. Beside the campaign at Truro, the surrounding villages were also reached and the tent was greatly used for the preaching of the Gospel of Christ.

There were now nine saints living in the district, meeting together for prayer and Bible study in our homes. During the third campaign we told Stan that the Lord was telling us to commence a local church to remember the Lord Jesus Christ in the breaking of bread, and to meet at Truro in His Name and for His glory.

Our dear brother Stan took us aside and made it very clear that we were to be quite sure that this was of the Lord, and that it was His will! Our brother was always straight and clear, and told us this exercise of hearts must be of the Lord, and our own exercise being the local brethren. The assembly at Truro commenced in 1967, and we broke bread in the Women's Institute Hall with our dear brother Stan and some other visiting brothers and sisters. We continue as an assembly to this day to the glory of God.

Colin Westaway, Par, Cornwall

Our earliest experience of Stan Ford was when Nora (my wife) was saved, as a teenager, through his preaching when she was on a visit to Liverpool in September 1946. On that occasion Stan was holding meetings in a public arena and his platform was a boxing ring! When she heard him proclaim the gospel, with particular emphasis on the love of God for a sinful world, she simply trusted Christ as her Saviour.

After we were married, we arranged an annual Bible-study weekend at our home in Cumbria. Stan Ford was the speaker at one of the first of those weekends, and following the Saturday evening service, to our great delight, our daughter, Anne, then thirteen years of age, was saved.

In 1986 we moved to our present home, and on Saturday 21st June we held a 'house-warming party'. We opened our bungalow to about one hundred and twenty of our friends and new neighbours. As Stan had been so much a part of our lives for the previous forty years, we asked him to address the company. Our lasting memory is of him speaking from Galatians 2.20. Hearts were touched that day as he spoke, with genuine feeling, of 'the Son of God, who loved me, and gave Himself for me'.

Eddie Stobart, Carlisle

Stan Ford was a man of intimidating appearance. With some trepidation we welcomed him to our house, but he immediately made himself at home. Over a period of some forty years, when in the area, he stayed with us. He would just walk in and up the stairs, saying as he went, "Same room, Mary?"

We had a rambling old farmhouse, which he enjoyed, and was always interested in the farming activities. If there was an axe and logs to chop he was in his element.

On one of his visits we had an elderly maiden aunt staying. When Uncle Stan (as he was known) came to lunch wearing a colourful shirt he said, 'What do you think of my shirt, Auntie?' 'A very nice shirt, Mr Ford, but not suitable for preaching in.' said Aunt. He was greatly amused and often referred to it.

On another occasion discussing various Bible translations, Harry Bedford, my father, said, 'Stan, I should throw that one in the bin.' 'Harry, I should take it out again,' was the reply!

Morley Bedford, Crediton

Stan Ford first came to Allerbridge for our Whit Monday Conference in about 1947/8. We then asked him for our Young People's Rally weekend in April 1951. This started a friendship that lasted right up to his home call. He would visit us over a weekend and stay four or five days into the week, with meetings for children and adults. His sense of humour was infectious, his singing was with much enthusiasm, although his timing did not always match ours! His ministry was always appreciated by local friends, and he would draw a crowd from over a wide area. We all experienced much blessing through his preaching.

In the early days he would use flannelgraph to illustrate his talks on men like Samuel, Jonah and Naboth. Also, he would give us up-to-date information of his visits around the world, including USA, the West Indies, and various parts of Africa, especially to Jim and Irene Legge in Botswana.

His preaching was of a very high standard, with series on Bible women, and other characters. On one of his last visits he spoke eloquently from John 13 and 14 – a table, a towel, a traitor, and a triumph. Eternity alone will reveal the tremendous help Mr Ford was to assemblies around the world.

Jeoff Burrows, Crediton

The children loved him and his stories. Even though his voice and size was very large and impressive, he came across as being tender and caring.

Stan never would say a bad word about a Christian brother or sister, nor would he listen to anyone else doing this – a most desirable quality.

I remember one particular meeting at Bethany Chapel in Augusta, Georgia, which was probably about 30 years ago. We had a visitor named Sal Ihba, an Italian living in the Ivory Coast. He was selling heavy construction equipment in Africa, and had come to us to discuss the purchase of some equipment of this type.

We invited him to the meetings at Bethany Chapel while he was in Augusta, and one night he went forward saying, 'There is a new Sal Ibha here tonight.' We were all very thankful at Sal's profession of faith.

Later, Sal sent his son, Juliano, to Augusta to work, improve his English, and get acquainted with the USA in general. While here, Juliano too professed to trust Christ as his Saviour.

John Smith, South Carolina

Stan Ford

They finished their course in the 90s

Gabriel B. Fyfe
1909 - 1999
"Hold fast the form of sound words, which thou hast heard of me, in faith and love which is in Christ Jesus."
(2 Timothy 1.13)

It is Friday evening and there are about fifteen to twenty of us, all in our teens and early twenties, scribbling as fast as we can in our notebooks while at the same time earnestly concentrating on the teacher before us. We are trying hard not to miss anything he says. His subject is summarised on the blackboard beside him in very neat and legible writing. We were here last week. We will make sure we are here in the 'crows nest' at the Grove Hall, Ealing next week. In fact we try never to miss these opportunities to listen to one of the most interesting, gracious, patient and friendly teachers we have ever known. He may be slight in stature but he is a giant of a man spiritually. To those of us who are young he is Mr Fyfe. To his own family and friends, 'Riel. But to many he is, and to those of us here he will become known affectionately as, 'GB'.

Gabriel Ballantyne Fyfe was born on 28th August 1909 into a Christian home and brought up in the nurture and admonition of the Lord. At school his great passion, like that of his brother Andrew, was playing cricket. He was in both the school team and a local one. Papers found after he died included detailed statistics on the results of these games showing runs scored, batting averages, boundaries etc and showed him at the top of the table. However all this was to change. While still teenagers he and his sister Margaret were approached and challenged by Alec Marshall, a Scottish evangelist, as they were leaving the gospel meeting at Elim Hall, Glasgow. After praying with them they were both gloriously saved. Very soon after he was baptised and received into fellowship. His great passion now was following the Lord who had saved him.

Under the godly guidance and encouragement of his Bible Class leader James Moffat, young 'Riel Fyfe spent all his spare time studying the Scriptures and attending Bible Readings. He quickly became engrossed in the Lord's work being active in the Sunday School and becoming secretary of the Bible Class magazine 'Knowing the Scriptures', which went all over the world with the object of building up young Christians. He was also involved in the annual Conference for Christian Youth attended by about 1000 each year and together with William Morrow started the Ayr Bible Readings.

GB's lifetime work of building up young men and women in a sound knowledge and understanding of the Scriptures commenced in those early years of his Christian life. Immediately after his marriage to Betty Proudfoot in 1938 he started a Bible study for young Christians each Friday night in their home when about thirty gathered for prayer and intensive study during the winter months.

As well as GB's personal work among the young, during the summer he was enthusiastic in tract band work visiting small villages. Open-air meetings were held at strategic points and gospel leaflets given to those in nearby homes and shops. Eventually he was responsible for a weekly open-air meeting in the centre of Glasgow where crowds thronged the busy street and listened intently to the gospel story. His keen interest in teaching God's Word was not confined to his local assembly but extended to meetings all over Great Britain. However when asked to go abroad for a series of engagements GB declined, feeling that there was so much to do in the homeland.

In 1941 he was posted to London, to a new sphere of service for which the Lord seemed to have been training him. His departure, with his wife Betty, was a great blow to their family and the saints in Glasgow. As the train left Glasgow Central, the platform was crowded with young people and the familiar hymn, "God be with you till we meet again" was sung with enthusiasm.

GB and his wife, Betty, were soon immersed once again in the Lord's service, meeting with the saints meeting at The Grove in Ealing. Their chosen home was within easy reach of the assembly and a local underground station with connections to all parts of London and the rest of the UK. These were essential factors in his local and wider service for the Lord, particularly as they never owned a car. For a short period GB did own a Vespa scooter and travelled all over London on it. However when another brother's greater need for transport became known it was given to him. GB laboured for the Lord in Ealing with zeal and enthusiasm for 56 years and served as an elder for over 50 of them caring for and encouraging the flock of God. During much of this time he also held a senior and responsible position in the civil service.

Like Daniel, daily set aside time to pray for the Lord's servants at home and abroad. His ability to prepare spiritual food for saints of all ages was clearly a gift he received from the Lord. He used this gift for God's glory and everything was done out of love for the Lord. His knowledge and understanding of the Scriptures came from many hours spent in the Lord's presence and with His Word. One brother remembers GB telling him that "the long journey on the Underground from Ealing to the office in Bethnal Green is spent in meditation on the Scriptures and when the train doors open at the destination it is like stepping into another world".

Upstairs, at the back of The Grove, was a room known as 'the crows nest'. It was there that GB held a Friday night Bible study class for young people from The Grove and elsewhere. They all received a solid grounding in the Scriptures, which has stood them in good stead throughout their lives – and some were saved at this class. There were no fancy methods, no gimmicks, no wasted time and no extras, just plain, clear, intensive study of the Word of God with a good balance between doctrine and practice. GB taught from practical experience and knowledge and was an authority on his subject. In his life he practised what he taught, he listened, he advised and corrected. His often declared motive was that each one "would gain, not just a head knowledge of the Scriptures, but an experimental knowledge of the Lord".

When encouraging young men in their public ministry, three key words he often used were brevity, clarity and sincerity. His own teaching style was an example of these principles and he always spoke ably using the richness of the English language, without the aid of notes and using only a very small Bible. Young people were constantly encouraged to "study to show thyself approved unto God, a workman that needeth not to be ashamed, rightly dividing the Word of Truth". He often commented that what was not learnt before the age of 40 would be a struggle to learn after that. The consistency of his teaching was remarkable. He never changed his doctrine or practice and was always able to substantiate his position from the Word of God. He was respected and loved by those he taught because he loved them and showed that love in many practical ways.

Often, having returned home late from a meeting, a young person would turn up at his home with a problem. He would always listen patiently, advise and pray with them. Nothing was too much trouble, he had time for anyone and everyone. He was approachable by all sorts – young and old, rich and poor, simple and sophisticated. Yet he was an outstanding example of self-effacement. At the least hint of praise he would become acutely embarrassed and endeavour to remove himself immediately from the spotlight.

While the Fyfes had no children of their own there are many that regard them as their spiritual parents. Their home was one of constant hospitality, laughter and fun. Many single young people who came to Ealing greatly valued the hospitality shown at 39 Byron Road. Indeed it was probably those who were younger in the 50s and 60s who best knew the other side of GB. It was the Bible Class parties at The Grove that revealed what fun the 'serious platform speaker' could be. He organised the games and made sure a good time was had by all.

GB was a great example in the matter of self-discipline. He was meticulous when it came to timekeeping always being early for meetings and never arriving at the last minute. While generally keeping good health he maintained the principle of 'keeping under' the body (1Cor 9.27). Two now older brethren remember going back to his house after a meeting on a cold winter's night and rather than walk the mile or so over Ealing Common expressed the desire to take the bus. GB's response? "Come on you chocolate soldiers what is wrong with you?"

Needless to say the two young men walked with him and have not forgotten the comment. Despite this self-discipline he would be tender with others and always made sure that his wife got a lift home in the bad weather. He was never known to get angry yet was never intimidated, always able to convince the gainsayers and with gentleness instructed those who opposed.

The Fyfes were always enthusiastic musicians and for many years Betty was the organist and pianist at The Grove. In his younger years GB was advised to stop his open-air preaching as it was ruining his singing voice. When faced with this choice the preaching took precedence. This enthusiasm for all things musical was passed on to the young people who were always encouraged to 'make a joyful noise unto the Lord' irrespective of the quality of the voice. During the Lord's Day evening hymn singing which he conducted after the gospel meeting, one of his favourites was, 'When the roll is called up yonder'. He taught the parts for this and it became known as 'The Grove Roll', sung lustily by all but none more enthusiastically than GB with great emphasis on the last lines 'I'll be there, I'll be there, I'll be there'.

In the early years of his time at Ealing, GB started monthly Bible Readings at The Grove. These were of great profit not only to the local saints but also to the many that came from further afield. His firm but loving control of these Bible Readings was of great benefit to all and he ensured that younger ones, perhaps overawed by some of those present, were able to make a contribution or ask a question.

GB was keen to encourage those with a developing gift for public speaking. A starting point for many was the open-air meeting held every Sunday evening on Ealing Green. His simple but effective method was to quietly come up behind a young man with the comment "you are on next". This was not a matter for discussion it was one of fact. Some still remember his advice when first asked to speak: "If you dry up give them some Scriptures and then get down." As always GB was the example to follow with his brief, clear and sincere declaration of the gospel message.

His firm example is still remembered by one of the young sisters who turned up on a snowy winter's morning for the

7.00am prayer meeting to find that no one had a key for the Hall. GB simply said, "Right, we will have our prayer meeting outside." So everyone stood in a circle in the snow and prayed.

In 1950 GB and the late James Scroggie commenced the Eastbourne Bible Readings, again out of a desire to teach young and old the truth of God's Word. The Readings started at Woodlands House Hotel, considering the book of Ephesians under the guidance of Harry Bell and A.J.Cricks. The format, which has been successfully used ever since, consisted of ministry of the Word from one of the two invited speakers who were there for the week, followed by open discussion morning and evening. As GB introduced the discussion period he would do so with his well known "we want animated and lively discussion, brethren". His firm authority, yet gracious manner, was sometimes required if a brother introduced legalistic views or ideas contrary to the Scriptures.

GB looked forward with eager anticipation to the annual Readings as did those who attended. The warm fellowship was a feature of the week. In this work Betty Fyfe was always hard at work among the young people, encouraging them to attend and ensuring that they had a 'fun week' as well as a time of spiritual profit and encouragement. GB's involvement as a founder convenor continued until ill health resulted in his retirement in 1990. However he remained a wise adviser till the end of his earthly pilgrimage.

In conjunction with the Eastbourne Bible Readings, GB was also involved in starting the annual London Convention which commenced in 1961 at the Friends' Meeting House and was then moved to Westminster Chapel. This was like an Eastbourne reunion with large numbers attending in the early years. In 1965, Young People's weekends were introduced at Hildenborough moving to Sunbury Court some years later and continuing until 1997. These weekends gave the opportunity, led by GB, for the young people to show their natural talents with recitations, solo singing, humorous sketches and even for bolder ones to imitate GB who enjoyed the fun.

In the midst of all this activity and a responsible job some long way from home, GB wrote many articles for magazines, contributed to commentaries, wrote a book on prophecy and travelled the country teaching and preaching. His earnest desire to serve the Lord resulted in him taking (what was unusual at that time) early retirement at the age of 60 and he was able to continue into his eighties when ill health took over. Throughout his busy life of service for the Lord GB's wife, Betty, was a practical and spiritual helpmeet and a tremendous support in all that he did. Their married life was one of partnership and a modern day equivalent of Aquilla and Priscilla 'always abounding in the work of the Lord' together. She was one to whom many young sisters went for help and advice. This they always received accompanied by much comfort and encouragement. When the Lord took her on 18th June 1984 this was a great loss to GB.

GB's concern for believers of all ages was evidenced when, in 1955, he and a number of other local brethren saw the need for suitable accommodation for elderly saints who had become unable to look after themselves. This resulted in the purchase of a large Victorian house in Ealing and its adaptation for this purpose. After much hard work Bethany Eventide Home was opened on 4th May 1957 with a full complement of 19 residents. He was a member of both the council, which had overall responsibility for the home, as well as the management committee to which was delegated the day to day running of the home. He was its chairman from 1979 until 1983.

GB had time for the residents as individuals also, caring for their physical as well as their spiritual needs. At the annual Christmas party he would bring his tape recorder, new technology at the time, so that the residents could recite a poem, tell a story or sing before tea and then have it played back after tea; a simple pleasure which brought much amusement and surprise to many. In 1987 the home had to be closed and sold as a result of new legislation but the proceeds from the sale went towards the building of a new one in Pamber Heath, Hampshire. This new home was opened in November 1992 and named after the old one – 'Bethany'.

During the 90s GB's health began to deteriorate quite seriously and his welfare became a matter of concern to many. Around 1995 GB was taken to view the new Bethany with the hope that he might be prepared to go there as a resident. His verdict on the way home was "it is a beautiful home but not for me!"

Eventually his health was so poor that he was unable to care for himself adequately, and with his eyesight almost gone he took up residence at Bethany in February 1997. From conversations with him we know that he was very happy there and appreciated all the love and care he received. It was from there that the Lord took him into His own presence on 28th November 1999. The Christ-like life he had lived since his conversion was obvious to all during his stay at Bethany.

Even in the last few weeks when he was too weak to communicate properly he would give the staff a little smile or gently squeeze their hand in appreciation of what they had done for him. Not only did the staff enjoy caring for him but they all, believer and unbeliever alike, genuinely loved him and shed real tears when he was taken from them.

Having throughout his life been well organised, and meticulous in matters of detail, GB left full instructions regarding his funeral arrangements. In them he says, "I desire that the grace of God be magnified and my blessed Saviour extolled." This was his constant ambition. The service of thanksgiving for his life commenced with, 'O for a thousand tongues to sing my great Redeemer's praise'.

GB Fyfe's spirit of humility would never have allowed him to say it himself, but the challenge of his life in particular to the young with whom he spent so much time is "Be ye followers of me even as I am of Christ".

Victor Michael, Maidenhead

Other Recollections

Gabriel Ballantyne Fyfe, or 'G.B.' as he was affectionately known, was characterised by three features

- A **G**iant in the Scriptures
- A **B**eloved brother in the Lord
- A **F**aithful servant of God

W Farquhar, Tayside

My earliest recollections of Mr Fyfe are as a small boy

listening to his preaching at the Gospel Hall where my parents were in fellowship. The message given was always plain so that even a child was able to understand the way of salvation.

Over the years that followed, he showed an interest in my spiritual development. On several occasions when I drove him to the station to get his train back home, his conversation was characterised by his being 'apt to teach', imparting short but useful words of exhortation and instruction.

He exemplified the interest of 'the elder' of 2 & 3 John, and found great joy in seeing his 'children walk in truth'. Immense help was given to me and many others in conferences and gatherings such as the London Convention, Sunbury Court weekends, and the Eastborne Bible Readings. In later years I became involved with him in convening these meetings, where his spiritual wisdom was much appreciated. His love for the saints, especially those young in the faith, ever characterised his service for the Lord.

Reg Carnall, Dorset

Many Bible students will particularly remember Riel Fyfe, or "GB", as he was affectionately known, for the Friday night Bible studies held at The Grove in Ealing.

Our brother had a concern for the consecutive teaching of the Word of God particularly to young people. Generations of the now not so young can look back and thank God for the occasions when they were able to comment on and discuss the Scriptures at those meetings. Riel had a particular interest in prophecy and the typology of the tabernacle. Periodically a model of the tabernacle would be carried by the appropriate parties and constructed as a practical demonstration to the Biblical truths expounded by our brother.

Jim Bustard, Ealing

The main association I had with him was in relation to the young people's weekends at Sunbury Court. He invited me to take five of the six sessions; he always took the final prophetical one himself as it allowed us to get away early and return home. The subjects for these occasions were always very varied and demanding. We often smiled at the way in which they were phrased as this revealed the very careful and meticulous mind he had when identifying and distinguishing spiritual matters. Examples of this are, 'Man's Tripartite Constitution - the relative functions of spirit, soul and body'; and, 'Does it matter much with what group of Christians we gather?'; and 'Are marriages made in Heaven?'.

There was always the right balance between the practical and the doctrinal. I benefited constantly from his clarification of things that differ and by his constant encouragement to develop my own personal style of ministry and way of delivery. Once, a young brother asked me to distinguish between the body, the flesh and the vessel. Taken suddenly by the question of the distinctions he required, I confessed that I didn't have a clue but Mr Fyfe would tell us. Without batting an eyelid he stood up and gave us five minutes on each with references to back it up!

Ken Rudge, St Austell

G B Fyfe grasped every opportunity, with his characteristic enthusiasm, to preach the gospel and teach the Word of God. Back in the early 60s a temporary gap appeared in ranks of the Sunday school teachers at The Grove assembly in Ealing. GB more than filled the gap, taking the role of Sunday school superintendent. As expected the singing took on a new vitality and both teachers and students were caught up in his infectious enthusiasm.

Tony Houghton, Hastings

Our late brother with his dear wife, Betty were involved sending relief parcels to Hamburg, Germany, just after the end of World War II. We had the privilege of seeing the joy in the faces of those who received these parcels. This demonstrated how the love of God constrained them to show such compassion and kindness to the saints in need.

As a fellow elder, Reil gave sound spiritual advice on oversight matters, and was loved and revered by the flock as a true shepherd.

As a result of Reil's rapidly deteriorating eyesight in his latter years, he attended Moorfields Eye Hospital, London. On one of these occasions, while waiting to be seen by a specialist, Reil spoke about the Judgement Seat of Christ, and said it was by our faithfulness to the Word of God that we show our allegiance and obedience to Christ, 'He that loveth Me, keepeth My commandments.'

Kurt W Jappe, Hanworth

He introduced to The Grove many outstanding teachers; he valued highly the gifts of other servants and used them for the blessing of all the saints. Jealousy was not a word in his vocabulary. 'Serving the Lord with all humility' was his sole aim in life.

His organisational capacity was remarkable; his zeal and energy never flagged. Those who worked with him speak of his consideration for their viewpoint, 'without thy mind I would do nothing' wrote Paul to Philemon, and such characterised him also. His extensive vocabulary, his knowledge of, and facility with the English language were hallmarks of his teaching. He enjoyed singing, and at his funeral service, so impressed were the undertaker's assistants that they joined in singing the rousing hymns our brother had chosen. Even in death he left an indelible mark.

Trevor Smith, Northampton

They finished their course in the 90s

Jack Gamble
1925 - 1994
"Addicted...to the ministry of the saints"
(1 Corinthians 16.15)

Jack Gamble's father came from farming stock in the north of Ireland. Between seasons he would travel to Scotland to join his uncles who were stevedores at the Glasgow docks. On one of these trips he was saved as he heard the gospel in a mission hall, following which he sold his farm and moved to Glasgow. Working at the docks he met believers who gathered with the assembly which had been meeting at 41 Craigiehall Street since February 1915. On days when no work was available for the dockers they would hold Bible Readings in the Gospel Hall, and through these contacts his father was taught truth which led to him being received into assembly fellowship.

Jack was born in Glasgow on 1st December 1925, the third of a family of five. He was a brought up in that area of the city where he would spend his life and it could truly be said of him that he was a Glasgow man. At a young age, like many teenage boys in the Ibrox area of Glasgow, he loved football and became an ardent Rangers supporter. Unknown to his parents he would slip away to Ibrox Park at the interval of the New Year's Day conference, hoping that his absence would not be noticed, to watch Rangers play Celtic

It was while playing snooker in the local billiards hall that God spoke loudly to him and convicted him of the need of salvation. Arriving home late in the evening, his father would often say to him, "Give an account of yourself!" On this occasion Jack said, "Dad, I want to be saved." He then confessed his sin and trusted the Saviour. Although only fourteen years of age, he was baptised and received into assembly fellowship in April 1940. By this time the assembly meeting place had moved, from Craigiehall Street to 33 Plantation Street. Later in 1970 a further move would be made to a new hall built in Harley Street. Up until a few years before his home-call he was in fellowship in this one assembly.

On leaving school at fourteen he started work as an office boy at Rolls Royce, the aero engine manufacturer, based in nearby Hillington. This led to an apprenticeship as a maintenance engineer. With the exception of his national service spent in the Royal Air Force, he remained with Rolls Royce, eventually rising through management until he became Plant Manager for the Group. Even then he was still referred to affectionately as "Big John". He maintained a strong Christian testimony throughout his working life. In times of industrial unrest, directors often complimented him on the smooth running of his department and asked, "How do you do it?" His reply was, "I still take time to walk through the workshops and speak to the men." He never failed to remember the days when he worked on the tools and he always had a genuine interest in those who worked with him and under his management.

In 1950 he married Joanne Wood from his home assembly, who had been baptised on the same evening as Jack. She remained his constant companion and staunch spiritual supporter throughout their married life and they had the great joy of raising their four children and seeing them all saved. The Gamble family, Jack with his brothers Frank and Bert and sister Ann, became well known throughout the assemblies in Scotland. He also had very close ties with his sister Nellie in Northern Ireland and many happy times were spent at the farm in Co. Antrim where his roots lay.

In the early days Jack Gamble's efforts were poured into the assembly at Plantation Street and it was the centre of his spiritual interest as he bore the burden of responsibility from an early age. Saturday night ministry meetings are common in Scotland today, but in the fifties, despite many assemblies arranging annual conferences, there were only a few Saturday evening meetings. Plantation Street had a regular Saturday night meeting and the proximity of the hall to the centre of Glasgow and public transport made it the ideal location for many to reach. The annual conference gathering held over the

New Year period was for hundreds, an occasion which could not be missed. They came from far beyond Glasgow with buses being run from many parts of Scotland and others travelling from the north of Ireland. Any who attended remember Jack as one of the prime figures at these meetings. Along with others he was busy, sometimes in the background, sometimes on the platform, but always active and concerned that all was going well. To an outside observer he seemed to be everywhere! Jack's guidance and support were evident year by year as he welcomed the believers on these happy yet holy occasions. Memories remain of hundreds being hushed to silence as the Word of God was expounded; of rousing exhortation and encouragement; of hymns being sung with a passion and fervour which added lustre to the gatherings. Crowded Bible Readings and ministry sessions were to be expected and those who did not come early would find themselves sitting on window ledges or round the platform at the speakers' feet. As a result the impact of these conferences was felt far beyond the local area and was a great influence for good in the Scottish assemblies.

Jack took an active interest in the work and problems of many who were serving in foreign lands. His contacts by telephone and letter made him a mine of information regarding the Lord's people world-wide. Rarely when asked about missionaries was he unable to give some information. He had an acute perception of conditions in many parts of the world. The writer well recalls asking him about a missionary who was little known, and receiving a five minute survey of this brother's work, the problems facing him at the moment, and an outline of the other assembly work in the country. It showed an impressive grasp of current conditions.

On the platform, Jack could appear to be an austere figure. He was large of stature and this, combined with his commanding manner, gave this impression to some. It also led to him (and his brothers) being mistaken for policemen! On getting to know him better, however, it became clear that he was a warm man with a big and sympathetic heart, quick to offer a word of encouragement to the young and to those who were going through difficult times. He was not taken in by insincerity but was quick to see spiritual potential in young believers which may not have been obvious to others. Many Christians, old and young, found him to be a trusted confidant and sought him out often for help and guidance in the problems of life.

He was a man of integrity who loved the Lord, His people and the Scriptures. The truth of the local assembly was dear to his heart and he revelled in speaking of these matters, hearing them ministered and in putting them into practice. He was also a sensitive man who felt things keenly but was never slow to see the humorous side of life. Often he would recount hilarious personal incidents both from work and assembly life.

Over the years many believers from around the world came to Jack and Joanne's house, and Bert and Isobel's next door, where they found hospitality and friendship. It was not unknown for the family to come home and find that unexpected guests were occupying their beds. Little value was placed on material things. Jack would often say, "Life is about folk, not things." He and Joanne used what they had for the good of others.

He found great friendship with believers from the North East of Scotland. In earlier years Gardenstown was a favourite holiday destination for the family, and happy times were spent with Chrissie Murray, known to many for her unique wisdom and warm heart. She and her husband, Johnny, did much to help the Lord's people. She referred to Jack and another two preachers, Jimmy Paton and Robert McPheat, as "The Three Hebrew Children".

Shepherding a local church and organising large gatherings is an invaluable service, but Jack's gifts extended further. On the platform he could preach the gospel and minister the Word of God with power. He spoke in a way which conveyed spiritual truth in easily understood language. No one could come away saying that the preaching had been "too deep" and yet the deep truths of God had been preached and expounded. No doubt the combination of Ulster blood with Glasgow roots helped! He often preached throughout the province of Ulster and attended the Lurgan conference for many years. Later he travelled extensively, to the Far East and North America. Trips were made to Malaysia, Hong Kong and Japan where his ministry was much appreciated. He well remembered on old brother in Japan listening to him and declaring with tears in his eyes, "He just thinks the way I do," amazed that a man from so far away could believe what he believed.

On taking early retirement from Rolls Royce, Jack was appointed a director of John Ritchie Ltd and a Trustee of the Lord's Work Trust. The fervour for which he was known was now turned to this new field of service. Although the Christian book trade and publishing were new lines of business for him he gave himself to them and proved of invaluable help to the work of John Ritchie Ltd. In the deliberations of the Lord's Work Trust his missionary knowledge was of great help. He made full use of the opportunities which this new service provided, never displaying a "party" spirit, and was able to develop his contacts on a world-wide basis .

In these later years, despite continuing health problems, Jack's participation in the work of the Lord did not diminish. Visiting him in hospital was an opportunity to learn from him of the background of others in the ward and of how they stood in relation to the gospel. These were not wasted days as he used the time to bring the gospel to his fellow patients. From his hospital bed he encouraged a brother to became an active tract writer. Even in illness he was thinking of the future and visitors left his bedside feeling added urgency to continue in the gospel.

For the last five years of his life Jack was in fellowship in the assembly which meets at Bethesda Hall, Linthouse, Glasgow, where his interest in the spread of the glad tidings was unabated. Even when it was clear that his strength was not what it once was, he accompanied evangelists going from door to door. He was a man who could relate to people and establish contacts with the most unlikely souls. Whether it was in areas of severe social deprivation or where material prosperity was enjoyed, he found no difficulty in speaking to the people. He was acutely aware of the changes which were taking place in society within the UK and the effect which these would have on the preaching of the gospel. He was not afraid to face up to the issues and recognise when changes of approach were necessary while still jealously guarding the scriptural principles of assembly testimony.

At length his health problems necessitated a heart by-pass operation. As he awaited the operation he was still looking ahead and concerned about the current issues affecting the testimony. He never regained consciousness after major surgery, and passed into the presence of the Lord on 4th May 1994. His passing left a great void in the family, in the assembly and in the greater family of believers in Scotland and beyond. It could truly be said of him, "The memory of the just is blessed."

John Grant, Bridge of Weir

Other Recollections

Their home was my "home away from home" for many years when I had to stay overnight in Glasgow during my frequent trips from Northern Ireland. Jack and I became close companions. Many nights were spent lying in front of a good fire discussing the scriptures and learning many things of everyday life. His advice and help to me was priceless. A big man with a warm heart is how I often describe him. One of the things Jack taught me as a young Christian was about giving time and money to the work of the Lord. This was something that I knew he lived for.

David McNeill, Ballyclare

When calling on the Rolls Royce Company at Hillington, Jack introduced me to the firm's Purchasing Officer. This man had the highest regard for Jack and respected him for his Christian principles, although he himself had no spiritual interest. I did business with that individual over many years and after Jack's death he would often ask after the welfare of Mrs Gamble and the family. Scripture says "do good unto all men especially to those who are of the household of faith", and in my experience Jack Gamble did just that.

Jim Harrison, Hamilton

Waiting on the coach to take us on our annual assembly outing, a local man who had been attending some of our gospel meetings said to me, "See that big man over there? He gave me a tenner and told me to buy myself some ice cream when we got to Rothesay! I don't even know him and yet he gave me this money! I'll have to give him back his change!" "Listen," I said, "I know Jack. He does things like that. That £10 is all yours. Put it in your pocket!"

I knew Jack Gamble from early childhood. Both of us grew up in humble circumstances in the dock area of Plantation, Glasgow, and both of us were saved as schoolboys. Years later he baptised my wife, Wilma, and me on the same evening, an occasion of great joy to him.

Sam Laughlin, Glasgow

Jack and Joanne were coming to a Baptismal Meeting at Plains but failed to appear before it started. They did however arrive late. At the end I said, "What happened, Jack, did you go off the road?" "Well, not exactly," he replied, "but my car is down the road wrapped around a lamppost - but no one's hurt" "Did you report it?" I asked. "I had no time, I did not want to miss the meeting! I just asked a passing motorist to take me to the Gospel Hall," he said. He always had his priorities right.

Jim Paterson, Plains

Many meetings and conferences shared over a period of almost thirty years only enhanced my appreciation of Jack's ability. It was a real joy to sit at his feet. A deep knowledge of the Word, a love for the Saviour and a caring shepherd heart for the saints lent a special warmth to him. His assembly convictions and a concern for divine truth made him a veritable tower of strength. In doubt or difficulty, I knew I could bring the burden to him - a courteous hearing always led to wise and balanced advice.

An able preacher and a wise counsellor, yet the memory that overshadows all is the picture of our brother in his favourite corner chair in his own home, with his big Bible open on his knee. Wife and family present, he would sit with friends from all over the globe. Question and answer, debate and discussion would range widely, but would all contribute to an increased delight in the Word of the Lord.

Jim Allen, Newtown Abbey

The natural warmth and friendliness which lay just beneath a somewhat austere public image, enabled Jack to get on well with all kinds of people. In true humility and with no sense of show he realised that all he was and had in every aspect of life came from the Lord. A keen student of the scriptures, he applied himself with dedication to the text of the Word of God. He encouraged younger men to read scripture itself before reading books about it. His skill in handling scripture was especially seen in the assembly Bible Reading. He could explain clearly passages of scripture but never failed to draw profit from the comments of others. He was adept at drawing together all the contributions. With diplomacy and often with a touch of humour he could smooth over any personal difficulties which arose in the discussion.

Alan Gamble, Glasgow

The assessment of Abraham by the Sons of Heth (Gen 23.6) is readily applicable to our brother. He constantly exhibited a grace and a gentleness commensurate with "a Prince of God". His Deportment was Acknowledged in his secular calling by all who dealt with him. His Dwelling was Acquainted (Job 21.28), for many found 72 Gower Street a haven of relief. His Dependability was Affirmed (Prov 17.7), enhanced by moral rectitude, as saints sought his godly counsel.

In a rich sphere of service that reached throughout the British Isles and to many countries beyond, all who heard him knew that as a Prince his Dynamic was Accredited (Gen 32.28). We cannot rightly value his work, his word, his walk or even his worship, yet we are assured that, weighed in the balances of the sanctuary, his Deeds will be Assessed and Awarded.

Thomas Bentley, Malaysia

There would be no one you would rather have with you in a fix than Jack. He was the most versatile of men. Whether motoring, domestic, illness, unemployment, bereavement he was available for advice or practical help, a friend in fair weather or foul. Although always busy, he would be among the first at your hospital bedside, his presence a morale booster. It was characteristic of him that he drove himself to hospital from the Breaking of Bread at which he contributed on the Lord's Day before his heart operation.

Jim McLatchie, Barrhead

106

Jack Gamble

Walter R. Gammon

1919 - 1995

*"Let nothing be done through strife or vainglory;
but in lowliness of mind let each esteem other
better than themselves. Let this mind be in you,
which was also in Christ Jesus."*
(Philippians 2.3,5)

I first had contact with Walter Gammon at Capango Mission Station, on the high central plateau of Angola, when he and his four brothers and their older sister, with their remarkable American mother and their English father came to visit their aunt Miss Annie Gammon. Walter, the third oldest of the six children (Joy, David, Walter, Theo, Alan and Philip), was around twelve at the time, while the writer must have been about nine. I remember being impressed by the tree-climbing abilities of the two oldest brothers (David and Walter), as there were some very tall fir and eucalyptus trees at Capango! A rather similar impression was made years later by Walter's skill at hunting in the African bush or on the broad plains. He was a person naturally endowed with quiet, resolute courage and practical ability of all kinds, but with no pretentiousness.

Born in 1919 in the Chokwe area of that Portuguese colony (as it then was) of missionary parents, Walter, along with most of his brothers and their sister, was to become a second generation missionary. (Sadly David died in his early twenties.) Their father Leonard was one of a family of whom four became missionaries in West Central Africa, having gone out from north Devon. The first of the four had died through a lightning strike within two years of arrival in Africa. Mrs Lillian Gammon, Walter's mother also came from a godly family whose forbears had emigrated from England early in the 1800s and who also had a keen missionary interest. It is not surprising, therefore, that Walter's thoughts turned in the same direction as he grew up.

But before that he needed God's forgiveness and saving grace in his own life. He was about six when his mother left him at home for her youngest son's birth. Then he became acutely aware of his need of salvation in order to be sure of meeting his loved ones in heaven. Young as he was, he repented of his sin and trusted the Lord Jesus as his Saviour.

Walter's schooling, along with that of his sister and brothers, was partly on the mission station where they mainly grew up, partly at Sakeji School in Northern Rhodesia (now Zambia), and briefly in Exeter in England. The "schooling" on the mission station was administered by a lady from the UK commissioned for the purpose. It may be of interest to some readers that Walter was a playmate and fellow pupil of the now well known Dr. Stephen Olford on that mission station in those days.

As Walter's faith and love for the Lord deepened, so did his exercise for the needs of the people of the land in which he had mainly grown up. The Lord was preparing him to serve where he was undoubtedly most at home. Walter also came to recognise the need for some suitable training, and accordingly applied for courses both at the All Nations Bible College and the London Missionary School of Medicine, both of which he in turn attended. It was at the former that an incident occurred which revealed the kind of person he was. He was on hands and knees scrubbing the floor of the dormitory when another student came up to him and with a grin on his face deliberately overturned his bucket of dirty water on the freshly cleaned floor. His tormentor said he did it to see if Walter could praise God in anything! His brother Philip said, "Did you hit him?" "No", he replied simply, "I thanked God and took courage."

As he sought definite guidance as to where the Lord would have him serve, Walter's father one day mentioned the circumstances of his missionary sister, Miss Annie Gammon (generally known as Auntie Nin), who was at that time serving almost alone at Capango Mission Station in Angola, of which she had been a "founder member" in 1905. She was clearly in need of help in her advancing years. Walter, after much prayer, applied for a visa for Portugal to study the language, but World War II had broken out, and he was refused permission to leave the country as he was liable for call-up for national service. He accordingly prepared himself to serve in the Medical Corps, but the authorities unexpectedly relented and informed him he was free to leave for missionary service.

It was around this time that an amusing incident occurred which he enjoyed recounting. Walter carried with him an intriguing foreign-sounding accent. One day, with war fever gripping the country, a policeman heard him speaking and promptly assumed he was a German spy and set about arresting him! Fortunately Walter was able to persuade him otherwise!

Commended from Culver Grove Hall, Stanmore & Fore Street Gospel Hall, Exeter, in due course he arrived in Angola to join his veteran aunt at Capango, where the African language spoken was Umbundu rather than Chokwe. He was to stay and work with her for some 15 years. Over those years he assisted in and at times supervised the medical work and the school work. The supervision in the earlier years of that period included overseeing the care of the boarders and the agricultural work which was part of their "keep". He also engaged in ministry of the Word on the mission station and in the villages within a radius of 15 miles where a testimony had been established and where basic school work was being carried on by African Christians under the aegis of the mission station.

In the meantime, further tragedy overtook the Gammon family in the untimely death of Mr. Leonard Gammon, whose long-standing deafness was probably responsible for his stepping one day in 1941 into the path of an oncoming car and receiving fatal injuries. Walter was thus left as the senior surviving man in the family.

Walter was not an oratorical preacher (though fluent in four languages), but his sincerity always shone through, as did his deep love for people. This love and concern was constantly demonstrated in his readiness to help others in any way he could, however inconvenient to himself. I remember being rebuked by an unusually candid African friend pointing to Walter's example when taking emergency medical cases by truck or pick-up to the Canadian mission hospital some 35 miles away. Walter always held himself and the vehicle in readiness for such calls, whereas (regrettably) I did not exercise the same degree of forethought, and was slower to get going!

His was a sweet, gentle, courteous, "meek and lowly" spirit, and was a person with whom it was always a joy to have dealings. Some, perhaps, judged him to be too magnanimous, but he was certainly never tolerant of wrongdoing or of injustice towards others. Along with this clear integrity of character went a ready sense of humour, and an ability to see a funny side to any situation where there was one! He was universally respected and admired, by African folk, by the government officials and Portuguese traders, as well as by his colleagues.

It was not until he was well into his thirties that the Lord provided a "helpmeet" for him. He first saw Anne Humenuk through a ship's porthole, and it was love at first sight! Anne was a missionary whose parents had emigrated to Canada from Russia, and who had gone to serve the Lord in S.E. Angola with a faith mission. It "happened" that while Anne was returning from a break in South Africa in June 1954 she was a fellow passenger with Walter's mother, who had come from South Africa to visit her son and her sister-in-law at Capango. Walter had gone to Lobito (Angola's second port) to meet his mother. The rest as they say, is history. Walter and Anne were married some six months later at Catota mission station. She severed her connection with the faith mission, and they were jointly commended from Bethany Chapel, Hamilton, Canada to the Lord's work in Bié.

In due course the Lord gave them one son and four daughters. Walter always loved children, and he was never happier than when amongst his own. The warm and close relationship which had characterised the family in which he had grown up was continued in his own family. The stable and godly home environment provided by Walter and Anne for their children has borne fruit in the five happy Christian homes of their offspring and their eighteen grandchildren.

As with many of the missionaries who served in Angola during the 1960s and 1970s, the colonial war and later the civil war made life difficult and even dangerous for those with young families. Schooling in English for the children had for several decades meant travelling anything up to 650 miles to Sakeji across the Zambian border twice a year. The railway was one of the early casualties of the war, and the roads became highly dangerous. Walter and Anne moved with their family to Fish Hoek, South Africa in 1967 to be near his "retired" mother, who had for some years been involved in the running of Wellwood, a home for retired missionaries and others.

Walter and Anne set up home near Wellwood. Walter soon found "doors of opportunity" in and from their new base, while Anne ran their home and cared for their young family, as well as being involved in outreach to women in the neighbourhood. Walter also became regional director for the running of the Emmaus Bible correspondence courses in the western section of Cape Province. He also ran classes at a reformatory school and a home for boys from broken homes. In Guguletu, a township on the outskirts of Cape Town, he had regular meetings for about 250 children, as well as helping in the assembly there.

In between he would pay visits to Zambia to meet with and encourage refugees from the Angolan war. He also paid at least five return visits to the Capango area, which, along with the other mission stations in the Bié/Quito province, had by then been flattened by the armed forces. In addition, he volunteered to be a Tear Fund co-ordinator on the Namibian-Angolan border when the South African army was heavily involved in the war between political factions both in Angola and Namibia. The Tear Fund representative in South Africa had been praying for someone to be found for the task when Walter, hearing of the need, stepped forward. Anne joined him there for a period of nine months, during which time they were close to the war scene, visiting "outstations" of Christians from various missions and encountering many folk from the Bié area. God greatly used them in their ministry to soldiers and civilians alike.

In 1994, while on a visit with Anne to Canada, Walter suffered a heart attack, which left him much weakened. His condition slowly deteriorated over the following year, and on Aug 28th, 1995, the Lord took him home. He slipped away quietly and peacefully. Many tributes were paid to him at the crowded memorial service at Wellwood Chapel, and many testimonies were given, and blessing received through his ministry quoted. One contributor described him as a great man. We ourselves who knew him well and were blessed by his life and warm friendship add a hearty "Amen", and affirm that his greatness lay in his humility and simple faith in the One he loved and served with all his heart.

Alan Adcock, Barnstaple

Other Recollections

Walter Gammon was ever a gracious fellow worker. One of my earliest memories of him was reading from the pulpit Bible in Stanmore assembly, Middlesex which had been dedicated to the memory of his brother David.

Well do we recall his so very timely visit to our mission at Mt. Esperance on our first term there in the 1950's. He came a considerable distance by motorbike from his mission to ours, over rough roads, to encourage us and seek our welfare. Our own co-workers Charlie and Winnifred Shorten were home on furlough at the time. He was a real breath of fresh air to our whole family. It was with little difficulty that we persuaded him to visit and teach at one of our outlying village assemblies. Having been born and lived in Africa in his early years he spoke the Bantu languages well. While an African elder was opening the evening meeting with prayer I was aware of Walter softly chuckling beside me. He later told me that the elder had been telling the Lord that the saints were going to get a meaty message from God's Word. Should any of them go home with a dry bone in his mouth they had only themselves to blame. His all too rare visits to our mission station were always refreshing and all very timely.

Ross Woodward, Ontario

Walter was always the model Devonshire gentleman from whom I never heard an unkind word about anyone, and about whom I never heard a derogatory word from anyone. He came to Angola as a missionary some six years after I did though he was born in the country and spoke Chokwe and Umbundu fluently.

With this background Walter grew up with a heart for Africa and its people and when God's call came he applied for recognition as a missionary, stating that his "place of birth" was in Angola. He was reminded that he was Portuguese by birth (his parents had not registered him with the Consulate as a British subject) and, as a Portuguese citizen, he had failed to do his two years' service in their army! After a barrage of letters from Echoes of Service, his parents, and others - as well as much prayer - he was finally cleared and given his visa as missionary.

While my wife and I worked with Ernest and Elizabeth Wilson among the Chokwe and Songo people at Chitutu, Walter trekked in occasionally six or seven days on foot, having meetings in all the villages he passed through, and then stayed a little while with us for fellowship. Ours was a very isolated place with only one dirt road in from the opposite direction, while east to Luma-Cassai took 8 to 12 days on foot. Those visits were rare and really enjoyed in such isolation.

Years later when we moved east to Luma Cassai to keep that work from closing and stayed for 22 years, Walter paid us a prolonged visit when he came to clear up his parents' belongings. His father had been killed in a car accident on his way up from The Cape to investigate conditions for return at the end of World War II. Again we were delighted to have Walter's company and help in a very difficult situation. He preached and ministered to great profit in the assembly on the mission station. He and I also tramped for days on end to visit isolated branch works and assemblies which had been sadly neglected for years, and to preach in pagan villages. Our only 'gear' was a food box and our sleeping bags, but we had a most enjoyable time of fellowship. Those days are gone but the results continue in hundreds of indigenous assemblies functioning without missionaries. This was always our aim.

D Boyd Long, Ballygowan

G. Harold German
1904 - 1990
*"Always abounding in the work of the Lord forasmuch as
ye know that your labour is not in vain in the Lord."*
(1 Corinthians 15.58)

Harold German was converted at the age of ten, the last member of his family to become a Christian. He was the youngest of a large family – ten boys and two girls. In giving his testimony, he always credited the salvation of his family to the prayers of his father and mother. He had no memory of his mother for she died when he was only eighteen months old but members of his family used to tell him that before she passed to be with the Lord, their mother gathered her brood around her bed, prayed with them and expressed the fervent hope that she would meet them all again in a coming day in heaven. His father was left to bring up that large family. He worked hard in the fields and his earnings in the early part of the century amounted to the meagre sum of 11/- per week (55 pence). The children were often hungry and ran barefoot during the long summer days. Their father was nevertheless a stalwart Christian who had a remarkable conversion and was a living testimony to what salvation can do in rescuing people from the gutter of sin. Harold used to say that his father was not very literate, but in the evenings, exhausted though he was after a day's toil, he was never too tired or too busy to conduct family worship. Thus, every night he would read to the family from the Scriptures and then commend them to the Lord in prayer. As a result of the prayers of both parents, the whole family were converted and formed an unbroken circle in the Lord.

Harold German was born at Bridford, a village in Devon, on 10th February 1904 and throughout his long life, he never lost his lovely Devonshire accent. When he first left school, he

117

worked in the fields, like his father for a time, then, at 16, he moved to Exeter where he worked in a transport business founded by some of his brothers. Here he continued for the next four years.

An evangelist arrived on the Exeter scene with a large tent in the early summer of 1924. The tent seated 2,000 and young Harold helped in this gospel campaign. Up till then, he had done little or no preaching but he came to be a considerable asset in personal work, dealing with enquirers in the small tent, alongside the main one. He seemed to excel in this type of counselling work and was instrumental in pointing many souls to Christ. The tent was packed every night and great blessing resulted.

When the campaign was over, the evangelist suggested to Harold that he might like to accompany him as he moved on to his next pitch for the rest of the summer season, this time at Derby. Harold asked his brothers for leave of absence from his employment and was told to go on to Derby as suggested. He was assured that his job – driving a steam wagon – would be kept open for him. The evangelist next invited Harold to labour with him during the winter months; which he also did. As a result, he never went back to his steam lorry in Exeter. Harold had begun to preach and found he was able to communicate with audiences. He had a natural aptitude which was consecrated on the altar of service.

This was but the beginning of days for him because, as the years rolled onward, he was to undertake the role of preacher responsible for gospel tent campaigns in many different towns and villages up and down the land during more than forty summer seasons.

In many parts of the country, the name of Harold German is inextricably linked with that of Fred Whitmore, an evangelist of the same age group. They were co-workers in a number of efforts over the next few years and their labours were greatly blessed. Those were days when the winds of God were blowing and the two young evangelists bestirred themselves. As a result, they were instrumental in planting a chain of assemblies at that time, particularly in Yorkshire.

The two young men first met at St Albans in 1925. Harold had been praying for a fellow-worker to accompany him in Yorkshire. Fred Whitmore wrote to say that he would be happy to join him in the Yorkshire tent. They joined forces at Ossett in 1926. It was apparently a lovely summer, crowds thronged the tent and there were many conversions. There was a mighty movement of the Holy Spirit and on the last Saturday of the campaign, when a baptismal service was held in a hall in Bradford, two special coaches were reserved on the train and these were packed to capacity.

For the next few years, they laboured in various parts of the country, including Yorkshire again, which seems to have been a favoured field of service.

In 1929, they bought a motor caravan to facilitate travel, provide them with ready-made accommodation and enable them to engage more readily in open-air preaching. This vehicle proved to be a useful resource, taking them to Wales and Northern England. Eventually, they made it to Scotland, campaigning first in Central Scotland, in the slums of Glasgow and Edinburgh. Then in 1930, they conducted a series of gospel meetings in a tent in Aberdeen and, eventually, found their way to Inverurie, sixteen miles north of Aberdeen, for a further six week tent effort.

This visit was to prove a defining experience for both of them for at Inverurie they met two young ladies who were close friends. Each preacher married one of them in 1932 and each evangelist conducted the marriage ceremony of the other. Harold, in a humorous aside, used to quip that Aberdeen was a well-known fishing port and it was on a visit to Aberdeenshire that he got hooked!

For the first three years of their marriage, Mrs German accompanied her husband on his many journeys throughout the country. Harold became increasingly well known as an evangelist and spearheaded many gospel efforts in different parts of the land, as far apart as Aberdeen, London and Devon. In the course of his many labours, he saw much blessing.

At the outbreak of World Ward II, Mr & Mrs German settled for a time in Kinross in order to be nearer to the Central Belt where there were many assemblies, large and small. In 1943, they lived for a while in Port Glasgow. A facet of his many labours, which is not well known, was a period when he worked among troops in the south of England before they embarked for Normandy. His family back in Scotland saw little of him at that time as security was very tight and he had to live in these staging camps. He was allowed home only between the departure of one group and the arrival of the next.

At the end of hostilities, Harold and his family moved back to Inverurie and then in 1956 to Aberdeen. He continued to be very active until well past the normal age of retirement and in his later years kept busy in the Lord's service both in the homeland and in Canada and America. He used to say with gratitude that in well over half a century of active service he had never once had to cancel a meeting because of illness – a remarkable testimony to the enabling power of God.

Mr & Mrs German's last home was just outside Inverurie and even from there, in his seventies, the writer has known him to travel the best part of 100 miles each way to take meetings on a Sunday.

Eventually, failing health on the part of both led to their taking up residence in Summerhill Eventide Home, Aberdeen. Mrs German passed away in 1988 and Harold, two years later. In his last months he often felt unwell and used to say frequently that he was longing for that day when he would receive a new body. On 13th June 1990, he entered the Lord's nearer presence which is an abode for the traveller, a rest for the pilgrim, a refuge for the stranger and a home for God's children.

Until well on in years, Harold continued to preach in his own inimitable way and with much acceptability. He never gave up that commission which he received in his twenties from the nail pierced hand of the Saviour. He was a very powerful preacher. His messages were delivered with clarity and conviction. He was a considerable orator. He could enrapture an audience. His style was robust, muscular, forthright and challenging. He always preached for a verdict. The writer recalls a brother of outstanding gift himself say to him once: "Harold German is one of the best preachers the assemblies have." Another brother during a campaign said in his own modest way: "Harold is worth supporting". Yet no one knew better than

Harold German that utterance is required as well as eloquence. He had both qualities to a remarkable degree.

Even between series of meetings, he would spend afternoons in the villages in tract and open-air work. Harold's car was fitted up with loudspeaker equipment as he visited unreached parts of the home area. By a strange irony, his car at that time bore the unusual but perhaps appropriate number plate – 'BBC 1'.

In compiling this remarkable record of service by Harold German which spans sixty years of active evangelism, one cannot but feel a sense of disappointment that Harold was not persuaded during his lifetime to write for future generations a detailed account of his work of faith, labour of love and patience of hope, showing what God can do through a life committed to His service, and providing a challenge and a stimulus for Christians of tomorrow.

Matthew Brown, Aberdeen

Other Recollections

In our home the name of Harold German is remembered with affection, since it was at meetings in his tent in a Kincardineshire village that he led my wife to the Lord. Tent work in summer months featured consistently throughout his long years of service for the Lord. From the south of England to the north of Scotland the tent was pitched and souls were saved. It was particularly through the 50s, 60s and 70s that I became involved in this aspect of Harold's work, since it was often pitched in and around Aberdeen. The tent had to be transported and erected, then at the close of the meetings taken down and stored. It was a privilege to assist in this along with others. Many happy times of fellowship were enjoyed and spiritual character strengthened on these occasions.

The preaching was memorable: *"The three knocks"; "The absence of Jesus on the return journey from Jerusalem";* and *"Remember Lot's wife"* to name but a few. It was also powerful preaching, as with deep stentorian tones and graphic illustrations it was delivered "not in word only but also in power". Like the unnamed brother Paul refers to, "whose praise is in the gospel", many of us in this part of the country salute the memory of Harold German.

Eddie Taylor, Aberdeen

Harold had a real heart for the gospel and visited many smaller villages in north east Scotland with his tent, one of which was Stuartfield where eight souls were saved in 1954. Later that year a conference was held for the first and only time in the village hall. The following year he returned to the nearby village of Mintlaw when again a number were saved.

Along with some local brethren Harold arrived at an annual fair held on a Sunday at a place known locally as "Aikey Brae". The intention was to preach the gospel, but the small group was stopped at the entrance by a police officer, who demanded to know what stance they had been allocated. Undaunted, Harold announced he had a booth reserved at the top of the hill and proceeded to take up a position on a grassy spot. One of the traders whose conscience was no doubt pricked, objected to the preaching. Harold's reply to this was that only a poor salesman could not make a living in six days.

Following these efforts in this part of Aberdeenshire a Gospel Hall was built in Mintlaw in 1959, and was opened with a conference at which brethren from nearby assemblies took part.

Robert Buchan, Peterhead

Mr German was a very modest person, but he possessed the rare gift of preaching lucidly and simply, and with a kindliness which appealed to his hearers. I recall an occasion when he preached from the three texts -

Rev 3.8: a door which is open, and no man can shut it;
Luke 13.25: a door which is shut, and no man can open it;
Rev 3.20: a door which is shut, but we can open it.

This preaching was characteristic of Mr German, and his message left a deep impression on me.

A sister told me of how nearly 40 years ago she listened to him speaking on the subject of baptism. She was 12 years old and the teaching based upon an acrostic of the word created a conviction which was only satisfied when she was baptised two years later.

James Brown, Peterhead

Recollections of the late Harold German take me back to childhood days in Inverurie where I was brought up along with the German family. Since he was away from home for much of the time in the Lord's service, we always looked forward to him returning to the assembly when he would preach the gospel and encourage the saints. We would watch the old pulpit shake as he preached with intensity and with great clarity. I recall one rather warm Lord's Day afternoon as he ministered the Word and one or two of the saints began to nod off. He remarked with a twinkle in his eye, "that we were too full of unbelief and new potatoes". He enjoyed holding open-air meetings and on the occasion of the annual conference he would often lead the march from the hall to the stance in the Square, singing as we marched.

He told us as when we were celebrating their golden wedding in 1982, that he never had to cancel a meeting owing to illness during over fifty years in the Lord's work. He would speak with joy of "eternity *with* Christ being a long, long time", but would solemnly add, "Eternity *without* Christ will be just as long." In 1975 he held his last gospel campaign in Inverurie along with Fred Whitmore, 45 years after they had conducted their first one here.

Robert Jamieson, Inverurie

Arthur C. Gooding

1917 - 1997

"Be ye also patient; stablish your hearts:
for the coming of the Lord draweth nigh."
(James 5.8)

Arthur Cresswell Gooding, known affectionately to his friends as AC (this distinguished him from his cousin Arthur of Kilmarnock), was a preacher who had an outstanding enthusiasm. Whatever the subject he was handling, whether expounding truth from the Tabernacle in the wilderness or explaining prophetic subjects, his enthusiasm for his subject was infectious. But he was not just an enthusiastic preacher, he had a deep concern for the spiritual welfare of the people of God. His exposition of prophetic truth was not with a view to satisfy mere curiosity, he wanted the truth of the Lord's coming to affect the lives of believers in the present age. The personal return of the Lord Jesus for the church, and His glorious, visible coming to the earth in millennial glory and power was a profound conviction that gave him a white heated passion for the subject. This resulted in his whole life and thinking being orientated by it. He believed that the coming of the Lord was a truth that would change an ordinary Christian into a daring witness for Christ. At the same time he was convinced that everything selfish would be destroyed by this truth, and a calmness and poise would enter the soul even when circumstances were disturbing and agitated.

Arthur's family background was one where the grandparents on both his father's and his mother's side were Christians. His father William Gooding, was born at Ipswich, Suffolk in 1885. His mother, Alice Mary Gooding, nee Keeble, was born at Stowmarket in the same year. The Goodings had six children, four boys and two girls. Arthur was born in July 1917 at Ipswich.

He was the third child and his parents named him Arthur Cresswell Gooding.

During a series of gospel meetings held by a Mr. Cameron in the local assembly at Ipswich, a number of young people were saved including Arthur's older brother Gerald and several of his cousins. This was probably the beginning of a serious work of God in his soul, but as yet he made no profession of faith. Before the meetings commenced he was diagnosed with scarlet fever and was put into the local isolation hospital and therefore unable to attend the meetings. His father wrote to say that many young people were being saved. This brought about a concern in his heart and he was most distressed that he was in hospital and not able to go to the meetings. He felt the Lord had put him aside, because he already had several opportunities to be saved. His father had warned him of the possibility of being left behind should the Lord come, but he had put the matter of salvation off, thinking there was plenty of time.

On leaving hospital he was at home one evening with his sister Winifred, the others having all gone to the meetings. He sat reading his Bible. After reading Romans 10.9 he asked his sister if it was really true. His sister answered, yes! "Well," said Arthur, "I am saved!" A week later thirteen were baptised including Arthur. The following Lord's Day those who had been baptised were asked to give their testimonies. This was Arthur's first experience of being on the platform. He was small and could hardly see over the top of the pulpit. He gave a moving account of his conversion, which left hardly a dry eye in the congregation. On Sunday afternoons his father would gather the children round the dining room table and teach them the Scriptures. In this way a foundation of scriptural knowledge was being laid in the hearts of his children.

The family moved from Ipswich to Exning near Newmarket for a period of three years. At this point Arthur began his working career. That was an important move for Arthur as it was during that period that he met Kathleen who would become his wife. Kathleen had been saved in London but was convalescing with an Aunt who lived at Newmarket.

When Arthur was seventeen the family moved back to Ipswich, and the next year his mother was called home. About this time Arthur went to Sudbury to work. In the assembly at Sudbury, a Mr. Micklewright showed an interest in Arthur and took him to the weeknight meetings at a village assembly and encouraged him to speak at the meeting from time to time. Arthur found that he was running out of subjects to speak on, and it was at this point he turned his attention to the study of the Tabernacle in the Wilderness. Out of a necessity to find fresh material to minister to the believers in that village assembly there grew a lifelong interest in this subject.

Many assemblies throughout Britain received spiritual instruction from Arthur's ministry on the Tabernacle, as he spoke on the glories of Christ illustrated in its various parts. Later he gave himself to putting the relevant Scriptures and pictures of the Tabernacle on 35mm transparencies, an effective way of teaching the truth of the Tabernacle visually and orally.

At age eighteen he stood as a Conscientious Objector and was given a complete exemption, during the second world war. For a short time he worked on the land, but then he moved to Stowmarket where he worked in a furniture store. He was in his mid twenties when he married Kathleen, their marriage was a happy and hard working partnership. They had one daughter Mary, and a son John. When he opened his own business at Stowmarket both Arthur and Kathleen worked hard and established a name for quality carpets and furnishings. At the same time he was heavily involved in the local assembly at Stowmarket where he served as an elder for fifty years. In spite of a busy business life and a heavy schedule of meetings they always found time to entertain the Lord's people. Many of the Lord's servants enjoyed the liberal hospitality to be found in the Gooding's home.

During the war years Arthur held children's meetings at the hall. Every week the hall was filled with children, many were evacuees from London, and after the war he continued the work among the children. Besides the children's work, for many years he was responsible for the assembly Bible Class. In this way the young people at Stowmarket were faithfully instructed from the Word of God.

When Arthur was eighteen, Mr. Harry Lacey visited the district with his prophetic charts giving a series of meetings on future events. Through this visit Arthur's interest was quickened in the subject and brother Lacey was a great help to him. Later, Arthur produced his own charts on roller blinds which could be pulled down as visuals illustrating, 'The Purposes of God in Creation, Redemption, and Vindication'; 'God's Dealing With Man'; 'Nebuchadnezzar's Image'; 'The Four Beasts' of Daniel 7, besides charts on 'Babylon the Great'. The charts were packed in a box fourteen feet long and heavy to manoeuvre, but that did not deter him from travelling throughout Britain with them, and taking them to Denmark, and the Faroes. He sometimes used the charts to give lectures aimed at the unconverted, and produced a leaflet to advertise the lectures entitled, 'Have You Been Fair To Yourself?' He visited the Orkney Islands ministering the Word of God among the believers in more remote parts, always seeking to encourage the saints wherever they were found. Arthur gave a lot of his time to the assemblies in East Anglia, he was happy to serve in small companies as well as in large gatherings.

In 1977 he was deeply concerned with the inroads of charismatic teaching among young believers throughout Suffolk. It was out of this exercise that with brother Eddie Honeyball of the Denston assembly a three-day conference of Bible Readings was commenced between Christmas and New Year at the Denston assembly. The mornings and afternoons were spent in conversational Bible Reading; the evenings were set apart for ministry. This proved to be of God and the numbers increased from year to year with good numbers of young people attending. It was these same young people who asked if a similar set of meetings could be arranged during the year. This saw a further weekend of Bible Readings over the May Day Bank holiday weekend. His concern for the assembly testimony evidenced his deep conviction that there was a divine pattern for the gathering of believers, and he upheld this throughout his life and encouraged others to search the Scriptures and find out the truth for themselves.

He made one visit to Canada for the Toronto Easter Conference. It was while they were there that Kathleen became very unwell, and Arthur was advised to take her to see her doctor when they returned to England. Kathleen was called home in 1980. Arthur was devastated but he continued the business in Stowmarket with his son John, also his service for God in the assembly and further afield never abated.

In 1985 Arthur married Bertha. Their wedding day photograph encapsulated the new happiness he had found with Bertha, a true helpmeet for him and for twelve years they served the Lord together. He was invited to minister the Word of God in Cork for their St Patrick's Day conference held at Bandon Grammar School. It was during that visit after the meetings were over that he took a stroke, and although making a recovery he was not able to do what he did before. This resulted in his active service for the Lord being hampered although not terminated. He continued to do what he could within the limitations the stroke had placed on him. Nothing daunted, if he could not engage in a wider ministry he would try and touch the neighbourhood where he lived. Arthur used a Bible study leaflet produced by the Marine Hall assembly at Eastbourne, and right to the end he distributed it to neighbours encouraging them to enroll as students.

The way in which his pilgrim days were brought to a close was fitting for a man who loved God's Word and found his delight in the law of the Lord. On 1st July 1997 after reading the Word of God at the breakfast table and before he could pray, the Lord took him home, just prior to his eightieth birthday. The results of the labours of this true man of God, whose service was motivated by a deep love for the Lord, will only be known when the Lord comes, 'to give to every man according as his work shall be'.

Eric Parmenter, Illminster

Arthur M.S. Gooding

1915 - 1999
"A living sacrifice, holy, acceptable unto God."
(Romans 12.1)

Many of the Lord's servants have commenced life in circumstances which, naturally speaking, offered little hope of spiritual success. This was certainly true of Arthur Maurice Salway Gooding who, though denied advantages that other young men had, was moulded by God into His faithful and trusted servant.

He was born at Gravesend, Kent, on 5th January 1915, the second child of Jack and Florence Gooding. His sister, Ruth, was two years his senior. Interestingly, his father included the name Salway in his son's name after Commander Salway RN who bore a fearless witness for the Lord at the beginning of last century. The following incident typified the commander's courage: as the coffin of a famous atheist was carried into Westminster Abbey he appeared from the shadows, quoted Galatians 6.7 'Be not deceived; God is not mocked: for whatsoever a man soweth, that shall he also reap' and then withdrew. At any rate Jack Gooding was impressed by the commander's daring witness and perpetuated his name in his son's.

Adversity came early in the life of Arthur Gooding. Tragically, his mother died when he was only a child of three. At the same time his father was employed as a travelling salesman and was more often than not absent from home on business. This added greatly to the child's sense of loss and resulted in him being committed to the care of his paternal grandmother. In these circumstances life proved to be hard for the growing child. Sadly, his father had little further involvement in rearing his son apart from terminating his formal education at the age of

131

fourteen. These were the early influences that, in the providence of God, were used to shape his character and prepare him for the rigours of manhood.

In 1929 Arthur was convicted of his need of a Saviour, cried to God for mercy and immediately received the assurance of salvation. Following his conversion he gave himself to the serious study of Scripture. So much so that within a year he had come to a definite crisis in his spiritual experience. Would he bow to the demands of Romans 12.1 and yield himself entirely to the will of God? Alone with God, at the tender age of sixteen, he responded by presenting his body a living sacrifice to Him. Consequently he became the willing and happy bondslave of Jesus Christ. His one remaining interest in this world was to please Him who had chosen him to be His servant. Thus, at the altar of Romans 12.1 he began a life of devoted service to the Lord and His people. This was the fulcrum upon which the whole of his life and service turned.

No doubt some who read these pages date their own surrender to God and His service to the time when they heard 'AMS' expound Romans 12. Often a hush fell over the audience as he appealed for greater consecration to the Lord. These were occasions when an abiding work was accomplished in the hearts of God's people and many were confirmed in their desire to serve Him at home and abroad - the 'Judgement Seat' will reveal how many.

During that same year he was contracted to serve a seven-year apprenticeship in 'Letterpress Printing' in Ipswich. This was a step that would have far reaching implications in Arthur's experience. It would influence the rest of his life and service for the Lord.

In the years following conversion, with the light of a single candle and a skylight window, he studied into the early hours of the morning. His steady progress and his ability to teach and preach became apparent to all who knew him. He spoke at his first conference when he was eighteen and two years later he was responsible with others for the care of the assembly. His weekends were filled with service. Saturdays found him engaged in outreach work in neighbouring villages where, along with those of like mind, he distributed gospel leaflets and preached at open-air meetings. Lord's Days were spent ministering to the believers and preaching in the small assemblies around Ipswich. As a young man he never took up 'hobbies' or engaged in 'worldly pursuits'. He found his recreation in study and service and was never happier than when engaged in them. For him, time was too precious to waste on 'pastimes'.

Although entirely committed to the Lord's work in and around Ipswich, he had a growing concern for those in other lands and was burdened about the need in Singapore and Ceylon (Sri Lanka). Seeking advice from a visiting missionary about going there to serve the Lord, he was counselled not to consider going while he remained unmarried. With no immediate prospect of marriage the door was apparently closed on missionary work. This disappointment and the problems he experienced as a 'Conscientious Objector' at the outbreak of war drove him to the Lord in prayer. He made a definite request that the way might open for him to use his professional training for the furtherance of the gospel throughout the world.

God heard and answered in a remarkable way. While he was praying, unknown to him, a letter was already on its way offering him a job in the 'Packing Department' of John Ritchie Ltd. in Kilmarnock. At peace and full of confidence in the Lord's will, he removed from Ipswich to reside in Scotland on 1st January 1941. En-route the train in which he was travelling was evacuated at Waverley Station, Edinburgh. In his haste to disembark he left behind a box his fiancée had given him before leaving Ipswich. It contained all his study notes compiled over the previous ten years. Unable to recover the box he arrived at Kilmarnock Railway Station with God and his Bible and no notes! He lived to prove that God and His Word were all that he needed for the exacting years that lay before him.

Before leaving Ipswich he had become friendly with Miss Hilda Wright from Braintree, Essex. Convinced that the life he had to offer a wife would be hard, and at times lonely, he was greatly cast upon the Lord as to the future of their relationship. As was their habit they asked for unmistakable guidance in this all-important matter of courtship and marriage. This they received and were duly married on 17th October 1942 and set up home in Stewarton, close by Kilmarnock. Throughout the years that followed she remained his loving and faithful companion, gladly bearing the difficulties and loneliness that he had so accurately predicted would be her lot as his wife. Shunning worldly ambition and the material trappings that attend it, they lived a simple life and were at times no strangers to hardship. During these years on three occasions he sold his library to provide for his family. He often remarked 'that without the sacrificial help and encouragement of his dear wife he would never have accomplished what he did in his work for the Lord'. Speaking of Mrs Wright, his mother-in-law, he commented with genuine affection that the love she lavished on him was the nearest he came to experiencing the mother's love that he had been denied as a child.

As we review these formative years of Arthur Gooding's life we should ask, "Does the Lord have a definite plan for our lives and, if He does, can we obtain knowledge of it?" In answer to the question we find on one hand a young man totally absorbed with discovering God's will for his life and on the other a gracious God gradually unfolding His purposes to him. Arthur Gooding believed and constantly taught that both the happiest place, and also the safest place on earth for the child of God was to be consciously in the centre of God's will. He had proved it for himself and he wanted all God's people to experience the deep joy of knowing it for themselves. Dare any of us settle for less?

United in marriage and also in the Lord's work, they were received into the assembly in Kilmaurs. From the first they threw themselves into the work there, conducting meetings for children and starting a Sunday School in the village. Two years later they moved to Kilmarnock where their three sons and daughter were born. Later that year they were received into the assembly, which meets in Elim Hall, Kilmarnock where they remained for the rest of their long and happy life together.

Although forced to leave school at the age of fourteen and thus deprived of 'higher education', Arthur Gooding proved to be a man of outstanding ability. While he never despised education, he was content with the knowledge that God had both called and equipped him for the service that had been entrusted to him. Never at any time did he feel disadvantaged by the lack of formal training, neither in the natural nor in the spiritual realm. His considerable achievements at home, in business and in the Lord's work stand today as a testimony to what God can do with a life surrendered to His will.

The ability he had shown in early years in Ipswich to teach and preach the Word blossomed during his years in Kilmarnock. He quickly established himself as an able and accurate expositor of Scripture. Consequently, as his 'gift' was recognised and appreciated, many doors opened for service and he was in constant demand for regular weekend assembly meetings and also for conference meetings throughout the British Isles. Apart from his heavy schedule of engagements, and while still in employment, he conducted many series of meetings for teaching the Word and also for preaching the gospel. The Lord's blessing was evident when many of His people were helped and sinners were brought to the Saviour. In partnership with his life-long friend and colleague Jack Hunter, gospel campaigns were held in Kilmarnock and today there remain in the assembly those who were saved at that time. Other successful gospel series were held in Barrhead, Newton Mearns and New Cumnock. Series for teaching are so numerous that it would be impossible to mention a fraction of them. Throughout those busy years he rose early, did a day's work, commuted to and from his meetings by public transport, sometimes arriving home in the early hours of the morning. He retired for the night weary but happy in the knowledge of a day spent in the service of God and all too conscious that the whole process would be repeated in the succeeding days and weeks.

At the same time, as an elder in the assembly, he shared the responsibility of caring for the saints in fellowship at Elim Hall - often an onerous and emotionally exhausting experience. He never complained of the heavy burden of responsibility that he was called to carry and was seldom discouraged in his service. Interestingly, he never possessed a driving licence and maintained that as a result, warmth was added to his ministry due to time spent meditating as he travelled by train or bus. Here, no doubt, was the secret of the powerful effect that his ministry had on the consciences of those who listened to him. Later in life Mrs Gooding passed her driving test and they bought a small car. Selflessly, she transported her husband to his many meetings. On one memorable occasion she broke from domestic duties to take him to the local railway station. Discovering that the train had already left, without hesitation she decided to drive him to his destination. Some four hours later, still wearing her apron, she telephoned her family to let them know she was safe and well in Consett, NE England and was on her way home!

It was during this long period of his life from 1941 to 1974 that the Lord answered the prayer uttered at Ipswich in 1940, i.e. 'that He would use him to spread the Word of God throughout the world through the printed page'. So for thirty-three years from his humble beginnings as packer until finally as Managing Director he served the Lord in the publication and distribution of Christian literature throughout the English-speaking world. By this means many in this land and beyond were saved and many others were established in the Faith. Another fruitful work that occupied him in those busy years was as editor or assistant editor of monthly magazines for the exposition of Scripture. He both edited and contributed to the 'Christian Worker', 'Believer's Magazine' and 'Assembly Testimony'. He was also a capable author and leaves three written works as examples of his considerable ability. His modest but invaluable volume, 'Straight Paths for the Children of God', is a compilation of articles written for monthly publication. 'Israel's 13 Judges' is a transcription of addresses on the Book of Judges while his exposition of John's three Epistles was a most valuable contribution to the Ritchie Series, 'What the Bible Teaches'.

While, for him, the door to missionary service closed around 1940, he never lost his interest in those who served in 'foreign fields'. As a Trustee of the 'Lord's Work Trust', he found himself in the privileged position of being able to maintain a deep interest in those who laboured abroad. He was also a founder Trustee of the 'Machermore Castle Eventide Home'.

He continued with John Ritchie Ltd. from 1941 to 1974 at which time he resigned as Managing Director of the company in order to give himself to full-time service in the Lord's work. It was during that time that his long and fruitful friendship with the late Jack Hunter was established. They worked as fellow-directors at Ritchies, laboured as fellow-elders in the assembly at Elim Hall, and as fellow servants ministered the Word and preached the gospel throughout the British Isles and beyond. Due to redevelopment in Kilmarnock Town Centre in the early seventies, it became necessary to relocate Ritchies in new premises. His final responsibility for John Ritchie Ltd. was to arrange for the transfer of the company to its new home at Beansburn. With that duty discharged, so ended thirty-three fruitful years of service for the Lord in the Printing Trade.

So, in September 1974, he went to 'full-time' service in the Lord's work commended by the assembly at Elim Hall and with the blessing of the directors of John Ritchie Ltd. Such a move had been on his heart for a long time but for various reasons, had remained unfulfilled. Now he felt free to devote his remaining years to what was always nearest to his heart - the edification of the saints through the ministry of God's Word. The Lord gave him a further twenty-four happy years serving Him and His people in this way.

The years from 1974 were spent travelling extensively throughout the English speaking world, principally to minister the Word of God and conduct 'Bible Readings' among the assemblies of the Lord's people. Frequent visits were made to Ireland, Canada and the USA as well as an expansive ministry on the British mainland. South Africa and Israel were also visited. It was during one of his visits to Canada and USA in 1993 that our brother's health was critically undermined. Returning home utterly exhausted and seriously ill, he was not expected to recover. He made a remarkable, though limited, recovery. Eventually he grew strong enough to undertake public engagements but never to the same demanding degree previously possible.

However, it was during these last years of his life that the assembly in Elim Hall was especially blessed by his contribution at their public meetings. This was particularly true when he rose to lead the saints in worship and prayer and also in his clear teaching in their weekly Bible Readings. Increasing weakness and almost complete blindness further limited him toward the end and, as was fitting, in December 1998, among his 'own people' at Elim Hall, Kilmarnock he addressed his last public meeting. The following week with Mrs Gooding and daughter Veronica he went on holiday. It was then that he succumbed to what proved to be his final illness. Returning home and in rapidly deteriorating health he was faithfully attended and cared for by his wife and family. During visits to the home his only real interest was the Word of God and the people of God. In his weakness his faith never faltered. Blind, he often sat in his chair motionless with his eyes closed. Stirring, he would remark "Don't think I'm sleeping: I'm reading my Bible!" Physically blind and yet in sight of the heavenly shore, his abiding interest was the knowledge of God and the Word of God.

And so, for Arthur Maurice Salway Gooding, the journey that commenced in a small room in Ipswich ended peacefully in Kilmarnock on Monday 3rd May 1999. The living sacrifice offered in 1930 was now wholly consumed. There remains for us the fragrant memory of a life totally surrendered to God. Having fallen asleep he passed safely home to be with his Blessed Lord, whom he had faithfully served for almost seventy years.

William Houston, Kilmarnock

Other Recollections

Not only his ministry made an impression. The writer remembers well that monthly Bible Reading in Cumnock at which many a servant was questioned mercilessly on important points of doctrine. When Mr Gooding came he would smile broadly, chuckle in that memorable way, and unflustered and patiently he would faithfully answer their questions. Younger men learned a lot about how to treat one's brethren, even when they are trying!

But his good-humoured dealings with his brethren did not mean that he glossed over points which might prove controversial. When the "High Leigh" controversy arose over how the work of God should be supported Arthur Gooding stood tall, opposing any tendency away from dependence on the grace of God.

Tom Wilson, Springburn

My first and lingering memory of 'AMS' was listening to this little man explaining the Scriptures in a way that I, a young convert, could understand. I listened to others and sometimes felt an interpreter was required! Not so with this man. His ministry ranged from Genesis to Revelation and was given with clarity and humility.

When he was preaching in a hall which had an amplification system, sometimes I would just listen to his rich tenor voice and wondered how such volume could come from so small a frame! His life could be summarised by Esther 10.3 since he was continually, 'seeking the wealth of His people'.

Brian Currie, Dunmurry

During his visits to Northern Ireland in the late 1950s, he carried out business for Ritchies during the day and in the evenings would often minister in Ebenezer Assembly, Bangor. His ministry made profound impressions on me in my early Christian life. I can still remember vividly his exposition of Philippians, his ministry on the life of Abraham and his "opening up" of the book of Amos. He had the great ability of making the sense of Scripture very clear. He was great company, and many evenings into the small hours he would talk about Scripture to help and encourage my brothers and myself in the things of the Lord.

He frequently attended the Lurgan Bible Readings, and we used to look forward so much to his reading, as we could be sure that it would be helpful and encouraging. His introduction of the passage was masterly, and it was at such times that his great knowledge of Scripture came to the fore. It was his custom to minister on the Tuesday evening, and he would direct his message to the sisters who had been busily engaged during the day in catering for the Conference. His great thoughtfulness and consideration for others were most apparent.

Denis Gilpin, Jersey

One of the first times the writer shared a Conference platform with brother Gooding was over 25 years ago at a New Year Conference in Cowdenbeath. He asked the two other speakers of their exercise and suggested that contrary to the accepted traditions in Scotland at least, the present writer, much the junior of his two experienced brethren should close the conference. Not for Arthur Gooding the idea that due deference required him to speak last.

The last Conference at which the writer spoke with him was again a New Year Conference. His eyesight failing, the passage was read for him. With consummate ease our brother then expounded the detail of 1 Thess 4.13-18. To the end he carried with him both what years of patient study had built in and evident love for his brethren which God had formed in him.

Tom Wilson, Springburn

I got to know him more intimately when we worked together in the publication of 'Assembly Testimony' Magazine, of which he was editor for some 25 years. His wise, perceptive and faithful counsel was appreciated. I asked him on one occasion to write a review of the changes among the assemblies during his lifetime. He replied, 'I am probably now the only man alive who knows the background of many assembly problems and they would be better dying with me.'

Brian Currie, Dunmurry

I became involved in the Lord's Work Trust shortly after his commendation to the Lord's work. Although no longer a trustee, he was always interested to know how the affairs of the Trust were progressing, and many times his advice was sought on important matters. He had a wide vision and appreciation of the Lord's work, and was acquainted with the Lord's servants at home and abroad. We still miss his wise counsel, but greatly appreciate the wonderful legacy he left behind.

Denis Gilpin, Jersey

In later years I came to know him personally and enjoyed the privilege of sharing ministry with him in a number of places. Other brethren of my age group found, as I did, that he was always helpful to younger men who were with him and gave encouragement.

Latterly I had the privilege of visiting him both at home and in hospital. One day he told me he was waiting for the Lord to take him home. We thank God for every remembrance of him and look to the day of rapture and reunion.

Jim Baker, Hamilton

They finished their course in the 90s

John Hawthorne

1920-1995

"Always abounding in the work of the Lord."

(1 Corinthians 15.58)

If ever there was a man who abounded in the work of the Lord, it was John Hawthorne, from his earliest days until the Lord called him home. He was a man who carried heavy responsibility in secular employment but was still busily engaged in gospel efforts, some of which meant many miles of travel. Being of slim build and enjoying good health, he was most agile in his movements, so when visiting from door to door, he almost ran rather than walked. His alert mind and his equally alert body meant that anyone who laboured with him and tried to compete was strained to the limit. His friendly approach when dealing with strangers was an asset to the gospel. Many will testify that they were impressed by his manner of approach, and his warm invitation to hear the message that resulted in their conversion. The absence of pride and his willingness to put his hand to give help wherever this was needed meant that he was not a mere spectator, whether it was in erecting of tents or in lending a hand in the kitchen.

One of the special favours enjoyed by our brother was that his parents were saved before he was born, and in addition to this, his father was a gospel preacher. This meant that often when other preachers were called 'Mr.' he was simply called 'John', so as to distinguish him from his father. His birth took place in Whitehaven, NW England, on March 2nd, 1920. His father was Scottish and his mother was English, and in 1922 they moved to Northern Ireland, so this gave our brother a wonderful blend of Scottish, English, and Irish.

When settling in Ireland his parents were in fellowship in

143

Ballyhackamore assembly, and John as a child attended the Sunday School conducted by the saints of that assembly. When he was 9 years old the teacher taught from the cleansed leper of Mark 1, and he became deeply burdened about his sin. In the gospel meeting, while Mr W. Campbell was preaching, he was saved through the words of John 3.16. Not only was a soul saved, but a life was also saved, for he never knew the evils of the world, nor was he mourning the wicked doings of the past, as alas, many have to do after conversion. Not until he was sixteen was he baptised, by which time his parents had moved to Mourne Street assembly, so it was into this assembly that he was received after his baptism.

A number of young brethren became interested in the district of Bloomfield in the late nineteen thirties, and among them was our brother John. He had a Sunday School class there, and helped in the gospel work that resulted in an assembly being formed in 1944. He was one of the foundation members of that company, and always had an interest in it until his home-call. His experience of assembly life at Bloomfield fitted him to be a help in the various assemblies among which he laboured in the Gospel. Although his full-time service necessitated his absence from Bloomfield assembly, this did not divorce his heart from it, for until his home-call, he was ever deeply interested in its welfare.

After leaving school he chose to work as a telephone engineer, and was employed by the A E I (Seimens) company, involved in the installation of telephone equipment in different new exchanges in Northern Ireland. Before he finished with secular employment he had become a manager, so it was no small sacrifice for him to leave his good position, and the work which he enjoyed, to become a servant of the Lord wholly dependent upon Him for support.

Mr W. McCracken and John's father were both preachers who were like-minded in spiritual things and enjoyed close fellowship with each other. Not only so, but both lived in the same street, so that they were not only friends, but neighbours as well. It is not surprising that John married the youngest girl of the McCracken family. This was in 1945, so just after the Second World War. They had three children, all of whom are saved and in assembly fellowship, so they had much joy in watching their spiritual progress, and their interest in the Bloomfield assembly. One outstanding feature of the Hawthorne home was its hospitality. Possibly no other home in Belfast entertained more of the Lord's servants, for most of those having meetings in Bloomfield, and in need of accommodation, found a home from home under the Hawthorne roof.

The most important feature of John's life was his interest in the gospel. For quite a time before he gave up secular employment he engaged in gospel efforts, so he was almost as much involved in the work as those in full-time service. Some were pressing him to leave the telephones and give himself wholly to the gospel, however, he was slow to make the move. In 1968, in fellowship with the Bloomfield assembly he went forth 'taking nothing of the Gentiles'. For 27 years he moved up and down the land telling out the message that was dear to his heart. He was a simple but solemn gospel preacher, with a good, clear voice, and a sharp mind, making him an interesting speaker. He was never long or dreary, but always had something definite before his mind, and with the help of God, he could drive home his point as a nail fastened in a sure place. He was blessed with a good voice for singing, and could not only sing the hymns, but knew the tunes of almost all of them.

Not every man can preach with brethren who are not of a similar temperament, but John was so flexible that he could fit into harness and yoke with any other preacher. For the length of time he was in full-time service, he was linked with a large number of fellow workers. Perhaps he was with Mr Tom McNeil longer than with any others, for they had many gospel efforts together. The present writer was with him in at least ten series of meetings, and enjoyed his fellowship every time. Only those who know the burden for souls that the true evangelist carries, can realise the strain associated with gospel preaching, and appreciate the many sorrows felt by him, over those who refused the message. In the mercy of God, not all reject the offer of salvation, so he had the joy of seeing quite a number saved during his years of service. Never at any time did he allow his zeal to outstrip his wisdom, for anxious as he was to see souls saved, he ever refrained from pushing sinners into a false profession. He believed that 'Salvation is of the Lord', and only what is done by Him will stand the test of time and eternity.

Whilst most of his labours were in Northern Ireland, from time to time he ventured further afield. On several occasions he laboured in the Republic of Ireland, and was well known to the saints of the few assemblies in that land. He ventured across to England for some meetings, but did not find the interest there encouraging. Scotland, Shetland and the Orkney Islands were also visited by him, so the lands of his mother and father shared in the benefits of his preaching. His brothers-in-law, Mr John and Mr Robert McCracken both laboured in Nova Scotia, so this aroused his interest in Canada. He visited it along with the USA on several occasions, and felt at home with the workers there. His furthest trip from home was to Australia. He was encouraged to go to the Perth area where a young couple from Northern Ireland, who knew him, sought to bring the gospel to the area where they had gone to reside. He found that pleasure-loving land to be unresponsive to the gospel, so left after a few weeks. Difficult as the work may be in Northern Ireland, yet in many other lands it is even more difficult.

John never considered himself to be a gifted teacher, and was content to be what he was fitted to be, a preacher of the gospel. This being said, he did quite often contribute to the ministry at conferences. His messages were pointed, short, and never dreary. When sometimes a meeting had become dull and heavy, he could rise with a fresh word at the end, which cheered the saints. He filled a niche that may never be refilled, for he was unique in that he had the courage to rise to the occasion, even when others would have given up in despair.

Few enjoyed better health than did John, for seldom was he off sick, nor did he ever complain of weakness, even though he was working so hard. However, in 1990 he required serious surgery for the complaint that eventually proved fatal. He recovered sufficiently to be back at the gospel, but in 1993 he had a relapse which the Lord used to call His servant home. During his illness he was fully aware that the end was near, but patiently bore the increasing weakness, and on September 2nd

1995 the Lord, who has the keys of death, opened the door and called him to Himself.

The funeral was from the Bloomfield Gospel Hall, but the large number that attended was more than the hall could contain, with more outside than inside. Although John was spared beyond 'the allotted span', those who knew him never thought of him as an old man. However, his work was finished, and the Lord who saved him and used him in His service had the sole right to decide when this time was reached. The Day will declare how much his work was valued by Him. May his example be a stimulus to all who are left who knew him, and all who read this brief account of his labours.

Albert McShane, Lurgan

Other Recollections

Anything John did, even in secular employment, he did it with all his heart, 'as to the Lord and not to men' (Ephesians 6.7).

While he was still employed we had a number of fruitful series of gospel meetings together, when precious souls were saved, later baptised, and added to assembly fellowship. It was evident to many that God had more important work for him than working with telephones, and encouraged him in this direction, subject to the will of God.

Later he laboured with other commended brethren with fruit and blessing, and was acknowledged as a great visitor of both saints and sinners, with excellent results.

He continued in the work, a diligent labourer until health failed and after a time of weakness, went peacefully 'to be with Christ'.

John Thompson, Lisburn

Our brother was a plain man, with a love for the souls of his fellow countrymen. His messages in the gospel were short and plain. Likewise at conferences, our brother could give a short encouraging word. He had a particular interest in areas where his father had laboured. This meant that often he was found in out-of-the-way places, and much away from home. He was highly respected in many homes and in different areas.

Over twenty years together we had some thirty eight series of gospel meetings, in Gospel Halls, portable halls, and in the tent when convenient. On the first time we visited the fishing village of Portavogie, we went for a walk along the harbour. The fishermen soon discovered that we were, what they termed, 'brethren preachers' when we asked if the fishing boat, the 'True Token' was around. On another day, when the tent was being erected in Portavogie, the local children came round to ask Mr Hawthorne what time the 'circus' commenced!

Thomas McNeil, Ballymena

The first gospel effort that I shared with our esteemed brother was in a tent in Belfast city in 1970. The city at this time had erupted in rioting, bombing, shooting, and murder, and many Christians in the various city assemblies had fled to the suburbs or to the provincial towns. I had obtained a site opposite the city centre railway station. The problems in the city were increasing, and many were questioning the wisdom of preaching in such dangerous conditions. However, we continued for six weeks. One evening I stood outside to watch the city burning, which was all so very sad, when dear John came out of the tent with his hymn book in his hand, calling me to come and commence. We saw a little blessing in salvation in those meetings, and this was the commencement of a partnership forged in a furnace of fierce rioting.

David Kane, Belfast

John came to the Orkney Islands twice to serve with me in the gospel. He was keen to visit the northern isles where his father had laboured before him. We preached together around the islands and on the Orkney mainland. One night a local man who had been a notorious former publican, shook hands with John at the door and said how much he had enjoyed the meeting. To this John's comment afterwards was that wicked old sinners had no right to enjoy a gospel meeting, and if they did it hadn't done them any good!

One day at breakfast the telephone rang, and John's face lit up. He said later that he thought it might be someone phoning to say they were under conviction and seeking salvation, or that they had been saved the previous night. He had the heart of an evangelist, and expected to see the Word of God working in human lives, and souls being saved.

A colleague in Ulster had been complaining critically to John that many evangelists in Ulster knew little about hard pioneer evangelism. One day, while visiting remote crofts on the island of Eday, tramping along a beach head-on into a force ten gale, John suddenly laughed, and shouted into the wind that if brother X were with us now he would really know what pioneer evangelism was all about!

Michael Browne, Bath

Approximately two years after I came into fellowship in the Bloomfield assembly, John began to invite me to take a little part with him in the preaching of the gospel on Sunday evenings in various places. To me, his earnestness and humility were obvious. He would pick me up in his car, and after a few words of greeting would settle down in almost complete silence until we reached our destination, however long the journey. His mind was totally on the meeting and his message.

On the way home we would talk about the preaching and the things of God in general. One particular evening on the way home, he said, "I wish every day could be like the Lord's Day, and my mind and heart on the things of God from morning until evening." I never doubted the sincerity of his words. As a young believer they made a deep impression on me.

William Mayhew, Belfast

John was one of a very few who followed his father as a full time evangelist, leaving a good position when family responsibilities were at their greatest. I can say that he was one of the most unselfish men I ever met, showing an interest in the labours of all his fellow workers. In fact, if he had a fault it was that he gave everyone the credit of being as genuine as he was himself.

At the close of a conference, in twenty minutes John could lift the meeting and give fresh ministry, with more condensed into that time than others who took twice the time.

Sam Ferguson, Bangor

149

It has been my happy privilege to know John Hawthorne in a close personal way since 1957. In those early years he was a consultant for the Telephone Company in Belfast where I also was employed as a young man just newly saved. John was a tremendous help to me at that time, not only in secular employment, but also in spiritual things. His kind, helpful manner and consistent, faithful testimony at work endeared him to all who knew him.

As a young believer I was greatly impressed with all aspects of John's life and marvelled how he could do so much so well. He held a very responsible position at work, was a loving husband and father in the home, and a faithful, godly elder in the assembly. Eternity alone will reveal the godly influence that John Hawthorne had on all who were privileged to know him.

Stanley Wells, Canada

John Hawthorne

Jack Hunter

1916 – 1994

"Who when he was come, helped them much which had believed through grace."
(Acts 18.27)

Jack Hunter was born on the 31st August 1916. His father and mother, William and Mina Hunter, arrived in Scotland from Limavady just after the turn of the century when work was scarce. They settled in an area of Coatbridge called Gartsherrie and lived in the houses near the blast furnace works in North Square. William and Mina at that time were unsaved and William was the Grand Master in the Orange Lodge. They had three sons, Glen, Jack and Robert and the boys would assist in holding the banner during the marching seasons.

In 1937 Jack Atkinson, known as the boy preacher, came to Shiloh Hall, Coatbridge for a series of gospel meetings and during these meetings William and Mina were saved. Jack, as a young man, had little regard for divine things but accepted an invitation to the meeting and on the second time of hearing the gospel was gloriously saved along with another young man by the name of Ben Bent. Jack was a proficient billiards player but upon his salvation gave the game up and focussed his attention on greater things.

On leaving school our brother had trained to be a barber but when the war years came he was a conscientious objector and was sent to work in a hospital in Glasgow. It was during this time he met his wife Margaret who worked in RS McColl's in the city. They were married in the house in Coatbridge by William Morrow, an overseer in the Shiloh Hall assembly.

Jack came into fellowship in Shiloh Hall assembly in which two men William Morrow and Moses Lonsdale were a godly influence, not only on him, but on the assembly as a whole.

153

The assembly at this time was large and thriving and when they would return from the open air they would have to sit on the platform because of the large numbers in the hall.

During this time many gifted brethren visited the assembly, among whom was the late W W Fereday and his ministry proved a real challenge to our brother in these early years. When Jack was first received into fellowship he was quiet at the meetings but soon he began to contribute in worship, prayer and ministry after the breaking of bread. It was during these times that our brother's diligence in the study of the Word and his desire to know more of divine things became obvious and he was encouraged by the overseers in Shiloh Hall assembly to develop his gift. In these early years our brother was also encouraged by the ministry of other young men of that time, namely the late John Lightbody and Robert Scott.

Our brother began moving out in the ministry of the Word and preaching the gospel throughout Lanarkshire in the mid 1940's and was invited to speak at his first conference at Porch Hall, Glasgow. Around this time a young Salvation Army officer came to Kilmarnock, and when in conversation with one of the elder brethren of Elim Hall she mentioned she had a brother in law who was in the assembly at Coatbridge and had recently ministered at Porch Hall. The brethren in Elim Hall made enquiries with the Porch Hall brethren about Jack and they commended our brothers' ministry. As a result Jack was invited to Kilmarnock where he began a life long friendship with the late AMS Gooding.

Following this meeting, Mr Gooding came to speak at the Shiloh Hall conference which in that particular year was held at Hebron Hall. After this meeting Messrs Hunter and Gooding had a long conversation and Mr Gooding invited Jack to take up a position with John Ritchie, the Christian Publisher. During his long association with Ritchie's he worked in despatch, cutting and typesetting, becoming a director with the company for many years.

During the time of his employment with John Ritchie he ministered to God's people throughout the UK and Ireland for a period of around 25 years. As an eminent teacher of the Word, and widely used, was a great deal of sacrifice involved, much travel and hours of study, so as to bring the people of God food convenient for them. During this period he also conducted a number of gospel campaigns with Mr Gooding, using a tent in the local areas of Onthank and Shortlees. A number professed faith in Christ as a result of these meetings. Our brother would be less known as a gospel preacher than as a Bible teacher but all his preaching came in much power. On three separate occasions when he was conducting a gospel meeting someone rose and came to the front and indicated that they desired salvation. One of these occasions was with the assembly in Forth where he was booked to conduct some ministry meetings. Having made these arrangements, the brethren in Forth had an exercise before God to change these to gospel meetings. One man who had heard the gospel on the previous two nights came out to speak to Mr Hunter at the beginning of the second hymn. At this point Mr Adam Aitken took the man to another room and before the meeting ended the man was gloriously saved.

After spending 25 years in employment at John Ritchie's, God called Jack to full-time service for Him. He was given the full warm-hearted commendation of the assembly in Kilmarnock, and in 1970 he was commended to the grace of God to serve in the ministry of the Word and preaching of the gospel. This gave our brother the opportunity to serve the Lord in a more extensive field. In the course of his service for the Lord he made 17 trips to USA and Canada where he was widely accepted and appreciated. His wide sphere of service did not, however, cause him to forget his responsibility to the local testimony where he served the Lord as an overseer for many years. Many assemblies from which such men come sadly seem to lose the benefit of their own brethren, but with our brother Jack there was constant concern for the local company. During one particular time of difficulty in the local assembly he cancelled some engagements and took his place again among the oversight and continued with this responsibility until the Lord called him home.

Jack Hunter will be remembered most for his ministry. He was a man of outstanding gift and a power of expression unique to himself. His ministry was expositional, devotional and practical.

The first time I recall hearing our brother preach was at a conference in Denny around 1972 speaking with AMS Gooding and F Cundick. On this occasion he spoke with great clarity from 1 Corinthians 12 on the subject of spiritual gifts and the baptism of the Spirit. During the 70's and 80's there was a rise in the popularity of pentecostalism and the charismatic movement. He appreciated the dangers these movements could bring to God's people, and throughout this period he gave much ministry on these subjects, endeavouring to clarify the issues in the minds of the people of God to prevent them being led away by such error. Giving this kind of ministry at such a time was not without cost and we know of at least two occasions when after having ministered he was confronted with exponents of this error. In this respect his courage has to be commended, willingly accepting the invitation to address such subjects knowing that many assemblies were being troubled and that opposition would probably be encountered. In other assemblies our brother conducted ministry entitled – 'Focus on Fundamentals'. During this time he would address subjects such as the virgin birth, at a time when some of christendom's so called teachers were trying to explain away this fundamental truth. He also spoke on the deity and humanity of Christ, presenting the truth of Scripture in a way which many who heard could quote even to this day. His ministry on the priesthood of the believer, the sovereignity of God and the church of God, laid a foundation for many young believers and only eternity will reveal the results of such ministry so faithfully given.

Sometimes after our brother's ministry, many of God's people resolved that things would never be the same again. Certain believers from different generations heard our brother speak from Genesis 22 and from that time they endeavoured to live a more consecrated life, making resolve that everything would be given to God. He would say that God's desire wasn't for Isaac's life but rather Abraham's heart. He would ask if God meant more to us than anyone or anything else in life and if everything was on the altar for God. This kind of ministry given with such power is rare and it penetrated the minds and consciences of God's people challenging them to live the kind of life where Christ is on the throne. Ministry given on the life of Nehemiah provided a real stimulus to believers, that even in the darkest of days God could move through one man with an exercise. One man with God is a majority and even when the wall of defence is broken down and all seems lost, God could move the heart of a monarch to bring about the spiritual prosperity of his people. His ministry was forthright and fresh. Coming from the sanctuary of the divine presence he spoke with great conviction and power. Often at the end of a meeting no one would move as the Spirit of God did his own peculiar work in the minds and hearts of the Lord's people.

There were different sayings he would use which many of God's people will recall with fondness. He would say, "I'm not here to read between the lines I'm here to tell you what's on the line." To draw attention to a particular verse he would say, "Drop your eye to verse...". His small Bible, his "come on now brethren", were all hallmarks of his ministry. He had an ability to hold an audience in wrapt attention as he sought to deepen their appreciation of the truth of God. Although he didn't have a great education, he took a real interest in words, their structure and background and this enriched his ministry. He told us that he spent as much time on how to say it as what to say. In addition to the ministry of the Word he regularly conducted Bible Readings in various places. These would often be in the company of men who themselves taught the Word and sought to explore the deep things of God. This served to draw out the depth of Jack's appreciation and knowledge of the Scriptures and showed the sharpness of his mind. It is known that as a younger man studying the Word he would often stay up long after midnight looking into the Scriptures and this kind of diligence bore much fruit in later years.

Another commendable memory of our brother was the relationship he had with young people. Even in advancing years he was invited and spoke at various young people's weekends and enjoyed teaching the Word to them. He had a real love for young people and this was reflected in the time he spent with them at meal times, out walking, enquiring as to their well being and taking a good interest in their spiritual development. There were young men whom he would call on the telephone when he was at home, enquiring of them where they had been studying or preaching, and giving encouragement and advice as to their service for the Lord. The saints at Winshill (Burton on Trent) speak of times when he came to that assembly in years past when there were young believers from non-christian families on whom our brother made deep spiritual impressions which moulded their lives.

He was one to whom you could go for advice. He seemed to have a good understanding of the problems young people faced and communicated with them in a way they could understand. He had a long association with us in the Carberry study weekends, and spoke there on numerous occasions. He was always very popular with the youth of the day and made impressions by both his ministry and conduct, which will be remembered for many years.

He had two sons, Harry and Stanley, both of whom have been used by God to help his people in various ways. He was a good father and a fatherly man.

In addition to his wide sphere of ministry Jack Hunter left us two commentaries, part of the "What the Bible Teaches" series. He wrote on Galatians and 1 Corinthians. In addition to this, much of the ministry our brother gave was recorded and several brethren have made this available to the Lord's people.

It would be remiss of me not to pay tribute to our brother's 'helpmeet', his beloved wife Margaret, a true companion and fellow labourer. For our brother to have served the Lord in such a wide sphere his wife must have spent much time alone and apart from her husband. Whilst many know and recognise the service our brother engaged in, not so many might know the sacrifices his wife made. Margaret's willingness to sacrifice in this way will most surely be rewarded in 'that day'.

In the early hours of July 23rd, 1994, our brother passed peacefully into the Lords presence, his course finished in fellowship with his God and his brethren. His funeral service took place from Elim Hall in Kilmarnock. Mr Gooding spoke with great fondness of him from 2 Timothy 4; "I have fought a good fight, I have finished my course I have kept the faith." Mr John Grant at the cemetery reminded us of what Jack used to say, "When I'm gone don't weep for me, I'll be in a better place."

The family of our brother Jack chose as a tribute the words recorded of Apollos "who when he was come, helped them much which had believed through grace" (Acts 18.27).

We salute the memory of a mighty man of God and thank the Lord we were privileged to know and love a truly faithful servant, whose faith we should surely follow.

Colin Hutchison, Stapleford

Other Recollections

'Uncle Jack,' as I affectionately came to know him, first stayed in our family home in 1953 when I was a young boy. This was the beginning of a friendship that would last well over 40 years. In the years that followed, the Hunter family came to stay with us for a number of summer holidays, and we paid return visits to Scotland. Jack Hunter had a profound effect on my life, even from those early years. His exposition of the Word in his unique, clear and challenging way helped to mould my spiritual life and future service for the Lord. I shared a number of conferences with him, and he was always ready to encourage. He was great in the home, and after my father went to be with the Lord, and eventually my mother could not cope with visitors, Jennifer and I had the pleasure of opening our home to this man of God, who had, in fact, married us some years before.

Alan Maunder, Cardiff

With regard to the many visits Jack Hunter made to Cork city and county, it can be said he was "a man sent from God". His first visit was in 1966, and thereafter he made in excess of a dozen trips to the county, especially to Skibbereen, Samuel Sweetnam remarks, "He was faithful in teaching us the Scriptures and on his first visit to West Cork in August 1968 with Mrs Hunter, his ministry is still remembered on Nehemiah, the building of the walls of Jerusalem." The saints found his ministry refreshing, practical and Christ exalting.

Believers would travel to Skibbereen from Cork, 60 miles, and Bandon, 33 miles, as often as possible and sometimes for ten days without a break, in order to hear our brother minister the Word. Many came to listen who are not in assembly fellowship and were always helped by the clear teaching of Scripture. It was often remarked how powerful a message and such a small Bible! When questions were asked about subjects that some may consider controversial, the writer remembers clearly with deep appreciation our brother's clear authoritative answers. He did a mighty work for God in this area and his memory lives on in many hearts. He was one of the Lord's choice servants sent for our spiritual blessing and instruction.

Wendell Webb, Cork

At St Monans Conference which was held during December, Jack Hunter had spoken on Prayer. Coming home with Isaac Cherry as the driver, the road was flooded and the car stuck. Isaac tried everything to get it started, but there was no kick from the battery. Isaac turned to Jack and said, "That message you gave us, is it just for the platform or does it work?" "Oh," said Jack, "it works. Let's put it to the test," and they all prayed. They turned the key and off went the car!

Jack Traill, Lesmahagow

Jack was my own personal hairdresser. He would remind me that my locks were getting too long and he being a barber would invite me to his house or he would come to me – just to cut my hair! These were opportunities to discuss the Scriptures and important these occasions were. But there was a deeper and more important reason, especially when our brother was called to the work, and that was to show me the necessity to have a deep personal interest in the saints in the fellowship. Jack was ever anxious as to how they were faring, what did I consider to be their spiritual needs, who were sick, did any need a visit. From this I was being taught the value of every brother and sister in a real shepherd's heart. Many times we would go together and visit some saint who was showing a lack of spiritual progress, or being laid low with a bout of sickness. Jack would have a word in season for each individual and present their need before the throne of grace.

Although Jack travelled far and wide refreshing the Lord's people, his affection for the assembly in Kilmarnock never waned. Nothing gave him greater pleasure than being at the

Bible Reading discussing with profit the passage of Scripture, and being happy to listen to the contributions of his brethren. To hear him express his devotion to the Lord as we met for the Breaking of Bread was ever Christ-exalting.

Louis Robertson, Kilmarnock

Jack Hunter was one of the few men who had the ability to "bridge the generation gap". He did this in a unique way in our own personal circumstances. When he conducted the marriage ceremony of our daughter Jane and her husband to be, David Park, both sets of parents had also been married by him in the late 50s and in 1963 respectively. We also felt very privileged to celebrate with Mr and Mrs Hunter and their family and a few friends their 'Golden Wedding'.

In his ministry and on a personal level he said many things that were of great help. When I first met with the overseeing brethren at Carluke he said, "Do not be rushed into a decision on any matter – wait, be patient, take your time." This was much needed advice as far as the writer is concerned!

We remember with thanksgiving much of what he said but perhaps what impressed us more was what he did. He and Mrs Hunter cared for his mother in her latter years, and all the years we knew them they lived in the same council house with no desire to "improve" their location. I heard him minister on many an occasion but it wasn't empty words, he practised the truth he preached. "Whose faith follow."

Peter Hinshelwood, Carluke

Joseph Jackson
1917 - 1995
"A man greatly beloved"
(Daniel 10.11)

Joe Jackson was born in County Durham in 1917, one of six children born to James and Isobel Jackson. At that time life in a mining village was tough. There were few luxuries to be enjoyed but Joe knew love and security and he had fond memories of those childhood days in Esh Winning. His parents were believers and from an early age he was taught about the Saviour both in his home and at the Baptist Chapel which the family attended. His father was a preacher and while Joe was still a young lad he would often walk several miles with him to other Durham villages when he had a preaching engagement.

Sadness came into the home when Joe was nine years old. His father died of smallpox at the early age of thirty nine leaving five children to the care of their mother. At this time there were great financial hardships but the family proved the unfailing goodness of God. They continued to attend the Baptist Chapel and it was there as a young boy that Joe realised his need of the Saviour. In simple faith he came to the Lord and was saved. He was later baptised as a believer, publicly confessing his faith in the Lord Jesus Christ.

Joe left school at fourteen and worked in the local dairy shop. He would often laugh as he remembered how he was so short that he had to stand on a box in order to see over the counter! He was encouraged in his spiritual life by godly men at Esh Winning and when he was sixteen he was asked to preach for the first time. With much fear and trepidation he managed to last eight minutes but he felt that he would never be able to preach again!

However, six weeks later he was once more asked to preach.

What he described as his first 'proper' sermon was on the subject of 'The Glories of Christ'.

Throughout his life this grand theme was always prominent in his reading, thinking and preaching. Joe's evident gift for preaching was encouraged and before long he was preaching in the open air in Durham city and in the surrounding villages.

When he was eighteen Joe travelled south to find work. He lived in lodgings at Wallington, Surrey where he began to attend the meetings of the assembly at Ross Road Hall. Through his reading and study of the Scriptures he felt convicted that he should sever all denominational links and meet with believers gathered to the name of the Lord Jesus alone, and so he approached the elders of the assembly with a view to fellowship. One of the elders who interviewed him was the late E W Rogers who asked him how he would know the gospel if he had only the first three chapters of the book of Genesis! This was no easy question for a mature Christian, let alone a young believer.

However, Joe must have given the right answer (he pointed to the wonderful promise of Genesis 3.15) and he was duly received into fellowship. Later he began to preach in assemblies in the locality and in the open air on Saturday afternoons with the village workers. Thus began a preaching ministry among assemblies that continued for the rest of his life.

When Joe came to the assembly at Wallington he met a young woman who had also come from County Durham to find work in the south. Joe and Ruth were drawn to one another and eventually they were married at Ross Road Hall in August 1940. Their married life was an example of mutual love and devotion that none of those who knew them would forget. Throughout the years Ruth demonstrated her love as a hardworking and true helpmeet, supporting Joe in all his work for the Lord as she managed the home and cared for the family. They celebrated fifty five years of happy married life just a few weeks before Joe was taken to be with the Lord.

As a Conscientious Objector Joe's wartime experience was with the Non-Combatant Corps ('the NCC'). Many lifelong friendships were formed at that time and it proved to be a period of spiritual growth and development as he read and discussed the Scriptures with the other believers in the NCC.

Joe returned home in 1946 and began work as a printer's cutter, a job in which he continued until his retirement. One of the advantages of this job was that it left his mind free to meditate upon the Scriptures throughout each day. In his tea and lunch breaks he could be found reading his Bible or a book on some spiritual subject. In addition he would often use this time to enlarge his knowledge of hymn tunes so that he could use a greater variety when he raised the singing at the assembly gatherings!

Joe took an active part in the assembly at Wallington where he later became an elder. He went out preaching the gospel nearly every Lord's Day and ministered the Word on several evenings each week and on Saturdays. On many occasions, after a full day's work, he travelled by bus or train all over London to preach and often did not arrive home to have his dinner until after 11 o'clock at night, starting out early for work again the following morning.

As a father Joe was certainly 'a man greatly beloved' by his family. The five children can look back on their childhood with great thankfulness to God for the wonderful Christian home in which they were brought up. It was a happy home where the sounds of laughter, jokes and games were frequently heard. It was also a place where one could hear the sound of hymn singing as they all gathered round the old piano. But the most important event in the family routine was the daily gathering for Bible reading and prayer. It was there that the children learned the vital importance of giving the things of God first place in their lives. He always maintained a close interest in all of his children and their families. He shared in their joys and sorrows and prayed daily for them all by name. Without doubt they owe more than anyone can tell to his prayers on their behalf.

Joe laboured among the people of God for almost sixty years in the assemblies at Wallington, Mitcham Junction, Sevenoaks, Weald and finally in Eastbourne at Marine Hall. In addition to this he travelled extensively throughout the United Kingdom preaching the gospel and ministering the Word. Over this long period he earned the affection and esteem of many hundreds of people who were helped by his ministry. He loved to be among the Lord's people at meetings and in the many homes where he enjoyed hospitality and fellowship.

Joe and Ruth's home was always open to the Lord's people and even in days of genuine hardship they maintained a liberality towards them. In a very natural way the conversation would be of a spiritual nature, whether the visitor was a visiting preacher of renown or the most humble saint. Here, too, his advice would be sought, the enquirer knowing that a wisdom which came from above would be passed on while every secret would be held fast.

Throughout his life Joe Jackson maintained a consistency of doctrine and conduct. He sought to maintain the truth of the local assembly as taught in Scripture without ever being hard or unloving and never wavered in doing so. His life was exemplary: he had a constant, quiet demeanour and there was no inconsistency between his private and public life.

Joe was a great reader and found it difficult to pass by a Christian book shop without going in to see if he could find any second-hand bargains, or simply to browse among the literary treasures. He read widely among the best of Christian writers from the Puritans to the present day. He was also well versed in the events that shaped the history of the church over the centuries. He believed that much was to be learned from a study of past events and he always enjoyed reading the biographies of the servants of the Lord.

Above all other books, however, Joe loved his Bible. It was his constant companion and he would use every opportunity to glean fresh truths from its pages. When he was reading his Bible he became so deeply engrossed that he would be oblivious to all that was going on around him. Even the noise and commotion of the family living room would not disturb his meditation on the Scriptures. He was a man who saturated his mind with the Word of God and this was very evident in his ministry.

Joe Jackson walked with the Lord for nearly seventy years and his love for the Saviour was reflected in his godly life as well as in his preaching. He preached from the heart. His ministry was always Christ-exalting. He could say with the apostle Paul, 'For to me to live is Christ, and to die is gain.' He faced his terminal illness with the same spirit of acceptance in which he lived his life. One of the last things he was able to say lucidly was that God never makes mistakes. As in his life, so in his death, he bowed to the will of Him who works all things after the counsel of His own will.

After a lifetime of dedicated service to the Lord he entered into his eternal reward in September 1995.

Robert Atkins, Haywards Heath

The Legacy
"The holy garments of Aaron shall be his sons' after him."
(Exodus 29.29)

What shall he leave his sons? Silver nor gold,
Nor heritage, has he, nor herd nor fold.
Not these can he bequeath, but this he can -
The holy raiment of a saintly man.

The fair example of a life well spent;
Of daily tendance in the sacred Tent;
Of ever-praiseful heart and reverent mind;
What nobler gift could father leave behind?

That son who, drawing near the Throne of Grace,
Can say, 'How well my father knew this Place!
How oft I've heard his voice in fervent prayer!'
Happy that son, that richly-dowered heir.

JMS Tait

Other Recollections
As a young man of 21, I moved to a printing firm where Joe worked. I had been told to 'seek out' Joe when I arrived. I asked around if anyone knew Mr Jackson who went to a Gospel Hall. Most of my colleagues were mystified until one lad, about my age, said, "I think he means 'holy Joe'!" Though spoken in wit, those words were, I was to learn, an apt description of our brother.

Joe was a guillotine operator, and at the top of it, at eye

level, there was usually a Bible verse that Joe could meditate on during the day. I spent many happy times around that guillotine putting question after question to my new-found friend, who answered with patience and interest. It was obvious to me from our very first meeting that Joe was a man that loved the Lord and the Book.

Paul Miller, Hildenborough

The first time I heard of Joe Jackson was through a brother called Jimmy. Jimmy had been to a conference, where there was one speaker in the afternoon session and one in the evening. Brother Jimmy was not too impressed with the afternoon session, and in the interval was expressing his thoughts to the brother sitting next to him, finalising his comments with the words, "I hope that the next speaker is better than that." When the evening session commenced and the speaker was introduced he was none other than the brother Jimmy had been speaking to, namely Joe Jackson.

When we moved to Percy Road where brother Jackson was in fellowship, he, his wife and family had moved into the assembly about eighteen months previously. He had left a large assembly to help a small struggling assembly.

Our brother was much used in the ministry of the Word, but such was his commitment to the assembly that he always was with us for the Breaking of Bread and the mid-week Bible Reading. This was much appreciated by the saints. His faithfulness to the assembly and the saints, as well as his cheerful countenance, still benefit the assembly today.

Reg Rowe, Mitcham Junction

Shortly after meeting Joe, he and his family moved to the village of Weald and lived in the flat above the Gospel Hall. Each Wednesday I would go over to the meeting as a visitor, and afterwards we would go up to the flat for supper. Many a night, for long hours, we would discuss the Scriptures together. Never do I recall Joe not having time or interest to talk upon spiritual things to us younger ones. Joe's answers were always considered and balanced, as was his manner of life and attitude to the Word of God. I can still see him in my mind's eye sitting in his armchair with he feet propped on the hearth of the fire, reading the Scriptures and communing with the Lord, then kneeling at the side of his chair to take us in prayer to God.

I remember the encouragement he gave me to get up and teach the Scriptures. I can see him listening with rapt attention as if he had never heard anyone teach the passage before. How encouraging that was. Afterwards he would always go over things you had mentioned in the meeting saying how much he had enjoyed various thoughts. Then, just at the end, he would correct some point or other in such a gracious and kind way that it was impossible to take offence.

Paul Miller, Hildenborough

In the early sixties there was a small assembly in Surrey where the situation became critical when one of the remaining brethren indicated that he was moving away. Joe was in fellowship in a fair sized neighbouring assembly, and I was in fellowship elsewhere some distance away, and expecting to move further away. For some time we had supported the small assembly by attending the midweek readings when we were free. At the time when this situation arose it was decided to hold a meeting for prayer and discussion about the future. Some thought that the assembly should close, but the matter was left open for further prayer and exercise. Knowing Joe and his concern for the interests of his Lord, I was not surprised to be told that he and his wife and children of varying ages, who were still at home, were intending to meet with the small assembly. God in His grace honoured the exercise; the assembly continues to prosper, and Joe and his family were blessed in spite of the fact that there were no other young folk associated with the assembly.

Tom Proffitt, New Haw

In 1983, when Joe and Ruth Jackson moved to Eastbourne and came into fellowship at Marine Hall, the assembly was very small numerically, about 15 in fellowship. Brother Joe, as we all knew him, was a great encouragement to one and all from the very outset.

The love he had for his Lord soon became apparent to those

in the assembly. All would enjoy our brother's appreciation of the Lord at the Lord's Supper when he would give thanks to God for His Son, and his ministry after the Breaking of Bread would always be Christ centred.

He was never far from his Bible. In his home the Scriptures were always on hand and once when he spoke at the children's meeting, our brother said that ever since a child he had a love for the Word of God.

Meeting with the Lord's people was a joy to our brother - he was one of few brethren who enjoyed "being on the door" simply because of the numerous visitors he met as they joined with us to remember the Lord.

Andrew Griffiths, Eastbourne

Joseph Jackson

James H. Large

1903 - 1995

"In quietness and in confidence shall be your strength."
(Isaiah 30.15)

James was born in the Cardiff area, to Christian parents, on 26th June, 1903. After leaving school, he was employed as an Insurance Officer for the Cardiff district. As a young man, before his conversion, he had noticed and admired a lovely young lady, Hilda Lacey, whom he knew was a committed Christian and she was to have some influence upon his seeking the Lord for himself.

Following his baptism and joining in fellowship with local believers, James spent most of his free time, with others, evangelising the outlying districts of Cardiff and the Welsh valleys. Indeed, it was largely as a result of these labours, under the hand of God, that the assembly at Dinas Powis was established.

He was also very much involved in the practical as well as the spiritual aspect of the setting up of this assembly: there are memories of paintbrushes and lengths of timber being transported by bicycle in order to help create a respectable meeting place.

In 1926 James married the aforementioned young lady who, in spite of considerable ill health over the years, was his true partner for nearly sixty years. They delighted in working together for the extension of God's kingdom.

On 13th May 1933 the assembly at Dinas Powis commended James to the Lord's work after which Mr. and Mrs. Large, with their small son Peter, spent several years evangelising rural areas of England using a caravan for a home while travelling. Times were hard and many tales were told of amusing, but always timely, ways in which the Lord provided for their daily needs.

It became evident that James was developing a gift for teaching and expounding the Scriptures and an invitation came for the family to move to North Devon, where a home would be provided, so that James could undertake the work of building up the small assemblies in Barnstaple and surrounding district.

Accordingly, about 1940, after much prayerful consideration and exercise of heart, Mr. and Mrs. Large and Peter took up residence in Barnstaple where James was involved in evangelising, teaching the Scriptures and encouraging the believers in the villages of that area. Many folk could testify to the benefit received from his ministry delivered, as ever, in his down-to-earth style.

The RAF station at nearby Chivenor was extensively used during the war years and many of the young men from the camp found a warm welcome and wonderful meals (in spite of wartime food rationing) at the large household both during the war and afterwards. There was always an open door for all who needed help and comfort.

During the early days of his work in North Devon, James would walk or cycle to and from meetings. On one particular occasion he was invited to attend a "get-together" where, much to his astonishment, James was presented with the keys to a car! What an enormous benefit this proved to be in the service of the Lord.

JHL felt an exercise and care for believers, particularly those young in the faith, who had been taken from their home environment to serve in the Forces, or for other reasons, and this led to the commencement of a Bible Correspondence Course which was used widely.

Perhaps, as a natural progression from this, the need arose for a magazine whose aim was to provide helpful and stimulating written ministry, together with reports of the Lord's work in the UK. The outcome was the launching, in 1945, of the Precious Seed magazine, and JHL was its first editor and continued in this responsible work until 1962. Of course, the commitment was very time-consuming and JHL was, as always, meticulous in its execution while still continuing to help and encourage the local believers, giving willingly of his time and gifts to any who were in need.

In the early 1950s, Mr. and Mrs. Large moved to Teignmouth, South Devon, where they spent a number of years. During this period, James was engaged in a teaching ministry which took him all over the UK as well as helping in the local assemblies and always encouraging believers in the work of the Lord. Again, hospitality was very warm and kind and many "waifs and strays" were cared for and sent on their way enriched by having been in the Large home.

In the early 1960s, Mr. and Mrs. Large went to live in Highgate, North London, where they kept open house for all, but especially for missionaries on furlough who needed to spend time in London for various reasons. They truly found a "home from home"! JHL also did a great deal of real pastoral work, visiting and encouraging the saints in addition to helping locally in the teaching of the Scriptures.

Their next move was to Seven Kings, Essex, in the 1970s and, again, they were helping and encouraging and showing hospitality. During this time, Mr. and Mrs. Large celebrated their Golden Wedding anniversary which was, in itself, a miracle as Mrs. Large had not been expected to live so long! They could both testify, with immense gratitude, to the great faithfulness of God over many years. They had so many kind friends and branches of family that they were persuaded to hold celebrations in both Seven Kings and Cardiff.

Sadly, Mrs. Large's health was deteriorating more rapidly and JHL, although very grateful for much loving, practical help provided by local believers, felt it time to consider taking up residence in a home where they would be given constant care as necessary. They therefore spent a short time at Newton Abbot (1982-83) before making their home at Auchlochan House near Lesmahagow where they settled very happily and it seems that both staff and residents benefited by their presence and they, in turn, received loving and efficient care.

James continued to be in demand in southern Scotland to teach and expound the Scriptures and encourage the saints. He continued to drive his car in the early months of their time at Auchlochan although he never travelled at more than 40 mph!

Mrs. Large's health steadily declined until her homecall in

1986. James had been absolutely devoted to his wife and he missed her sorely. He said he felt that his right hand had gone but he continued to be active in the Lord's service and, in fact wrote his books on Abraham (published 1986) and on Jacob (published 1988).

His own health was deteriorating by that time and he became housebound and, subsequently bedridden, but he continued to be interested in others and in the work and Word of God. He never wanted to cause trouble or inconvenience to anyone and was deeply grateful and appreciative of the loving care he received at Auchlochan and, no doubt, those who ministered to his needs were blessed by his example of patience and endurance. The Lord called this faithful servant home in November 1995.

James was a reserved and self-effacing gentleman who had no "small talk" and, although he might have appeared to be unsociable, he always had time to give to folk who needed help, advice or a listening ear. His advice was often just sound commonsense but he had a way of imparting it that was acceptable. He made people feel that they mattered, as individuals, to God.

He used to comment that "teenagers" were not a modern cult; Daniel was a teenager! It was this kind of understanding that endeared him to many and opened minds to the teaching of Scripture.

James enriched the lives of many with whom he came into contact during his long life and he had a remarkable rapport with younger people and considered it very worthwhile to encourage them. He was balanced, calm and fair in all his dealings and a true example of steadfastness. He had a quiet but unshakeable faith and absolute confidence that the purposes of God would be fulfilled in spite of opposition. He kept abreast of world affairs in order to be able to communicate with people on their own level. Although considered to be poor in this world's goods, James was rich by God's standards.

We acknowledge and thank God for his life and his example of unstinted selflessness shown during seventy years of service for his Lord and Saviour.

Brian Lacey, Cardiff

Other Recollections

It was in the early 1950s that JH Large made the first of many visits to the north east of Scotland, and he often stayed with my parents. I now reflect with deep appreciation on the privilege I had as a young man to establish a lasting spiritual friendship with this saintly and godly man. It would have to be said that his first visit was something of a culture shock as he did battle with both climate and dialect. "Have I given the right reply?" was a question frequently on his lips.

Passing over the many years of true spiritual help he gave me, his last visit to our home, when he was well into his eighties, confirmed in my mind his devotion to his Lord and to the saints. He was writing his very helpful book on Jacob, and on one occasion my wife took through to him a cup of coffee and a biscuit. Returning some time later to remove what should have been an empty cup, she found he had not even been aware of her bringing it to him, the coffee and the biscuit still untouched. This brought from him the suggestion that some kind of timer would have to be on the table.

Eddie Taylor, Aberdeen

My earliest recollections of him in our home when I was very young are of a kind, gracious, interested, gentle man. He and his wife were a devoted couple - to each other and to the Lord.

I stayed with them for a number of weeks in London and observed their daily godly living. His characteristic quick, sharp manner was complemented by his wife's chatty, motherly kindness. Sometimes she would be talking and be unaware of time. With a twinkle in his eyes, he would, in his inimitable way, say "Now, my dear ..." They adapted their mealtimes to suit me, and before leaving for work, there would be family devotions. His prayers were wide-ranging but specific; he had a great interest in the Lord's work everywhere. He was a man of few words, but what he said was always so full of meaning. They faithfully witnessed to all who crossed their path, and the weak and wavering in faith were encouraged to go on. Their self-sacrificing service and warm hospitality were appreciated by many, "and myself also".

My most abiding memory of Mr J H Large is of a discreet

man of wise counsel. When visiting him in Auchlochan towards the end of his life, it was refreshing to see still the same interested concern for others which had characterised his life. The so-called declining years were rich in written ministry from which so many of the Lord's people have benefited.

Ruth Hatt, Basingstoke

As a newly married couple fresh from Ayrshire facing the unknown of London and a new job, the kindness and care of Mr Large and of course "Auntie Large" remain fresh in our minds to the present thirty years on. The provision of space in their home and a place in their hearts for a young couple with a new baby was fullsome and sacrificial and typical of them.

I had the opportunity to drive Mr Large to his many speaking engagements in London for a period of some four months. His ministry was always fresh and relevant and delivered after much prayer and deep preparation. One morning I passed his study door and heard him "preach". I later discovered that he rehearsed his ministry on tape and listened to it himself to ensure its integrity before taking it to the Lord's people.

He was a man of great kindness who lived close to God and had therefore a deep empathy with the needs of men. His interests in the issues of the day even in later life, enabled him to take into the sanctuary an understanding, which ensured quite a unique pointedness to his ministry.

Ian Grant, Aberdeen

Mr Large was a master of illustration, and this ability ensured that his ministry was not easily forgotten. I recall one occasion at Cheshunt when he had been dealing with the necessity for a closer walk with God. He concluded his ministry by recalling a dull day in Scotland, and a bright day in England. (There was nothing particularly significant about the two locations!) In Scotland, a flock of seabirds had flown over him as he was out for a walk, but had it not been for their cries, he would not have noticed them. They cast no shadow. But in England, on a sunny day, a butterfly flew over him, and there in front of him was its shadow. "You see," said Mr Large, "when you walk in the light, every dark shadow shows up clearly, and we can then make the necessary adjustments in our lives. But when we are not walking in the light, all sorts of things can be happening to us, and we just don't realise that they are taking place. Keep yourselves in the light of God's presence: it is the only safe place to be."

He was also full of good advice to young people. As a young and inexperienced preacher I once asked Mr Large what he thought about repeating sermons. He replied, succinctly, "It's a poor greyhound that runs only once!"

John Riddle, Cheshunt

Mr Large was often one of the speakers at the "Bloomsbury" meeting in London, held on Saturday evenings of February and November, before and after the last war. I was seldom missing at these meetings and always enjoyed Mr Large's ministry, including his dry humour. It was therefore a great pleasure, that, when I came to live at Auchlochan House in Scotland, to find him here. At his suggestion, he and I managed to get some brethren together for weekly prayer and Bible study. He also kept a committee together until his health deteriorated, to arrange evening epilogues for the residents.

Cecil Green, Auchlochan

David Mawhinney
1915 - 1992
"I know that my redeemer liveth."
(Job 19.25)

Redemption - its cost *"precious blood"* (1 Pet 1.19).

It was Friday, 7th March, 1930. David Mawhinney, a fifteen year-old schoolboy and farmer's son, sat under the ministry of the gospel in his home town of Magherafelt, Co.Londonderry, Northern Ireland. The messages of preceding evenings had come home to David's heart in Holy Ghost power, teaching him that he needed something to fit him for the world to come. He had learned too, from God's Word, that that 'something' could never be attained by personal merit or effort. In God's sight he was a needy and bankrupt sinner, in possession of nothing wherewith to procure the salvation he so desperately needed.

David listened intently to the message and that night the glorious gospel entered his darkened heart. Another, the Lord Jesus, had purchased salvation for him at Calvary. There, upon the Cross, its mighty price had been paid, not in an earthly currency such as silver or gold, but in precious blood. Furthermore, that payment by the Saviour had been enough to satisfy God and was sufficient for the salvation of his soul.

But David felt he needed something more. If only he could have a word of assurance from God, a word whereby he might know that this great salvation was his personal possession. Before that meeting concluded the longed-for word was given. It seemed to come from heaven and was spoken with simplicity and clarity, "He that believeth on the Son hath everlasting life" (John 3.36). This was the very word for which he had waited. David appreciated that in it was divine promise; in it was certainty. In simple faith he stepped out upon it; God was true to His promise and David entered into the joy of knowing that he was now the possessor of everlasting life.

David Mawhinney in that meeting was saved for eternity. The cost of his salvation had been very great, but had been paid for by a loving Saviour in precious blood. He had been redeemed.

Redemption - its claim *"not your own. ..bought with a price"* (1 Cor 6.19,20).

It was early 1938. The fifteen year old schoolboy who had been redeemed had meantime left the shelter of his parental home in Co. Londonderry and had gone to the city of Belfast to serve his time in business. He had now entered his early twenties and life stretched out before him, holding great promise. Then that word redeemed confronted him again. It had assumed a new meaning and now seemed to demand something from him. "I am redeemed. I have been bought and paid for with precious blood. I am no longer my own. This little life that stretches out before me is no longer mine. It too has been redeemed and belongs to another."

David Mawhinney felt that God was calling him. God wanted his life. Furthermore, lost souls were calling and their cry he could not silence. What would he do with his life? A battle raged within. David took that battle into the presence of God and there it was settled. Something of that inner struggle is reflected in lines which he wrote on Sunday, 20th February, 1938.

Yes - a cry as of pain has come to my soul,
It has echoed and echoed 'till echoes do roll
Over mountains and valleys, o'er plain lands and steep
'Till my faith sees the wandering of the poor lost sheep.
"Oh! do come and help us," 'tis the cry I have heard,
If you love your Saviour, His love would be shared
By us who are dying in want and in shame,
If you tell us of Jesus, we will trust in His Name."
Yes, this cry is heartrending, it must be obeyed,
And a life all for Jesus is the sacrifice made,
The cross may be heavy, its weight be untold,
But one soul for my Saviour is more precious than gold.
Oh God, give me a heart, both faithful and brave,

To help lift the burdens off many a slave.
Then all for my Saviour I'll willingly give
And henceforth, to Thee alone shall I live.

David Mawhinney felt that he could no longer hold on to that which did not belong to him. His life, henceforth would be lived for the One who had purchased it upon the Cross with His precious blood and from that moment David set his heart on Central Africa.

The path which God had shown was now clear and David prepared to follow. However, the advent of World War II prevented his immediate departure, but in July 1946, accompanied by his wife Sadie and eighteen month old daughter Helen, David set sail from Belfast for Africa's dark interior, to the country then known as Northern Rhodesia, to Dipalata, Chitokoloki, to Lumwana, and there that life which had been **redeemed** was poured out for God.

David dearly loved Africa. He loved the African bush and he loved the African people. To tell the message of the Saviour to those who had never heard was a great delight. To witness the transformation, as men and women turned from darkness to light and from the power of Satan to God, brought a deep satisfaction to his heart. But David's supreme joy was to see believers, some but a short time delivered from heathendom, gather in collective testimony to the One who had wrought such mighty change in their lives. Life in Central Africa was certainly worthwhile.

Life in Central Africa, however, was not without its problems and its disappointments. Nevertheless, the One, who at the outset had pledged to David His Word, "Lo, I am with you alway" (Matt 28.20), never once failed to keep that promise and was with him all the way. The compensations far outweighed the disappointments and over thirty years were spent among the Lunda and the Lovale tribes. Those years yielded rich spiritual harvest.

Redemption-its consummation *"the redemption of our body"* (Rom 8.23).

The year 1978 brought great changes. David, stricken

down with severe rheumatoid arthritis, was obliged to return home to his native Northern Ireland. Leaving the land and people of his adoption and the work so dear to his heart was not easy. God had called him aside. Many wondered why.

God, however, was still at work in David's life. The work of God for David upon the cross for his salvation stood glorious and complete. The work of God through David in Central Africa also stood a shining testimony to the grace and power of God. But now God was doing a work in David, a day by day transformation of his life. Those nearest to him witnessed that transformation – it was glorious. The trial brought forth the pure gold. At times the heat was intense but God watched over that process and He knew His purpose best. In addition to rheumatoid arthritis were the problems of failing eyesight, bronchiectasis and coronary heart disease. The overall course was increasing disablement and suffering. The outward man was perishing, yet the inward man was renewed day by day (2 Cor 4.16).

A short respite for two and a half years (1980-1982) enabled David to return once more to his beloved Central Africa. It was a time of great need among the believers there and David's ministry was timely, a ministry of correction where there was error; a ministry of healing where there was division; a ministry of exhortation, edification and comfort.

The closing years of David's life brought increasing limitations. His spirit, however, was not bound and soared above his physical weaknesses. Many little assemblies in the homeland were enriched by his ministry. Many young lives were moulded and guided by his prayers and personal encouragement. David, wherever he went, carried with him a fragrance of Christ. It was indeed a privilege to be in his presence.

Lord's Day, 14th June 1992 brought to a close David's earthly sojourn, his limitations and his suffering. On that morning, quietly and peacefully, he passed away from scenes of earth into the presence of his Redeemer. There he is today, in conscious bliss and is "at home".

David's earthly account closed that morning - nothing will be added to it and nothing can be altered. That record is on high and one day will be opened out again in the presence of his Lord. David had only one life to give and he had yielded it, without reserve, to the claims of his Redeemer and he never took it back.

David's worn-out body was committed to the grave in a little nearby cemetery in the village of Broughshane, Co. Antrim, and there it rests, awaiting the morning of redemption for it too has been redeemed. That morning of redemption will break at the coming of the Lord and will be glorious, a morning without clouds, a morning of realisation. Not until then shall the consummation of redemption be fully known, but when that day breaks, in a clearer and purer light, David more perfectly shall know the wonder and wealth of the word "redeemed".

When in heaven I see Thy glory,
When before Thy throne I bow,
Perfected I shall be like Thee.
Fully Thy redemption know.
My Redeemer
Then shall hear me shout His praise.

Jack Strahan, Enniskillen

Other Recollections

David Mawhinney was a lifelong friend of our family, so we were pleased to welcome him and his wife Sadie to the assembly in Broughshane when they came to reside in the village for their 'retirement' years. For David, that meant less than two years.

In his later years David suffered much from arthritis, and his eyesight became very poor, but in spite of this he was regularly at the gatherings of the Lord's people. He used to sit and 'talk' the Scriptures, sharing his understanding and appreciation of spiritual things with an endearing warmth and intimacy. Even when his failing eyesight meant that he could no longer read, he could still discuss the Scriptures in depth for he knew them by heart and could quote them extensively and accurately - a challenge and encouragement to us all. He had a rare affinity with the young and showed a keen interest in their lives and spiritual development.

We benefited much from David's presence with us, both in the home and in the assembly, until the Lord took him home. His earthly remains lie in the garden village of Broughshane, until the day dawn and the shadows flee away.

Robin Strahan, Broughshane

I had the pleasure of introducing him to John Britton of Warrington, an outstanding spiritual personality in Lancashire. They became firm friends and enjoyed much fellowship together. In his latter years I was able to meet him from time to time on my visits to Ulster. The last earthly memory I have was in sharing a gospel meeting with him in Ballymena. By then he was an ill man with failing eyesight but still able to preach and present Christ with a sweet and winning way.

Jim Baker, Hamilton

David was a warm-hearted friendly brother well learned in the Scriptures and richly gifted to minister the Word in a simple gracious manner. He had an intense interest in younger brethren to whom he was a great source of encouragement.

David "had hands for everything" which was a tremendous asset in Zambia where vehicle and electrical spares were most difficult to obtain. He was in all things precise and methodical – an accomplished master of improvisation. He could work wonders in Zambia, and later at home, with strong elastic bands cut from motor car inner tubes; for example a replacement for the conventional metal spring to keep the garden gate shut. Prior to returning finally from the field his brother-in-law sent him a sketch of rooms in a house near Adam Street Assembly, and David, in Zambia, prepared a detailed plan and specification of necessary modifications which were completed in time for their return home.

Francis Regan, Belfast

David Mawhinney

Sydney Maxwell
1919 - 1993
"accepted of...his brethren, seeking the wealth
of his people, and speaking peace to all his seed"
(Esther 10.3)

Shortly after I began serving my time as an apprentice in the aircraft factory of Short & Harland's, Belfast, I was introduced to Sydney Maxwell by a close friend of mine, the late Jack Wylie. From the moment we met, somehow we were linked in an affection which the passage of time neither dissipated nor disturbed. Sydney was of tall and slender build; a young man with impressive potential for either worldly greatness or for God. Thankfully the latter was fully realised by the grace of God in his life, as several years before I met him, he had come to know the Saviour through the preaching of John McKendrick.

It was a delight to hear him relate the story of his conversion through Isaiah 53.6. He went in, as he would say, at the first "all" and came out at the last "all". In the freshness of his youth he exuded a sincerity and a sweetness of manner that won not only my confidence, but also those who would come to know him in the Lord. Constantly he diffused an aroma of a deep, genuine piety, anxious at all times to be unspotted from the world and to live godly in Christ Jesus. Virile and warm-hearted he engaged enthusiastically in the spread of the gospel. Associated as he was with a Testimony Band, his intense desire to see souls saved marked him as a man destined for greater things. His fervency exerted a charm over my spirit, and as a result, a captivating friendship ensued which was to enrich every moment we were together and extend undiminished for the fifty-four years we knew fellowship in the Lord. Meeting him when I did, when I was five years his junior, I observed his free and earnest spirit was prepared to respond to teaching from the Scriptures with candid and inquiring interest. True, my new-found friend moved freely and widely in pursuit of the interest of the Kingdom, yet I sensed that his spirit was fettered by denominational barriers.

Gradually in our youthful encounters, I plied him with material from which I was deriving the utmost help. Sydney was then in Baptist circles and I was being greatly helped by ministry on the assembly, written by the late Hawthorne Bailie. This honoured teacher was answering a Baptist Pastor's assault on assembly truth. This provided me with useful material for Sydney. Just at this time, Sydney was attending meetings held by his local Pastor, who was seeking to disprove the scriptural viability of the assembly. I supplied Sydney with questions which I suggested he put to the pastor. On doing so Sydney came into work the next morning with absolutely no answers to the questions I submitted. Somehow, under God's amazing help, for I was only 15 years of age, my simple efforts brought increasing light which was greatly augmented by his attendance eventually, at a Bible Class we held during the lunch period in the factory at which many brethren, including Mr. Joe Milne (Venezuela), attended. Initially he resented the fact they were all 'brethren'. Of course, had he written his objection, the word brethren would have carried a capital B!! I retorted, "And what would you expect them to be?"

In December 1939 I had Sydney attend his first conference. The Belfast Christmas Conference that year was held in the YMCA Belfast, and among others, Mr. GMJ Lear (Argentina) ministered the Word of God. Brother Lear was the first to rise that afternoon and opening at Leviticus 23, then Numbers 28 and Deuteronomy 16, he submitted a useful outline on the Feasts of Jehovah. His points were lucid: The Time When (Lev 23), The Manner How (Num 28-29), and The Place Where (Deut 16). It was the third point God was to use mightily, for, at the close of the day spent in His courts, as we left the building and walked into Wellington Place, Sydney, with tears in his eyes, said, "Tom, it is the assembly for me."

These words continue to burn in my soul for they were truly

prophetic. Early in the New Year of 1940, Sydney took his place amongst the saints gathered to His name at Francis Street, Newtownards. On informing his father that such would be his association, he met with severe opposition to the extent that he was told, if that were the case, he would have to leave home, for he was deserting the family's religious persuasion. My mother offered him a room in our home in Belfast, but that was not necessary for his father, when it came to the point, relented. Later he had the joy of seeing both his parents trust the Saviour. The Lord always honours them that honour Him. Over half a century elapsed in which our beloved brother lived out the reality of his decisive step. In a most devoted manner and with a thoroughly disciplined mind he gave adequate expression by life and lip, in movement and in ministry, to the strength of the conviction that brought him to the place where God had put His name.

Not long after this Sydney was twice hospitalised for surgery. When we first met I noticed he had a limp. He explained that his ankle was giving him trouble as result of a kick he sustained while playing football. Eventually he had a steel insert which straightened and strengthened his ankle effectively. Then he had to have a kidney removed, from which he recovered quickly and as result, he usually referred to himself from then on, as a one-cylinder preacher!

Brother Maxwell went on to grow in grace and in the knowledge of our Lord and Saviour, Jesus Christ. His application to the study of the Word of God characterised his manner of life and round of interest. This became clearly manifest in his efforts in the gospel, as he was used widely throughout Ulster in preaching. A series of gospel meetings was conducted by several younger brethren, among them Bob Neill (South Africa) and Reginald Jordan (Belfast) who also worked with us in the aircraft factory. These meetings in the Flush Gospel Hall were well attended and saw some blessing. One night Reggie opened the meeting and then Sydney took over. Reggie was sitting, as it would be, right under Sydney's nose! The people were crowded into what was not a very large hall. Sydney opened with 2 Kings 5 and preached, of course, on Namaan the leper. In his way through the message he came to the point where

Namaan resisted accepting the prophet's advice to go to Jordan. Sydney, ably imitating ably Namaan's reaction, launched into a tirade on dirty, stinking, filthy Jordan!!! Everyone in the hall got the 'implication', Sydney apart. We all had to stifle our laughter, yet Sydney pressed on oblivious that the mention of Jordan would have any reference even by inference to Reggie!

Often we preached together and he would say, "Go ahead Tom and preach your best, and I will come in with a sound word afterwards." Eventually after several years of close fellowship together, he shared with me his exercise relative to the work of the Lord in North America, Canada in particular. It alerted me to the fact that, soon I would be without my dear brother's company and companionship. His going forth would bring about a temporary end to the happy times we spent together around the Word of God and its proclamation throughout our favoured province.

It was in 1948 that Sydney with his beloved wife Sarah, affectionately known as Cis, and family, left the shores of his native land for Canada. There began what turned out to be, along with the United States of America, the sphere of his many exploits richly owned by God in abundant blessing to both saint and sinner. He was used in the salvation of many precious souls throughout the whole of North America. Many too would be led into paths of obedience as he ministered the Word of God and taught truth that directed their feet to the place where God had put His name. Having a razor-edge type of mind, he excelled in Bible Readings and scarcely allowed if ever, any deviation from the truth he held so dearly. Many of those with whom he served so industriously, are like himself, safe home at last. There are not many left who could tell the story of his exceptional ability and eager aim to see the testimony established on every shore he was permitted to reach.

Throughout the intervening years, I would only see Sydney as occasion served. He being in North America and I in Malaysia, opportunity of serving together was no longer a regular feature. However in 1972 he invited me over to Vancouver where he lived and for several weeks we joined in cordial service together. Other occasions since brought us to various areas and one of the most memorable was the 100th celebration of Toronto's Conference. Tragedy befell brother Sydney and his wife, when their eldest daughter Margaret was killed while on vacation in California. This had its own remaining effect on our dear brother, as he missed her keenly.

Right up unto the end whether in presence or in absence my dear brother, fellow-worker and fellow-helper, never failed to cheer my spirit, comfort my soul and consolidate my service. Like Joseph he was a good man for he sustained to the last a deep unadulterated affection for his Lord. His love for Him was strong, sincere and truly sacrificial (Luke 23.50). Like another Joseph, he maintained an unshaken fidelity to the truth which he learned in earlier days moving his feet to the assembly of God (Acts 11.24). No one can but rightly discern that he had a remarkable affection for the Book. He gleaned much. He gave much. He guarded much (Matt 12.35).

Many souls today will thank God that Sydney had also an insatiable appetite to spread the glad tidings of God to the souls of men. He truly was a bearer of 'good tidings' (2 Sam 18.27). Nor can it be denied that he had more than a passing affection for his beloved wife and family. We think of the life he lived before them, the love that he had for them and the legacy he left to them (Prov 13.22).

The night he boarded the cross-channel boat, before taking his further journey across the Atlantic to the sphere of divine appointment, with hundreds gathered to wish them well, we joined in singing, as the ship carried the treasure away into the darkness, "We'll all gather home in the morning." It is so that we will on that fair shore and in the morning without clouds, unite in praise to Him who bought us with His blood and brought us nigh to God and to one another in our Lord Jesus Christ. It is this that nerves us on as we tread the remainder of the road home without the brother beloved we knew as Sydney Maxwell.

Tom Bentley, Ballymena

Charles W. F. McEwen

1899 - 1992

*"I press toward the mark for the prize of
the high calling of God in Christ Jesus."*
(Philippians 3.14)

A man in his late fifties strode purposefully across the Plymouth banking hall to the Securities counter where I was working one Saturday morning. The Administration Manager came over to me and asked, "Who was that earnest-looking man who was speaking with you?" I replied "That was my father, Sir!" That unbelieving banker had intuitively discerned and expressed what might aptly summarise my father's approach to life "an earnest man". The focus of his life was an earnestness for God, for the preaching of the gospel and the upbuilding of believers.

Father was born on 12th January 1899 at Ottery St Mary, a small east Devon town, into the family of an evangelist, John Knox McEwen, who will still be remembered by a number of older readers, and his wife Alice Mary (nee Fowler). He was the younger of two sons. Soon after his birth the family moved to Exeter where his parents remained until their homecalls in 1944 and 1950. Because his mother was not robust in health and his father was often away for long periods of time, including repeated visits to North America and particularly Nova Scotia, there was usually a lady companion staying in the home. One of them was of a rather severe disposition and from all that I can gather, father had a strict upbringing. Part of his education was at Mount Radford School, Exeter, then under the Headmastership of the late WE Vine. As a boy he enjoyed soccer and he organised a Saturday game for which he was appointed team captain, but his father then forbade him to attend. One can imagine the reception at school on the following Monday when his team members turned on him for not attending the match, especially with his being the captain of the side!

Along with his parents he attended the Fore Street Gospel Hall in Exeter (destroyed in the German blitz in 1942) and it was there as a teenager one Sunday evening that he turned in repentance to God and put his faith in the Lord Jesus. God had been speaking to his heart for some while. He had a particular scare when, coming down from the attic bedroom where he slept, he found no one in the house. His immediate thought was that the Lord Jesus had returned and taken his parents and he had been left behind. The truth was that an overnight guest had had to make an early departure and my grandparents had accompanied the visitor to the tram, leaving father alone in the house!

On leaving school he commenced work for a Christian who ran a house-furnishing business in Exeter, but his training was interrupted in 1917 when in the First World War he was called up for National Service. He appealed as a conscientious objector and at a tribunal on 28th February he was exempted from military service on condition that he undertook "work which not being under military control is nevertheless useful for the prosecution of the war and under conditions approved by the tribunal". His stance aroused some opposition, not least from his older brother who was serving in the Royal Air Force and later rose to the rank of Squadron Leader.

Father was sent to Northern Ireland to undertake farm work in the Newcastle area of County Down. Conditions at the beginning were fairly severe, though later he moved to Ballywillwill where he worked for the Wright family. At Newcastle his zeal in the gospel began to develop and he used to preach on the promenade. There too he became firm friends with Mr and Mrs D Bond Walker; also the McNeill family, including Ruth, later to be Ruth Bingham, beloved mother of Derick. His experiences there were used by God to develop character and to prepare him for his life's calling.

He was deeply devoted to his mother throughout her life and missed her sorely. When eventually he returned home after three years, he took her on his knees (she was quite a frail little woman, though a great prayer warrior) and sang:

He is not a disappointment; Jesus is far more to me
Than in all my glowing daydreams I had fancied He could
*   be.*
And the more I get to know Him, so the more I find Him true
And the more I long that others will be led to know Him too.

In 1921 father moved to Tavistock, South Devon, near the border with Cornwall. He began working for the late Charles M Bond in charge of the office, first in Mr. Bond's ironmongery business and then in his motor engineering business. For the next six years my father threw his efforts into the work of God at the Tavistock assembly, especially among the young people there, and in preaching the gospel. He frequently crossed over into Cornwall to preach in the open air and after six years he sensed that God was calling him to work full-time in gospel preaching. Mr. Bond wrote of him, "His ability and integrity leave nothing to be desired; regularity, punctuality, accuracy and the conscientious discharge of duty were among his many strong points." In 1927 he was commended to the work of God by the Tavistock assembly and Fore Street Gospel Hall, Exeter (the elders there wrote that "he has been engaged in gospel work and the Lord has greatly used him in the salvation of souls") - I still have the letters of commendation!

In 1928 he made his one and only visit to the USA where he joined up with his cousins, Sam and Hugh McEwen, who were both preachers there. This handsome young cousin from England was quite a heart-throb to a number of American ladies! Resistant to their charms he returned to England where he had come to know a Miss Gladys Godsall who worked for Pickering and Inglis whose London shop was in Paternoster Row.

Gladys was an eager young woman and marched with the Pilgrim Preachers in gospel witness as well as being active in her assembly at Willesden in Sunday School work, etc. She and her sister Lily were visiting Torquay on holiday and joined with the local believers who were holding an open-air witness. I am told that they were invited to sing a duet and they sang "Oh why not say Yes tonight". Father was preaching at this same meeting and as he had quite a good singing voice, he sang "It may be the last time you'll ever hear the call"! There was no double entendre in the choice of songs, but a friendship began and they later became engaged. They were married in October 1933 by the late JB Watson at King's Hall, Willesden.

Father and mother set up home in Exeter, but every year from May to late September they went to Cornwall in a caravan and moved from village to village, father preaching and both of them distributing gospels, tracts and especially copies of "The Traveller's Guide". Cornwall has been called an evangelist's graveyard. But he persistently walked mile after mile, encouraging the small groups of believers he met, as well as witnessing to unsaved people. In the winter months he travelled more widely in gospel preaching and Bible teaching. On 11th January 1936 news came to him while in a series of gospel preaching in Harbertonford, a village outside Totnes in South Devon, that he was father to a baby boy, born in London where my mother's parents lived.

In my early years my parents continued to go to Cornwall with their caravan and I have faint memories of being with them on the harbour wall at Mevagissey, where father was preaching in the open air on the September night in 1939 when war was declared. I was unaware of the reason for the hush that came over the small crowd of fishermen and others who were listening, but I knew that something serious was afoot. I can guess too that the opportunity was taken to stress the urgency of responding to the message of the gospel. The visits to Cornwall came to an end and soon after, as I began school, mother was no longer able to travel with father and she was grounded in Exeter. She accepted the often lengthy periods of loneliness without complaint, including the time of the Luftwaffe blitz on Exeter. She was always an enthusiastic encourager of her husband. During the latter part of the Second World War, a number of Polish prisoners of war were stationed outside Exeter. Father, along with a few other local Christians, began a regular programme of visiting the camp and distributing tracts in Polish and preaching where they could.

Throughout his life I could never get my father to disclose how he survived financially. His answer to occasional questions was always along the lines that he could "only speak well of God. He is faithful and He has always met my needs." He lived in the confidence that God could be totally trusted to do so in the future. My parents were very conscious that the gifts they received from God's people were often the result of sacrifice. It was therefore incumbent on them to use those monies responsibly and also to give of those monies themselves - but always with great confidentiality. Indeed confidentially was a quality which Father highly valued and keeping the confidences of those who came to consult him was a matter of the utmost importance. Perhaps that is one reason why many people did in fact come to speak with him.

Like most of us, he had his own idiosyncrasies. He was meticulously concerned about punctuality; being late was impressed on me as being unacceptable. He always sought to reply to any letters he received by immediate return. He would dash to the front door to grasp the incoming post, open it at once, and soon after breakfast he was in his study penning a reply. The envelopes he used were ones he had received and patched them up with Croydex paste and labels! Throughout the time that I lived at home there was no telephone or radio.

When he was away on preaching tours it was his habit to write every day to mother and likewise she replied by return. It was said by Mr. James Hutchinson, a partner in the gospel, "Charlie, if you're ever found dead, it'll be with a pen in your hand writing to Gladys!"

He was never a lengthy preacher and for that reason, among others, I suspect he was often very acceptable. His style of preaching was usually alliterative with a generous scattering of illustrations. Sometimes he would be quite pointed, though not in what today would be considered by many as the outrageous style of his own father's preaching. An old Devon farmer said to my father more than once: "Ah, Charlie, you're not half the preacher your father was"! The truth was that my father was of a much gentler disposition than his father, although by no means lacking in fervour for the gospel. Much time was spent in his study and there were times when I burst in as a child to find him on his knees in prayer. He prepared his messages with great care and his

Bibles were carefully marked with copious notes. Most people would have needed a magnifying glass to read them!

Father's sphere of preaching began to spread more widely with visits to Scotland (from one of which he had to return home in 1944 because of the death of his 91 year old father); also Wales and to various parts of England. For many years in the summer months he would regularly be found with a marquee sited in a West Country village and holding gospel meetings, preceded during the day by an extensive visiting programme. He was also an assiduous visitor to hospitals and homes where people were in need of comfort and encouragement. Every spring for almost the rest of his long life he made a visit to Largs and Ayr to attend Bible Readings. These were highlights of his year when he met so many friends and fellow-preachers, as well as enjoying the exposition of Scripture.

In 1948 he was invited by the elders of what was then the Buller Road Gospel Hall in Exeter to lead a gospel mission in a tent. He felt unsure of doing this alone and, with the agreement of the elders, invited Mr. James Hutchinson to join him. There began a partnership in preaching which lasted over many years and in a variety of locations. The Lord blessed in that tent mission so much so that the elders invited the two evangelists to come back again two years later. In subsequent years regular invitations came to preach in Northern Ireland with James Hutchinson. Some of these meetings continued for many weeks and one I recall particularly was when they were at Ballymena and saw God's hand in the conversion of a considerable number of souls. Also for years they preached together in open-air meetings on the promenade at Newcastle, Co. Down, the very place where he had preached as a teenager in his "exile" to Northern Ireland.

He had no hobby of relaxation as such, but he could be frequently found in his study, clipping from a variety of Christian periodicals articles which he considered of value and sermon illustrations. He would then file these in cabinets under alphabetical order of subject matter. Likewise his library of books was in alphabetical order of subject and author. Near the end of his life he had given almost all these away. His exercise came from walking and even well into his eighties he would set off at a brisk pace to walk into the city centre.

Father deplored extreme legalism and an attitude which despised Christians associated with other groups and he strongly advocated what he saw as a "balanced standpoint". He would, however, have been regarded as strongly loyal to his understanding of New Testament church principles. He was among the founder members of the "Precious Seed" magazine and remained on the organising committee well into his 80s. Though by this time no longer involved in gospel missions, he would still preach and give devotional messages in numerous assemblies in and around Exeter.

The time came in the 1980s when father began to suffer a number of ischaemic attacks which caused him to fall and the doctor said that he must no longer drive his car. I was deputed to tell him and he was not happy to receive such a message, saying that the doctor had not told him! Sense, however, prevailed and the car was sold. Mother had for a long time been very deaf and she was also suffering from angina. In 1983 they found the maintenance of their house too much for them, so they moved to a flat at Whipton, Exeter. At the same time they transferred their membership from Belmont to the assembly at Whipton Chapel.

In 1991, when they really needed care, my wife and I expressed a willingness to provide for them in our own home in West Sussex, but this was far from their roots and so many friends and assemblies which they knew well and enjoyed visiting. Others in Northern Ireland encouraged them to move there to a new retirement home which was being built at Ballymena, where father had often preached and had many good friends. So in October 1991 they said their final farewell to Exeter and flew to Belfast. In January 1992 they moved into Prospect Nursing Home in Ballymena and my father was to preach again at the Cambridge Avenue assembly. Although now 93, his voice, though quiet in conversation, rang out with vigour and clarity.

Only four weeks after moving into Prospect, Mother was taken into hospital where she passed away after surgery and heart failure. The loss for father was immense and whilst the local Christians were most supportive in visiting and other acts of kindness, he steadily weakened. I think he had cherished a secret hope of living longer than his father and this wish was granted. He had told me, on the last of my regular visits to see him, that he was now ready to go Home and on August 23rd he passed away peacefully. Jim Hutchinson, who had been a faithful and supportive friend, officiated at the funeral services of both Father and Mother. And so a long life had ended, lived with earnestness and devotion to his Saviour and Lord.

John McEwen, Leamington Spa

Other Recollections

My first acquaintence with Charles McEwen was as a small boy attending the gospel service in our local assembly. I was glad when "Charlie Mac" preached because I knew the service would be all over within the hour - he was not a long winded speaker!

Charles always had an interest in my spiritual development and became a father figure in my life, my father having died when I was 16. As a family, we feel the debt we owe to Charles and Gladys McEwen for their prayers is incalculable.

Blessed with a good sense of humour, Charles had a fund of witticisms suitable to the occasion. After attending a meeting where a brother had gone a little over the top with his typology, Charles commented, parodying the words of the well known hymn: "Wonderful things in the scriptures I see, things that are put there by you and by me"!

When visiting the little assembly in the East Devon fishing village of Beer, he would tell us with a twinkle in his eye: "Having our potatoes boiled in beer on Sunday"!

Michael Partridge, Barnstaple

His ready wit gave instant response one day, as he and I worked on the promenade in Largs, Ayrshire. It was General Election time, and a person was hopefully handing out bills by, or about a local candidate. He passed one to Charles who said, "No thank you, my Man's in!"

Archie Murdoch, Glasgow

Periodically he would invite me to his home for a meal after which we would sit down together and talk. He was a good listener and the counsel he gave was always sound and biblically based. He regarded our time spent together as being mutually helpful and would say, "Iron sharpeneth iron".

As a young man, at times I nervously made a contribution at our Sunday morning meeting. He would telephone me to express his appreciation of the word passed on. That simple but sincere act greatly heartened me.

Ronald Baker, Exeter

Knowing of his increasing frailty he was asked by his Doctor, a believer, why he could not ease up on preaching. He replied in Paul's words, unhesitatingly, "Woe is me if I preach not the gospel." His presentation of the gospel was direct, powerful and yet always winsome. One of the choice sermons we recall he preached in the eventide of life was entitled "The Gospel according to Christ's enemies" -

Never man spake like this man.

This man receiveth sinners and eateth with them.

He saved others, Himself He cannot save.

Ivor Harris, Taunton

In 1953 Mr Charles McEwen joined Mr J.G. Hutchinson for gospel meetings in Ballymena. During the time of the meetings, the preachers stayed in our home - and what a happy time it was! The children really loved 'Mr KEWEN' (as they called him) and many practical jokes were played on one another.

Charles was very gracious, extremely considerate, always careful lest he should embarrass anyone. He was never idle - ever busily engaged in his varied interests - Bible study, proof reading for 'Precious Seed' or other publications, letter writing to missionaries, praying for and helping others. His preaching was clear, simple and direct. He was not interested in place or prominence, but walked humbly with his God.

J S Wallace, Ballymena

Over many years when travelling from Exeter to Bristol by car for the 'Precious Seed' committee meetings, ten minutes into the journey Mr McEwen would bring out his little black book which went with him everywhere. He would then proceed to give all the latest news of the assemblies; the births, deaths, and marriages. Most dear to his heart were those who had come to faith in Christ, for he was an evangelist. Then he shared a Scripture that had been very precious to him, and finally a point of doctrine to discuss. All too soon we arrived at our destination.

Desmond Gahan, Stoke Gabriel

I had not met Mr McEwen when he wrote and asked me to join him in meetings in a large tent in Exeter. Although I felt I should go, it was with some measure of trepidation, for I had often heard his father who was a fearless, penetrative preacher, who at times seemed severe. I was not long in Devon until I learned what the local Christians said was true, "he had his father's truth and his mother's grace."

As we travelled, prayed, and preached together I learned he was a faithful steward of time, truth, and treasure. He was very appreciative of all that God gave him, and he would not take a glass of water without giving thanks for it.

His love for the gospel was very great and the assembly position was very dear to him. He was grieved when some would want to make unscriptural changes. This led to his involvement in the magazine 'Precious Seed'.

While steadfast and loyal, he often said, "If you take a moderate stand it is more easily maintained," and would quote Proverbs 8.20, "I lead in the *midst* of the paths."

James G. Hutchinson, Dundonald

In the mid-fifties a close friend of mine sought his advice following an encounter with a stranger on a train, who had commented adversely as my friend read his Bible, indicating he had once been an evangelist among so-called brethren churches, but now believed it was all "rubbish". My friend was somewhat shaken as the statements were made with some vehemence.

On consulting Charlie he was taken aback, not merely because the stranger was well known to him, but because he took from his pocket a card with the names of many for whom he prayed daily - the stranger featured there! Who can tell whether one day this man, the subject of such consistent prayer, returned to the Lord?

Ivor Harris, Taunton

Charles W. F. McEwen

Robert M. McPheat

1933 - 1990

"for my name's sake hast laboured, and hast not fainted."
(Revelation 2.3)

Robert McLean McPheat was born at Airdrie in Scotland on 13th November 1933, the third child in a family of six. In 1947 a Mr Wilding had gospel meetings in the nearby village of Greengairs and a school friend of Robert's, John Clelland attended and was saved. He then spoke to Robert at school about his salvation and having expressed an interest in this matter they both went into the school gym where Robert accepted the Lord Jesus as his Saviour as a young lad of fourteen. He subsequently was baptised in the Hebron Hall at Airdrie and received into fellowship in the nearby assembly at Plains. During his early years at Plains he appreciated the help he was given by the saints there, and in particular by brother John King whom he spoke of lovingly as his spiritual father.

In 1951 he came to Newtongrange in Midlothian, at that time a large coal mining area, to work at the Lady Victoria Colliery, travelling home each weekend. He married Margaret (Greta) Robertson, who was in fellowship at Plains, in January 1953 and they were commended to the assembly at Newtongrange two months later, setting up home in Mayfield, a nearby village where the assembly is now located. During all his service for the Lord both Robert and Greta maintained a close fellowship with Jim and Mary Paterson from Plains, and Robert made many visits to the assembly at Plains to minister the Word of God and preach the gospel. From the beginning of their marriage, Robert and Greta used their home to provide hospitality to the saints, and we have many happy memories of fellowship enjoyed there, especially discussing the Scriptures. Robert served faithfully as an overseer in the assembly and his guidance and care was greatly valued at a time when the testimony was faced with many difficult problems.

It was evident in those early years that the Lord had gifted Robert in preaching the gospel and teaching the Word of God, and in October 1967 he was heartily commended to the work of the Lord by the assemblies at Plains and Newtongrange. His first meetings after commendation were in Northern Ireland where he was warmly received and where he often made many visits over the years to preach the gospel and minister the Word of God. At this time the assembly at Newtongrange had obtained a site to erect a new hall at Mayfield, and the first meetings at his home assembly were in 1968 in a tent pitched on this site. During these meetings the local SNP candidate, Andrew Sharp, professed faith in Christ. The tent was also pitched at a nearby village of Pathhead where brother Wilfred Glenn from Northern Ireland shared in the preaching. This was the first time we had met brother Wilfred and we will always remember him earnestly preaching with tears running down his face and repeating frequently

"Tomorrow hath no promise that it can give to you,
Tomorrow is eternity just hidden from your view."

Oh that we could have our heart in the preaching, like the Lord Jesus as He beheld the city and wept over it. Wilfred was later to serve the Lord in Brazil from where he was called home as a relatively young man.

These meetings were encouraging with many local people attending, and during this effort two elderly ladies, Mrs Mills and Mrs MacDonald, both widows in their eighties, trusted the Saviour. It was a joy to subsequently see them obeying the Lord in baptism, and being received into fellowship at Mayfield. Later Robert purchased a hall in Pathhead; to continue to build on the interest shown in the village, and this was used weekly for children's work and for monthly gospel meetings. Though he had felt that he was not gifted in children's work it was a thrill to see the response of the children in the work at Pathhead; they loved him and were queuing at the hall door some time before the meetings were due to start. During this time the tent was also pitched in the nearby villages of Ormiston and Tranent. In the first week of the meetings at Ormiston vandals damaged the tent, but Robert managed to obtain the village hall to continue the meetings. It was because the assembly was so small at Tranent that Robert was exercised about having gospel meetings there, the tent being pitched on the edge of a car park. In both Ormiston and Tranent there was not much response from the local people but the gospel was faithfully preached in both these places. Sadly not long after the meetings, the assembly in Tranent closed.

He had a great love in preaching the gospel, sounding it out with his powerful voice in a solemn yet winsome way. He had a lovely voice too for singing and appreciated good singing in the meetings. He was always interested in hearing new tunes for hymns and often when having a time of hymn singing in the home would introduce us to different tunes so that we could try them in the meetings.

Another of his outstanding features was his interest in young people. He was quick to encourage when he observed any spiritual progress being made, and likewise would gently yet firmly draw alongside and warn if he felt there were features being shown that would harm spiritual growth.

He was a person who was easy to confide in, knowing that he would respect that confidence and go out of his way to help in a personal way. He said latterly that he felt it an increasing burden to try and identify with the many difficulties and problems that many of the dear saints expressed to him, matters that they oftimes felt were almost too heavy to bear. Because he was away from home in his service for the Lord, he stayed with many of the saints, and since his death many have mentioned to me that it was a joy and privilege to have him in their home. He would quickly set them at ease and would become part of the household.

He seemed to have that unique ability too of assessing the calibre of individuals and assemblies, and would not be afraid to convey either personally or by ministry his concerns about any matters that he thought should be corrected. His gift in ministry took him to England, Canada and the USA where he endeared himself to the saints with his heart warming yet searching ministry. In ministry he loved to speak on the person of Christ, and few who attended the conference at Larkhall in

Lanarkshire not long before his homecall will forget his ministry on the burial of the Lord Jesus. Brother Alf Wilson, himself an able teacher of the Scriptures, said after listening to this address, " That was more than ministry, it was worship." He also would enjoy using character studies in ministry, making many pointed practical applications from the lives of those in the sacred page. Many times we listened to him and have been captivated when he highlighted things that we hadn't noticed, but have experienced the searchlight too of the Scriptures as he applied divine truth practically.

One noticeable feature during his service for God was that he did not engage in any written ministry, as he always said that he was happier preaching than writing. It came as a surprise therefore to discover after his death that he had at the request of brother Dennis Gilpin written on the life of Joseph. It has been a joy to see this book recently completed and made available to the saints under the title "Joseph – a fruitful bough".

As with all faithful servants of Christ it is their earnest prayer that they will see fruit from their labours in preaching the gospel, and Robert had the encouragement of seeing many accepting the Lord Jesus as their Saviour, among those being his own family Simon and Joy, whom he pointed to the Lord when they were young. They are both married and continue faithfully in assembly fellowship.

During the last two years of his life, ill health restricted him from engaging in sustained series of meetings and from travelling further afield. He would engage nearer to home in weekend meetings or in four subsequent Lord's Days for ministry and gospel preaching. It was a joy and privilege to share with him on some of these occasions at Port Seton, Musselburgh, Shields Road, Motherwell; the last being Wednesday evenings for gospel meetings at Meadowside in Dundee in March 1990. He said at the end of these meetings that though he had preached in many places over the years he would always treasure these last times together in the gospel, adding that he wouldn't be here much longer. We had always been close over the many years we had shared fellowship together, and it became obvious with matters that he talked about that he appeared to anticipate that his service was drawing to a close.

He had enjoyed a close friendship with Denis and Margaret Gilpin from Jersey and it was while he was on holiday there that the Lord called him home suddenly on 25th July 1990, a noble and faithful servant of Christ who is greatly missed.

Robert Miller, Mayfield

Other Recollections

With Robert at a conference in Galston, we had just come out of the prayer meeting and before we went up onto the platform Robert turned to me and said, "Do you not feel like Samson when he said 'O Lord God, remember me I pray Thee, and strengthen me I pray thee, only this once'." (Judges 16.28). This has been the cry of my heart oftentimes since.

Mr Malcolm Radcliffe, Ayr

God had endowed Robert with a unique gift of wisdom and sympathetic understanding to encourage and advise many of God's dear saints faced with various problems. Robert put mothers at ease immediately, as he took children on his knee and played around the floor. He was a giant, yet could get down to gain a child's affection. Hearing of his death my own little granddaughter said through sobs and tears, "He was my favourite preacher".

Jim Paterson, Plains

On one occasion his sense of humour was special. After a ministry meeting, he presented me outside with a package and gave explicit instructions that it had not to be opened until we got home. To our surprise, when the parcel was opened, it contained a newly killed hen that needed to be plucked – a procedure with which I was unfamiliar. When I phoned to thank him and to indicate the predicament, he burst into uncontrollable laughter and informed me that there were many things in life we still had to learn.

John Frame, Glasgow

I was nineteen when the assembly at Gourock had two weeks of consecutive ministry meetings with Robert on the life of Moses and the Song of Solomon. At the end of the first night he said to me, "Learn to tell the difference between a nice man and a good man." I discovered what many others already knew, he had the very unnerving ability to read the hearts of the saints. As the meetings continued into their second week I knew I had met a 'good man' who had my spiritual welfare at heart.

Robert Thomson, Bishopton

In 1989 my wife and I were very exercised about full-time service and we were looking to the Lord for guidance. Robert came to Bridge of Weir for our conference weekend in November and his ministry spoke very loudly to both of us. I particularly remember the warm and compelling word after the Breaking of Bread when he exalted the Lord Jesus by drawing our attention to the priest with his hand full, the psalmist with his heart full and the home at Bethany where there was a house full of worship. We both felt that this was the word from the Lord for which we were waiting. Doubts however, still clouded our minds and we looked to the Lord, Gideon like, for a second confirmation.

At the end of that year Robert was speaking at the commendation meeting for Malcolm Radcliffe. Although it was a dark, wet stormy night, we decided to go. As we listened to Robert it seemed that he was speaking only to us. He knew nothing of our thoughts, or even of the effect that his previous ministry had had on us, but his words reached our hearts. He addressed the very fears which we had and urged us to put our trust in God. On our way home from that meeting, and in the days that followed, we determined to go forward. It was some months before I could speak to the brethren regarding commendation, after which we decided we would let Robert know how telling his teaching had been. Before that, however, he had gone home to be with the Lord.

John Grant, Bridge of Weir

The man's transparency and discernment were outstanding. Even in correspondence it seemed he could just see where we young Christians stood and his letters were full of wholesome instruction. I had often seen him off at harbour and airport but the last time I did so he put his hand on my shoulder and giving me the straight look in the eye he said "Ivan you're a man now! The most important thing is to be a man of God."

Ivan Gordon, Glengormley

As a scribe, he was a master in the art. His letters were pithy, balanced sometimes with a little humour but always containing words of encouragement and warming our affections to the person of Christ. I quote from a letter received a few months before his homecall – "The cold is my worst enemy (apart from self). I long for the heat and summer (Heaven will be better)".

John Frame, Glasgow

Joe Merson

1921 - 1996
*"...the ministry which I have received of the Lord
Jesus to testify the gospel of the grace of God."*
(Acts 20.24)

A correspondent from Shetland wrote, "I am glad to think that you are likely to put in writing something of our late brother's labours for the Lord..." In a sense, what was said many years ago about no less a person than John Nelson Darby may be applied to Joe Merson – he was, "As unknown and yet well known". It is a matter of regret that full-time servants of the Lord who circulate widely over a cycle of many years should so soon be forgotten as they slip into a vague twilight of hazy recollection.

Joe Merson was among the youngest members of a family of nine children, five sons and four daughters. They were brought up in a home where the name of God was greatly revered, in the small village of Sandend (near Portsoy), on the Moray Firth. From early years, they knew the way of salvation but Joe's response was negative as he drifted more and more into sinful ways and regrettably, this included a growing fondness for strong drink.

One night, Joe was on his way home, very much under the influence of alcohol, when he missed his footing and overbalanced into a ditch which had quite a lot of water in it. Such was the drunken stupor which gripped him that he was unable to muster the co-ordination – mental and physical – in order to extricate himself. He lay there for most of the night. Eventually, he sobered up and was able to make his way home. This terrifying experience had a marked affect on him because, for a long time afterwards, he was the victim of congestion of the lungs. It also directed him to the grim

215

realisation that, had he drowned that night, he would have been lost.

In his search for salvation, Joe sought out a Christian in his native village and they had many conversations. One evening, deeply troubled, Joe went out for a walk along the braes as far as the ruins of an old castle, about two miles away. There, at Findlater Castle, Joe bowed his knee and received Christ as his Saviour. His life was completely transformed as a result. After a few years, he felt the call to serve the Lord full-time and was commended to this work by his local assembly.

The present writer first met Joe soon afterwards in the summer of 1949 when he and the late Harry Burness co-operated in a campaign, centred in a gospel tent at Keith which was then the administrative capital of Banffshire. Keith was a hard place with a large percentage of Roman Catholics and the work was difficult with a very muted response. There was then a small assembly in Keith and one remembers the Breaking of Bread meeting being held in the burgh court room with its plush red benches lending a solemn dignity to the proceedings.

The Aberdeen Gospel Van frequently journeyed to Keith to give help during that campaign. The writer well remembers hearing Joe preach for the first time. He seemed to be very much "feeling his way" and gave the impression of being still wet behind the ears. However, this very soon changed. Within a year or two, Joe had obviously burned the midnight oil and it was obvious that he had a good grasp of the Scripture and a growing understanding of the Book. He also quickly developed a growing competence as a preacher of the gospel and as a minister of the Word. Thus, he progressed very rapidly from strength to strength. He conducted campaigns in many parts, series of ministry meetings and a growing number of conferences.

Joe visited the Shetland Islands, some 180 miles north of Aberdeen, frequently over many years of active service, first invited by the late James Moar in 1951. Thereafter, he went to Shetland many times, year after year, addressing both gospel and ministry meetings. In those days, it was common practice to have gospel services in cottages and in farm kitchens during the winter months, as well as in halls. Joe's preaching was greatly blessed. He also joined Mr Moar in districts where there was no assembly using Mr Moar's bus which seated 30-40 persons. He and Joe would visit in the district during the day and then have a gospel service in the evening. This sphere of activity proved very fruitful.

Some of the highlights of Joe's service as a preacher were in Ayrshire where he was a frequent visitor. An early visit was to Dailly. The small assembly was keen to have a gospel campaign but they were unable to support an evangelist although able to offer hospitality. Joe volunteered to go and his visit was a great boost to the small assembly. Another occasion was at Glenburn, Prestwick. Interest there was good and the period of the campaign was extended, with eight professions of faith being made. Another time, at Stevenston, sixteen professed under his preaching. In the course of many visits to various places, he preached in halls, tents, portable halls and in the open air.

Joe travelled extensively to many parts of the British Isles, including Northern Ireland. He used to say frequently that nobody could pray like the Irish! His work also extended to farther fields. On several occasions, he went to give help in Guyana where his brother-in-law, Alex Sutherland, was a missionary. He also visited Trinidad and went even as far as Alaska!

Several corespondents, writing of Joe Merson, have singled him out as a man of prayer, a preacher of great earnestness, a student of the Scriptures and an evangelist with a deep yearning for souls.

Joe passed to be with the Lord very suddenly on 11th December 1996. He had gone out in his car to do some visiting but appeared to have taken ill and to have drawn in to the side of the road where he was found dead at the wheel. His wife who had suffered very poor health and increasing debility survived him by only five months. They had no family.

Matthew Brown, Aberdeen

Other Recollections

I first met Joe Merson in the home of my parents when he and the late Harry Burness came to Forres to conduct a series of gospel meetings in the late 1940s, commencing a long association with this devoted servant of God and his dear wife Mary.

Joe's gospel preaching was with much fervour and sincerity, ever reminding his audience of the awful consequences of rejecting Christ as Saviour. Many souls were saved through his preaching. He had many jotters full of messages which he always wrote out before he preached them. He never lost the joy of his own conversion and loved to tell of the day when he accepted Christ as his Saviour in the ruins of Findlater Castle in Banffshire. His ministry was very practical and easy to be understood. Many saints today still remember his words of encouragement and help. Joe felt keenly the responsibility of preaching, and when the pressure of preaching was over he sometimes would relax and play his mouth organ in the home where he was staying.

On one occasion while Joe was visiting in Forres he saw a house for sale that he fancied and as soon as he got back to our home he told Mary. Her quick reply was, "Have you prayed about it, Joe?" That was the end of story. Mary was a true helpmate, latterly suffering from severe arthritis. Only the Bema of Christ will reveal the full service rendered by this godly couple.

Sam Matthews, Forres

Joe's faith and prayerfulness extended to the details of life as well as the service he rendered publicly. One day he accidentally locked himself out of his car and was in a real fix. After trying in vain for a while to coax an entry, he came into the house and got down on his knees and prayed about it. As he rose up he noticed a small pair of scissors on a low table beside him. "Do you mean me to use these, Lord?" he asked. He did and successfully turned the door lock open, retrieved his keys - with a "Thank you, Lord!" and got on his way.

Bert Cargill, St Monans

Joe Merson travelled widely in the furtherance of the gospel, and many who read these recollections will have heard Joe speak of his visits abroad. Along with my uncle and aunt, the late Mr and Mrs Allan Little, I accompanied Joe on a visit to France in 1953. Joe did not speak French which led to some amusing situations. However these minor difficulties did not affect his willingness and his ability to speak by interpretation and distribute gospel leaflets, although on one occasion he mistook a letter box for a post box and inserted a letter to his wife Mary through it! My limited ability to converse in French was severely tested as together we stood at the door and tried to explain to the rather bewildered occupant of the house the reason for the envelope lying on the door mat. "Don't tell anyone back home about this," Joe said, which thing I observed, at least for a few months!!

On a more serious note, I recall the first time I met Joe was in the town of Beauly. He had recently gone out into the work of the Lord full-time and had joined the late Harry Burness who was having meetings in the workers' camp at Cannich where they were building the Glen Affric Hydro Electric Scheme. This was a tough apprenticeship, but stood him in good stead for the days ahead.

Eddie Taylor, Aberdeen

Jack Noble

1915 - 1989

*"He was a good man, and full of
the Holy Ghost and of faith"*
(Acts 11.24)

Jack Noble was born in Maxwelltown, Dumfries in Scotland on December 21st 1915. He grew up in Portadown, Northern Ireland, the place where his mother moved to after the death of his father in the battlefields of France during World War I.

As a young man Jack commenced work in Corbett's drapery store in Portadown. Jack's great interest was amateur dramatics, at that time involved in elocution and acting. When he was 17 years old, Mr DL Craig came to the Gospel Hall in Portadown for a series of gospel meetings. Jack and two of his friends, who were his regular companions, attended these meetings. During the course of these meetings both his friends trusted the Saviour. Jack was deeply troubled about his soul, however the series of meetings ended without him getting saved.

The following Monday morning after the meetings had ended, Jack arrived at his place of work to find a letter waiting for him there. He recognised the writing as belonging to one of his friends who had been saved. He did not open the letter immediately but waited. Later that morning he went upstairs to the tea-room which was situated above the drapery shop. He opened the letter to find the following words:

"For God so loved Jack Noble that He gave His only begotten Son for Jack Noble, that if Jack Noble believed in Him (God says) he will not perish but have everlasting life" (John 3.16).

Underneath the verse these words were written:

'Jack are you going to make God a liar?'

Jack reread the verse very carefully for the second time and in that tea-room that Monday morning he bowed his heart and believed God. This was the turning point of his life.

Mr Craig had commenced more gospel meetings that very Monday evening in a place just outside Portadown. The brethren from the Portadown assembly had hired a bus and were going out to support these meetings and Jack accompanied them. Someone had told Mr Craig that Jack had been saved and so at the opening of the meeting without any warning Mr Craig announced that there was a young man in the meeting who had just got saved that very day and he (Jack) would tell them how it happened. Years later Jack told me, although he did tell the audience how he had trusted Christ, he never really forgave Mr Craig for springing this on him so suddenly!

For some time leading up to, and during the time of the gospel meetings in which he got saved, Jack had been rehearsing for a play in which he had the leading role. The play was scheduled to take place a few nights after Jack's conversion. Jack was in a dilemma, he did not want to act but the time was too short for someone else to learn the part to replace him in the play. He went to see the brethren in the Portadown assembly, and they, after waiting upon God, advised him to fulfil his obligation.

Jack went and played his parts that night and when the final curtain came down he went out through one of the rear exits of the building and leaning against the wall he wept his heart out. The glitter and thrill had gone out of acting – he had tasted something better. *'The joys of earth can never fill the heart that's tasted of His love.'*

From then on he was engaged in assembly life, having a great love for the gospel which he never lost.

He later went to work in another drapery store in the town of Larne, and very soon became the manager of that store. During his time in Larne he was actively engaged in children's work, open-air preaching and gospel campaigns in tents. During one of the gospel series in Broughshane, several members of the Strahan family were saved. He often said to me that one should continue in their daily secular employment until the demands of the Lord's work were so great that you could not do both. Jack Noble was a living example of this belief. His burden for lost souls deepened until the brethren in the assembly at Larne commended him to the work of the Lord full-time in December 1946. In January 1947 he went out to serve the Lord in St Kitts in the West Indies. On January 8th 1948 he married Sadie McCullough who became his faithful helpmeet in the service of the Master.

They laboured together in St. Kitts in association with the late Charles Brown, Tom Morrell and Mollie Creeth and saw the Lord's hand in blessing. After six years of faithful service in St. Kitts, Jack and Sadie moved to Antigua in 1954. There they joined the late Les Crossley in gospel work and in the planting of assemblies. There are three assemblies in Antigua and two other halls which were built for gospel work and are still continuing today.

When they were on furlough Jack had many fruitful series of meetings in the gospel in the North of Ireland, Ayrshire, Lancashire and Staffordshire where he is still remembered with deep affection.

During their time of service in Antigua, Jack developed a chronic eye disease caused by the strong ultraviolet rays of the tropical sun, therefore Jack and Sadie had to return to Northern Ireland in 1972 accompanied by their family of two sons Eric and Drew and daughter Grace.

It was just after this that I had my first opportunity of preaching the gospel with our dear brother. We shared a series of gospel meetings, which were held in a portable hall outside the town of Newry, close to where I was living at that time. We saw some fruit of our labour in the salvation of souls. This was the start of our friendship that was to last until God took our dear brother home.

In January 1976 Jack and Sadie emigrated to Canada, first settling in Toronto and then some months later moving to Guelph. Prior to this in September 1974 I joined our brother for a very fruitful time in the gospel in Bracondale assembly in Toronto. Over the next few years we had gospel meetings in the Canadian towns of Windsor, Sault Ste Marie and Bolton. In many ways Jack was a spiritual father to me, teaching me a lot in the ways and the work of God. He was one of the most encouraging and selfless men I had ever met. If ever you admired or made an appreciative comment on an article, for example, a Bible, a pen or a book he possessed, the next time Jack came to visit you he presented the item to you as a gift. His kindness and thoughtfulness helped many a person and he was an inspiration to those whose lives he touched. His uppermost consideration, however, was the winning of souls for the Lord and the building up of God's people.

In November 1989 once again we shared another series of gospel meetings this time in the Shetland Islands, a place Jack had visited on a number of occasions previously. We returned home to mainland Scotland on December 4th and I took Jack to Stranraer for him to get the ferry back to Northern Ireland. When I bade him farewell little did I know that it would be the last time we would be together down here. Following his return home Jack took a number of meetings that week. On December 8th in Limavady he spoke from John 20, emphasising the words of the Lord *'So send I you' (v.21)* and quoted *"Bye and bye when I look on His face, I'll will wish I had given Him more."* Within 24 hours his account on earth was closed and he was with his Lord.

When I heard of his sudden homecall I felt, and still do feel, like Elisha did when Elijah was taken from him. I have lost a spiritual father, a true friend and a brother beloved.

Following his death, his wife Sadie whose hospitality and kindness my wife and I have enjoyed many times over the years, gave me Jack's model and chart of the Tabernacle. Our brother had encouraged me in the study of this great subject and I am glad to use the model and chart in the exaltation of the One whom our brother Jack Noble trusted as a young man of seventeen years old and served so faithfully for 57 years.

Malcolm Radcliffe, Ayr

Other Recollections

Jack Noble was a great encouragement to young men to use the gift that God had given them in service. His labours with Mr. Whitmore around Manchester in the 60s taught us how to reach out to souls. A direct challenge while having tent meetings in the city created in me the desire to serve God full-time. Jack simply said, "This is your gift, and this is your calling, leave everything for God." He warned me of the trials but like others whom he encouraged to go to the West Indies, I took up the challenge to serve God. On my first visit to Canada, Jack was in tent meetings at Portage La Prairie. As usual, he had young people preaching with him each night. When the brethren asked me to preach one night, Jack stood down. He wanted the young men to have the opportunity to serve God. This encouraging in spiritual things meant much to Jack.

Norman Mellish, Stoke on Trent

I knew Jack well, particularly in the mid and late 40s when he worked in Whiteside's Shop in Larne and before he first went out to St. Kitts. I trusted the Saviour when he preached the gospel in the village of Broughshane in April 1945. During the war travel was difficult, and Larne to Broughshane is about 20 miles. Jack got to the meeting each evening, travelling partly by bicycle, partly by train, and sometimes partly by taxi (there was a limited radius for taxis during the war). Oftentimes he stayed overnight in my parents home, and was a close friend of the family. These were fruitful gospel meetings for two weeks.

Jack Strahan, Enniskillen

He married us in 1957. He visited us in Trinidad in 1963. Just before he arrived a large barrel filled with foodstuffs arrived. During his visit we had our 6th wedding anniversary and Jack gave us $60 which was a very large gift in those days. Another time when he visited us he must have noticed that we had an old aluminium kettle on our gas cooker. The next visitor from Canada brought us a brand new electric kettle from Jack.

He kept a little note book, not for recording the faults of the Lord's people, but to record ways in which he would be able to help. When he returned to Canada he loved to go shopping for bargains to fill the needs he had previously written down.

Daniel Ussher, Limavady

Engaging in a gospel series we had been preaching for the first three weeks on the theme, salvation was not of works but by grace alone. A couple of religious people had been attending quite often and we decided to visit them. After calling on them we spoke regarding salvation and the work of Christ. The wife said to Jack, "Indeed we just try to do our best and hope for heaven." Afterwards, driving down the road he said to me "Wherever have we been preaching these last three weeks?"

Albert Aiken, Lisburn

In April 1945 Jack came to Broughshane to spend the Lord's Day. He preached the gospel that night with power, and it was with deep exercise of soul that a further three nights were announced. It was to be a spell of meetings that those who attended would never forget. The presence of God filled the place as he preached of the coming Judgment and of refuge to be found in Christ. It was the period of compulsory tillage, and heavy snows that winter had delayed the ploughing season, but people left their ploughs and came indoors, unable to focus on temporal things. The meetings were extended to last for two weeks and many young people, among them three of my brothers and my future wife, were convicted of their sin and turned to Christ for salvation.

Jack wrote a poem shortly after these meetings, acknowledging his co-workers in the gospel and looking forward to eternal rejoicing together. The last verse runs as follows:

A parent's tears, a teacher's prayers
Will certainly have reward,
So together my friends of the Braid we'll rejoice
In The Beautiful City of God.

Robin Strahan, Ballymena

Jack Noble was well suited as a missionary in the West Indies. He had an outgoing, charming personality, with a ready smile and quick wit. The West Indians loved him, and during his time in the islands many were saved through his preaching.

Jack never knew his father, who was killed on active service as a despatch rider in the First World War, days before he was due home to be decorated for bravery. Jack had a life-long desire to see his father's grave in one of the cemeteries in the north of France. Friends in the south of England arranged to take him and his wife, Sadie, to visit the grave in 1989. On finding it, Jack was visibly moved and happy that his desire had been satisfied at last. A month later, almost to the day, he was called home.

Jack loved to preach, and was preaching the night before his sudden home call, during which he stated that 'the Lord's servant is immortal until his work is done'. Jack's work on earth was done; the Lord called His servant home.

Ray Dawes, Westcliffe on Sea

James Paton

1914 - 1999

"Every one that was in distress, and every one that was in debt, and every one that was discontented, gathered themselves unto him."
(1 Samuel 22.2)

James Paton, or "Jimmy" as he preferred to be called was one of a family of seven, four boys and three girls. He was born in 1914 and reared in a Christian home, and in early life lived in Ardrossan, Ayrshire.

He was led to the Lord by his beloved mother at the age of fifteen. She bought him his first Bible, "a Newberry", and helped him to purchase a Strong's Concordance, as Jimmy said that he might "Read to Know; Feed to Grow; and Study to Show". His mother also had a special light fitted at his bedside which he used to conclude his night's study, when he became overpowered by sleep at his desk.

In secular employment he was a slater and plasterer, until he was enlisted for military service, but he registered as a conscientious objector and had to appear before a tribunal, as a result of which he was sent to work on a farm. Unfortunately his employer was a hard man, and Jimmy had to pay a price for his convictions. He travelled a good distance to the farm by bicycle and worked long hours, which sapped his energy, without receiving food to give him the energy for the hard work he was forced to do. In course of time he suffered much physical discomfort with sores all over his body, yet he never refused or complained to his taskmaster of an employer. His local GP was a good friend of the family, and often received a bowl of soup from his mother. He seeing the state of Jimmy's health, forbade him to work, and appealed to the tribunal judge to have him relieved of his farming duties. Eventually he was allowed to leave the farm on health reasons, and return to his original trade as a slater and plasterer. Needless to say he bore a good testimony for his Lord to those he worked beside and also to his employer. It could be said of Jimmy, that like His Lord, "He suffered but threatened not, and when he was reviled, he reviled not again."

He spent his early life in assembly fellowship at Ardrossan. A godly couple by the name of Mr. & Mrs. Redmond had a great influence in his life, especially as he began to move into public ministry. Mr. Redmond was a good man but was unable to do the jobs that were needing done in a working class home, so Jimmy willingly helped and was much appreciated for it.

Mrs. Redmond in earlier days had been connected with an evangelical mission in Glasgow, and was kept busy singing and preaching. However through reading the Scriptures she was convinced that the place where the Lord intended all believers to be associated with was the church of God in the locality where they lived. She therefore joined herself to an assembly on the west side of Glasgow. As he worked in their home, she told him how these convictions were formed in her life. These talks formed similar convictions in his heart, not simply opinions in his mind. Andrew Boreland, said, "A person will argue about their opinions, but will die for their convictions."

As Jimmy moved out more into public ministry these truths had to be stated, for ministry should answer to need, and not cater for taste.This caused those who formerly had a love for him to turn their backs on him, thus bringing a great deal of sadness to his heart. But in light of the fact that one day he would stand before the Judgement Seat of Christ, he willingly bore the reproach, rather than suffer loss then. His prayer was that the Lord would give the necessary help to speak the truth in love, "in meekness instructing those who would oppose".

His parents moved from Ardrosan to Stevenston, and there he was in fellowship with a godly man by the name of Willie Neilly. There is no doubt Willie could have gone on to make his mark in the world of education, but he chose to leave school early and work in the coal mines, in order to supply means for his widowed mother to support and raise her family. He taught Jimmy the value of spending time, studying his Bible with the help of the Holy Spirit, digging below the surface to find the hidden treasures, as well as discovering the amazing accuracy of the Word of God. For example he pointed out the difference in the word "for" in 1 Tim 2.6, where it states "for all", and in Matt 20.20, it is "for many". In 1 Tim the "for" means "on behalf of", that is the availability of the work of the Lord Jesus Christ "for all", which is the truth of propitiation, the message in the gospel for the sinner. In Matt 20, the "for" means "instead of" many, which is substitutional teaching for the saints to enjoy. If we fail to distinguish the difference we are in danger of preaching universal salvation, and failing to impress the need to enter in and be saved.

About this time he met William Gaw from Dreghorn assembly, and was charmed by his clear, loving, passionate appeal as he preached the gospel. He also taught Jimmy how to help the distressed and downcast saints, but most of all Jimmy remembered him for his prayer life. It was evident he was in intimate relationship with God.

Jimmy once said, "I hardly dare start to write of the support I received from the woman whom the Lord chose to be my wife, who for 46 years was a true help meet to me. As to our marriage it was not only in the Lord, but certainly for the Lord. We wrote to each other, our letters crossing in the post, and the contents of each contained the same sentiment. I had indicated to Elizabeth that as long as she didn't stand in my way if called to the service of the Lord, I would be happy to be married to her, and the contents of her letter to me confirmed these very things. I never needed to alter my ministry to accommodate her lifestyle. Her hair was neither shorn nor braided, her dress was neither costly nor immodest. Her way of life was godly."

All of their married life was spent at Beith and it can be truly said their door was ever open and the table spread to express kind and happy fellowship with God's people from many parts of the world, as far away as Canada, America and Africa. They had a tremendous testimony locally. Jimmy preached the gospel and ministered God's Word in many parts of the British Isles, as well as Canada and America, and was also very much appreciated in Ireland. He was a big man physically, but whilst he ministered God's Word with conviction, he had a soft heart. Many a time did his lips quiver with affection for his listeners, as he appealed to them to apply God's Word to their hearts and lives.

Turning now to a later time in his life, when he was being invited to help in ministry meetings, he met and was greatly helped by having fellowship with two brethren, who were in many ways "opposites". The first was John Douglas from the Ashgill assembly, in Lanarkshire, who was a coal miner. His text book was his Bible, his study was a disused hen house, his teacher was the Spirit of God working in his life. His university was the assembly. The secret of his power was a godly life and fearing no one but God. Most of his ministry was based on pictures and principles taken from the Old Testament which confirmed New Testament teaching. He had a very sharp mind which made him outstanding at Bible Readings. Jimmy said he never heard anyone more able than John was as he contributed, and made excellent use of the contributions of others. Young believers were amazed and encouraged as he made much of their little and simple statements, which he developed and enlarged upon to the benefit of all present. Jimmy himself always took time to converse with young believers who were in the audience at the various meetings where he spoke, to encourage them to study God's Word, and be like the Bereans, to search the Scriptures.

It was John Douglas who invited him to speak at his first Saturday night ministry meeting which was at Ashgill, and later his first conference was also at Ashgill. He was much helped of God at those meetings and much appreciated by many of God's people as he faithfully ministered the Word of God, both in season and out of season (2 Tim 4.2), i.e. "where it was much needed, but not wanted; and where it was wanted, but not so much needed."

The second brother who had a great influence on Jimmy was Mr. Willie Trew, who lived up to his name. He was one of those rare class of brethren, who could be described as living with God and visiting men! Jimmy certainly was greatly benefited by spending time in his company, as well as listening to his delightful ministry. He was one of those rare brethren who was not only interested in preaching the gospel to sinners, but also in ministering God's Word to saints. He greatly impressed and helped Jimmy and others by his accurate and interesting exposition of the epistles, especially in relation to the character of the assemblies, and their activity in each locality.

The example of these two brethren, as well as their counsel encouraged all to give more time to reading and studying the Scriptures, enabling them to help according to the measure of the grace given to them. Jimmy personally said that he followed these two servants afar off!

After his beloved wife was called home, our brother Jimmy was persuaded by his son George to live with him in Hamilton, in 1993. He was then in fellowship with the saints at Sheilds Road assembly Motherwell until he moved into a flat at Auchlochan House in 1997. He then came into fellowship with the saints at Bethany Hall Ashgill, where his fellowship and help was very much appreciated. Even when in Sheilds Road he was brought each midweek to the prayer and Bible Reading meetings at Ashgill where his help was greatly appreciated. He was very much at home among the saints there. He said a few weeks before the Lord called him home, "I wish our brother John Douglas was here for me to finish my days with him in the little assembly at Ashgill."

It pleased the Lord to call him home in February 1997. A large number of believers from many places throughout the British Isles attended his burial service, showing the high esteem and respect he held in the hearts of those who knew him. The service was taken by Alex McLean, Peterhead, who was one of his bosom companions. His seat is empty; and his presence is very much missed.

Alex Aikman, Ashgill

It is fitting to conclude with the following poem of which Jimmy was the author:

Psalm 90.12
"So teach us to number our days,
that we may apply our hearts unto wisdom."

Help me, my God, to know my time, how short it is!
Lo, measure it by days not years, by steps not miles.
'Tis but a sunrise; a sigh; and a sunset, with a tear;
And thus we come and go, we live and die.
Help me, my God, while time is, to fill each moment
With Thy wisdom, love and grace;
With pilgrim feet to tread the heavenly road,
With steady pace,
Till time is past, and time no more shall be! Eternity!
J Paton

Other Recollections

James Paton, or Jimmy, as he was known to most of his friends, was one of the true working class theologians that the assemblies movement has produced.

His parents' home in Ardrossan, was a happy and hospitable scene of Christian kindness. What he saw there he practised all his life. On moving to Stevenston he started in business and was loved by his workers and by the poor of the community. Some might say that he was not a good business man because he could not bring himself to charge a proper fee for work to the widows and the destitute, and when some other tradesmen failed to pay their dues he would not take legal redress. As a result of his tender conscience he could not continue in business.

He lived his life under the eye of his heavenly Master and would rather suffer than do anything that violated what he knew his Lord's mind to be. I believe that it was this that gave weight to his teaching. When Elisabeth died she had two pounds in her purse and Jimmy told me with tears streaming down his face that he could not give her any more out of their pensions because she was so tender hearted she would give it all away.

"Being poor yet making many rich" can, I think, be a just epitaph to Jimmy Paton as the following story of Jimmy as the legendary baker illustrates. Without the extra money to give expensive presents to the families of their many friends who were getting married, they decided to make them their wedding cakes. The unbelievable skill that Jimmy expended on these beautiful cakes showed a true labour of love.

Jim Bertram, Kilwinning

Jimmy (as we were allowed to call him as boys) was as much at home in the kitchen as on the platform, and many a 'meal' we received from both places. He was the man with the broad smile and the big heart. The warmth of this dear man and his beloved wife were greatly enjoyed by many at their home in Beith. His immense knowledge of Scripture was reflected both in his teaching gift and in homely chats around the fireside. He always put across his point in a lovely way, and on occasions you knew exactly for whom it was intended.

He had a love not only for people but also for the gospel, and was instrumental in bringing the Ayrshire Tent to Beith several times. After those meetings many of us heard gospel truths expounded as never before.

Coming home from a meeting one night he was stopped by the police. After a friendly exchange with the officer, it was he who was exhorted to spend his time catching criminals rather than stopping men going about the Lord's business! The Lord's business was what he lived for, and many of us have cause to thank God for the influence on our formative years of the man who allowed us as boys to call him Jimmy.

Ian Wallace, Kilbirnie

Jimmy had a great variety of ministry to meet a great variety of need among God's people. Behind the ministry was a man of feeling, with a heart for the people of God. His ministry was fresh and when his subject was the Person of Christ he was in a class of his own. With choice vocabulary and clear unbroken runs of expression he would thrill our souls. At Harley Street Conference one year he spoke on Hebrews 11 and there was not a dry eye in the hall. The Levitical Offerings too were handled with the utmost skill. Latterly he wrote on this subject for "Words in Season". Jimmy was also greatly respected and his ministry greatly appreciated in America, Canada, Northern Ireland, England and Wales.

He was a great help to younger men who were interested, but he did not suffer fools gladly. He would spend hours teaching young men to value the local assembly and to put their all into it. It was a burden with him as he believed this was a much needed ministry, and the local assembly was where the real value of a brother lay. Jimmy, with his beloved Elizabeth, worked together to this end in unstinting hospitality, building up the local assembly, and bringing many of the Lord's servants to contribute in ministry and Bible Readings for the benefit of the local company.

He was unique in many other ways, a great man who could get down to the children. He was staying at a home where the father of a young boy had a thick head of hair. Looking at the lad and noting his curiosity at his father's head of hair and the visitor's bald head, he said to the lad. "Do you know the difference between your father's head and mine?" The lad shook his head. "Well," said Jimmy, "your dad's hair has grown up through his head, and my head has grown up through my hair!" He was loved and respected in every home he visited, putting mothers at ease, always taking time to talk to the children and just fitting in to the home life.

On visiting him in Auchlochan House he was always ready to give some thoughts on his meditations. Jimmy, apart from being a good cook, was also known for the 'tablet' he made for the residents and friends. Once when the fire alarm sounded Jimmy was missing at the assembly point. Someone ran up to his room to check and was told, "I can't come right now I'm stirring the tablet!"

Jim Paterson, Plains

James Paton

Tony Renshaw

1930 - 1997

"But his delight is in the law of the Lord;
and in his law doth he meditate day and night."

(Psalm 1.2)

Tony Renshaw was born in the mining town of Mansfield, Nottingham on 29th September 1930.

He first heard the gospel while on National Service at Aldershot in the south of England. An Army Scripture Reader by the name of Andrew Purslow faithfully preached the gospel which was a message he had never heard before. Despite arguing vociferously during the meeting about being called a "sinner", he was profoundly affected by the graciousness of the preacher who, as he was leaving the barracks, put his hand on his shoulder and said, "It's all in love you know." He left the building deeply troubled and wept bitterly.

A short time later he was surprised to hear from his cousin Jean, a Baptist, who assured him that he had been much in her prayers. Those prayers were answered during a train journey which gave him the chance to reflect upon his life and the One who loved him profoundly. The crowded railway carriage knew nothing of his inner turmoil as he made his way to the toilets and there, in the privacy of the cubicle, in distress, he confessed his sins and was gloriously saved. To the day when he was called home, he never forgot the joy of that moment.

In the Lord's goodness he was directed to a small assembly at Radford Street, Mansfield, his home town, by Mr Purslow. Dear brother Harry Shimmin and a small group of believers made him very welcome and for the first time he saw a local assembly functioning for the honour and glory of the Lord Jesus Christ. The simplicity of the assembly gatherings and the love of the believers all made a profound impression upon him. He never lost his love for the assemblies of the Lord's people and sought to be a help and a blessing in those early days at Radford Street. He believed passionately that what brought pleasure to the heart of Christ was to have His rightful place in the assembly and simple obedience to the Word of God.

He was invited to his first conference and was thrilled as he listened to the late Mr Harry Bell expound the Scriptures. By now he was devoting more and more of his time to the study of the Word of God. His unsaved parents could make nothing of what had taken place as he withdrew from the Church of England and declined to continue his former activities of cinema, theatre and concerts. With mounting concern, they watched him pack his bags and move to Guildford where he had been offered the position of Public Health Inspector. From there he transferred to Stockport Town Hall in 1956 and about this time was received into the fellowship of the assembly meeting at Brownwood Hall, Wythenshawe. It was about this time that he met Elizabeth Dixon who became his wife on 8th March 1958, and whom he lovingly called "My Bet". She became a devoted helpmeet for him in all aspects of the work.

In Wythenshawe which, at that time, was the the largest council estate in Europe, he gave himself wholeheartedly to the work of the assembly. To understand the remarkable contribution he made to the lives of so many for the last forty years of his life, it is necessary to understand three things about him: he was a man of prayer, a man who loved his Bible and a man who loved the assembly of the Lord's people.

He saw in the lives of Mr Joe Gill and Mr Willie Morrison a practical outworking of what he had been taught on the platform. He worked in happy fellowship with the assembly seeking to involve himself in all its activities. This involved work in the Sunday School for many years. It soon became apparent that he had an ability to communicate the gospel very clearly to children and young people. The result of this was that he spent a certain amount of time for many years using the long summer holidays from Salford College of Technology to speak at Sunday School camps, children's campaigns and school assemblies. It was a joy and privilege to listen to him preach the gospel to teenagers and, although small of stature, he very rarely had discipline problems.

He gave a great deal of time to this work and his preparation was always meticulous. He loved to keep in touch with the children who went right through the Sunday School at Wythenshawe, and even those who sometimes got into trouble with the police would receive a visit from him in the various institutions where they were placed. He loved the children and young people of Wythenshawe passionately and many of them found a place in his prayer list and were prayed for every week.

With increasing responsibilities in the assembly at Wythenshawe and constant travelling around the UK to give help in the ministry of the Word, time was often at a premium. He could see the hand of the Lord overruling in His own wonderful way when at 55 years of age, Salford College of Technology offered him early retirement. With the wholehearted commendation of the assembly at Wythenshawe he therefore commenced the last chapter of his life of service.

Nothing gave him greater pleasure than to be preaching the gospel in whatever situation it pleased the Lord to make possible. Gospel tent work was very close to his heart as was open-air work of any kind. We can remember the effort involved for him to preach on a Saturday morning in the precinct at Wythenshawe after he had commenced treatment at Christie's hospital, Manchester, and would have been advised to stay indoors. His love for the lost souls of Wythenshawe was so great that nothing at all would stop him occupying his place outside the butcher's shop and powerfully present the Lord Jesus Christ as the only Saviour of sinners. Whatever the weather, if the Lord gave him strength, he would always be there and preached as if he would never preach again. One sensed at times that the grandeur of the message he preached almost overwhelmed him and it was not unusual to see him in tears as with an open Bible he pleaded with the ungodly to repent and trust Christ before it was forever too late.

It was a tremendous privilege to live under the same roof with him for 27 years and see the key to his usefulness in his service for his Lord and Master. He was primarily an "intercessor". We very rarely disturbed him during the first part of the day before he left for work in Salford, for he regarded prayer as of such vital importance that nothing should in any way hinder his time spent in the secret place.

He would often say to us, "If you can't stand your own company, you ought not to inflict it upon anybody else"! He regarded prayer as hard work and devoted himself to it. It was in the secret place that he prayed in detail for all the many activities of the assembly and every single member by name. This gave character to all his service which was appreciated by so many. He believed passionately that the Christian life involved many acitivities but none is more important than prayer. We may serve the Lord in many different ways but prayer is the most effective of them all. Indeed prayer is essential to them all. A man may be a better gospel preacher than he is a distributer of tracts. A sister may be more effect on the door step than she is when teaching in Sunday School. But it is not valid to say that a Christian may be better at personal evangelism than he is at prayer, or better at preaching than he is at prayer. For if we fail in prayer we shall fail in everything else.

His ability to put pen to paper and express his thoughts in writing was a work that he took very seriously and his writings were a help and blessing to many of the Lord's people. He saw this as an opportunity to perhaps be a help to some dear believer in difficult circumstances, whom he would never have the privilege of meeting this side of heaven. For over thirty years his articles appeared in various magazines and, since his homecall, many have said what a help and blessing his written ministry had been. In this as in all his service he desired that "He must increase" and shunned the approbation of men.

His love for the gospel was reflected in his interest in missionary work in general. He prayed in detail for missionaries in many countries of the world and until just shortly before his homecall used the Daily Prayer Guide to focus his prayers upon the activities of many of the Lord's people. In his ministry he would often urge the Lord's people to visit a different country each day of the week by praying for the Lord's servants overseas. This left an indelible impression upon his family and those close to him.

The work in the continent of South America held a very special place in his heart and he was thrilled when his doctor gave him special dispensation to make his only visit to Brazil at the end of 1996 and see something of the work in the state of São Paulo. The work in the little town of Casa Branca was still in its very early stages but we will never forget the contribution he made during his 10 week visit when he sought to involve himself in all the activities of the work (there wasn't yet an assembly planted at that time). It thrilled his heart to see that the assembly principles which he had sought to encourage in his homeland could function just as well in the interior of South America and function perfectly.

He watched with tears in his eyes as the firstfruits of the work in Casa Branca obeyed the Lord Jesus by passing through the waters of baptism. The first baptismal service to take place in the hall in Casa Branca was a memorable occasion as a young converted Roman Catholic publicly obeyed the teaching of the Word of God in spite of the opposition of many of his family and friends. With gratitude he watched first generation believers beginning to find their feet spiritually and moving towards the local assembly. The young believers in this small provincial town were drawn to him and listened to him expound the Scriptures by interpretation in his own inimitable way. This short visit forged a link with them and he prayed for them until just a few days before the Lord called him home in October 1997. In fact, a young girl came to the trust the Saviour as a result of his homecall.

He was essentially a very disciplined man who preferred to judge himself than judge his fellow believers. It was unheard of for him to speak ill of other believers and he would not tolerate criticism of any kind under his own roof, believing as he did that "every idle word" would one day to assessed at the Judgment Seat of Christ. A man of wisdom and rare spiritual insight, his counsel and advice was sought by many of the Lord's people from far and near. One of his greatest qualities was his appreciation of the Lord Jesus expressed in his prayers and his ability to raise the level of worship in the Lord's supper, with his tremendous insight into the passages concerning the life and death of the Lord Jesus.

That the Lord kept him in peace of mind and heart during his long illness was a comfort to all who loved him so dearly. It was a joy and privilege to share with him in his closing hours down here and to watch him being removed from a scene of suffering to a sphere of unspeakable bliss, "absent from the body, present with the Lord".

The staff at the Adult Leukaemia Section of Christie's hospital, Manchester, who cared for him so faithfully, grew very attached to him during his long stay in hospital. They acknowledged to his immediate family that rarely had they seen one accept with such dignity all his sufferings. It was a tremendous testimony to the truth that the One who saves is able to keep to the uttermost.

Andrew Renshaw, Brasil

Other Recollections

Tony was my brother in Christ and brother in law because he married my sister Betty. We were both in the same assembly at Wythenshawe, Manchester. When we moved to Norfolk he often came to help us and he was appreciated by all ages. He regularly spoke at our Young Peoples' Easter Weekend and was respected by the young people for his ministry. He was also not afraid to 'let his hair down' and we all remember him giving a speech which was full of mixed metaphors. For many years he spoke at the Senior Camp for young people on the North Norfolk coast.

Tony had the ability to make the Word of God come alive and the rare ability to stop speaking while we were hanging onto his every word.

David Dixon, Norfolk

First and last impressions of Tony Renshaw were of one who spoke, preached and prayed - with a deep conviction that it was right and it was important and that the Lord would hear.

He was endeared to believers in North Staffordshire through the ministry of the Word and with his involvement in the camp work. The camp work demonstrated his capacity to relate to young people. He had consummate skill with the flannelgraph, and was able to convey a message simply but with real substance.

In 1993, Tony was responsible for the North Staffordshire Tent Campaign at Clayton, Newcastle under Lyme. This he later described as the happiest experience he had ever had in gospel preaching. His diligence in outreach to both children and adults and alertness even at midnight to 'visitors' at the Tent site was a real inspiration to those who were with him!

Derrett S.Watts, Newcastle under Lyme

At one of the Manchester conferences, Tony was preaching about the importance of giving priority to prayer, and particularly first thing in a morning. Tony was always very practical in his ministry and on this occasion talked about the use of the alarm clock. Being well aware that many of us might be tempted to just switch the alarm clock off and then doze again, he recommended that we always make sure the alarm clock is well out of reach, so that we have to get up to switch it off, then at least we increase the likelihood of spending precious time alone with God first thing each morning. Tony was a man of prayer and I believe he lived out his own ministry.

Colin Raggett, Botswana

Tony was a man of peace (Romans 12.18); of prayer (Colossians 4.2); a man prepared (Colossians 3.23); a man of purpose (2 Timothy 3.10).

Tony sought, without relaxing his principles, to live at peace with his brethren. Tony was disciplined and orderly in his remembrance of others. He said little about his own prayer life, evidently assuming that his brethren were as devoted to prayer as he was.

Tony never thought lightly of addressing a meeting; he was painstaking and thorough in his preparation. He kept all his addresses filed under subjects, yet he was never repetitive in his ministry. There was a purpose to his service and he was conscious of the dignity of the work to which he had been called.

Alex Morrison, Manchester

Tony was a man of prayer who believed in prayer for spiritual success and he earnestly practised it daily. When he became the chairman of the Lancashire Gospel Tent committee he insisted that instead of an opening prayer, we had prayer first in which all could participate. The practice continues to this day and his influence is greatly missed.

Richard Parnaby, Fleetwood

During a number of years we worked together visiting a number of schools in Warrington with whom I have contact. Tony was one of the first of the Lord's servants to conduct assemblies in some of these schools. He was very popular with both the staff and the children and his well illustrated stories gripped the attention of the children so much that large companies of more than 200, including some infants, listened with rapt attention.

Harold Cooper, Warrington

Tony was a gifted man who had a unique way of comparing and contrasting two scriptures, often in the Gospels. You would ask yourself why you had not seen such truth before, it seemed so obvious now.

For over 25 years he taught in the Sunday School, always giving loyal service and help. During these years he addressed Open Schools in many places, spoke at countless parent's evenings and prize givings, gospel meetings, and open air testimonies. He was involved with the Manchester and District Sunday School Camps for many years, conducting morning and evening devotions. He took the Lancashire Gospel Tent, the Staffordshire tent, and gave morning and evening devotionals at such places as Charterhouse, Meadowcroft, etc.

Almost the last recollection of Tony was of him standing with his wife Betty and two or three other brethren in Civic Centre, Wythenshawe, to preach the gospel. Tony was already receiving treatment for leukaemia, and on this occasion he asked that he might speak first, and then after he had finished his message that he might quietly leave us, and go home because standing too long caused him distress.

Alex Morrison, Manchester

Tony Renshaw

Alex Ross
1903 - 1997
"A workman that needeth not to be ashamed"
(2 Timothy 2.15)

While the name of Alex Ross is always associated with Aberdeen, he was in fact an Aberdonian by adoption.

He was reared in the small village of Cowie, near Stirling in Central Scotland. It was a mining community and, as was common practice in those days, youngsters on leaving school followed older members of their family by going to work in the coalpits.

It was during this period in 1920, to be precise when he was seventeen years old, that he was converted through the efforts of his older brother, Robert, who had been saved only a fortnight before. A preacher of the name of William Duncan was conducting a gospel campaign at the time. Alex attended the meeting one night and was invited to his brother's home for a cup of tea at the end. Soon afterwards, a knock at the door heralded the arrival of the preacher who, on being introduced to young Alex, asked if he was saved. On finding he wasn't, the preacher then asked if he would like to be. After explaining the way of salvation, he turned to John 3.16 and asked Alex to insert his name: "For God so loved Alex Ross that He gave His only begotten Son for Alex Ross that if Alex Ross believed in Him Alex Ross should have everlasting life". That night he saw it so clearly and was saved. He told the story in more detail in later years in a little tract he wrote "How God saved a Coal-Miner".

Conditions were hard in the coal-mines, wages were low and employment uncertain. Trouble spread from the pits to other major industries, such as steel, engineering and transport in 1926 and culminated in the General Strike. Great bitterness, hardship and recrimination followed.

The result was that Alex Ross packed his few belongings, tied them to his bicycle and left home in search of work. He spent some time in the Highlands working as a labourer in road-making and bridge-building. When that project was completed, he was paid off and, as the General Strike was not finished, he felt guidance was given to him through a scripture in which God said to Israel, "Turn you northwards" which brought him to Inverness. He stayed there briefly when again he was moved by a sense of Divine guidance on reading Genesis 12.9: "And Abram journeyed going on still toward the south". Alex resolved to do likewise and this prompted him to head for the city of Aberdeen, where he arrived on his bicycle in July 1926.

On his way to Aberdeen, he found a Christian conference at Craigellachie on the banks of the River Spey. He stopped off there and was given over-night accommodation as the conference lasted two days. For many years after that, when Aberdeen was packed with visitors from the south of Scotland, Alex used to arrange a bus to take believers to the Craigellachie conference. He used to advise visitors that it was a beautiful run and had the bonus of good ministry.

Within a few days, he was able to find work, labouring on a building site, digging trenches for laying water-pipes. He continued in this job until the work was completed but it was only casual and again he found himself unemployed. This led him to begin on his own account; buying fish from a brother in one of the Aberdeen assemblies and then selling the fish from door-to-door out of two baskets. From this humble beginning he progressed to a retail shop and then to set up as a wholesale fish merchant. The Lord prospered him in mill and in market, in field and in store-house. Throughout the years of his business life, whether on the Fish Market or in his premises, with colleagues and clients as well as his staff, Alex maintained a clear uncompromising testimony as to "Whose he was and Whom he served". In the local assembly at Holburn there is at the time of writing a dear sister in happy fellowship who was saved as a result of being one of Alex's employees.

Alex's association with the assemblies never wavered, and his more than fifty years in happy fellowship in the Holburn assembly was a testimony to this. Throughout this period he was an active and enthusiastic member in all aspects of its testimony. He had a great love for children's work both in Sunday School (he was superintendent for a number of years), and in local authority school outreach work. These were ways by which he expressed his genuine zeal in the gospel, whether in the context of the local assembly or in the towns and villages of the shire. In earlier, as well as later years he actively supported mobile gospel van work and had an unmistakeably clear voice for open-air preaching. There would be no embarrassing silences waiting on a brother to step forward if Alex was present. Many recall with affection, fellowship with him in the open-air. On the subject of gospel van work, it is worthy of note that, immediately after the war quite a few young men were keen to help small assemblies in the local area. Alex Ross rose to the occasion by purchasing a suitable vehicle which was festooned with appropriate gospel texts and equipped with loud-speakers. He handed over the vehicle licensed and insured. For a number of years then, and another thirty years at a later date, the Aberdeen gospel van was active in support of North East assemblies.

One of the great interests he had throughout his Christian life was the work of the Lord in other lands. This led him to forge lasting bonds with many of the Lord's servants both by correspondence and by personal visits to them. He was responsible for bringing many missionaries to the assembly and to the wider attention of other assemblies in the area. He saw a missionary conference commenced in the local assembly which continued for many years, thus promoting missionary interest in the city.

There were at least two other tangible legacies from Alex's Christian life which have benefited the Lord's people. He was keen to make use of his pen in reaching out both to believers and unbelievers. Early in the Second War, he took over a Bible shop known as the North of Scotland Bible and Tract Depot in the centre of Aberdeen. It was understood to be in financial difficulties and it was genuinely believed that Alex rescued it from almost certain closure. He sold it after the war and it has been a CLC shop for more than half a century. Considering the shortages and restrictions that the war imposed, it probably brought in little financial gain but it gave him the opportunity to publish tracts and other items. His first effort was a gospel magazine called "The Northern Trumpet". Other tracts and pamphlets followed and in later years published a few books, including "Choice Gems from the Psalms" published on the occasion of his diamond wedding in 1988.

Alex when he was well into his eighties was very thrilled when a friend told him that he was given a tract one afternoon by a lady standing at the street corner in one of the Cotswold villages. The recipient who belonged to Aberdeen, was able to tell the dear lady that he knew the writer well. This brought pleasure to all three persons involved; the tract distributor; the author of the tract and the recipient. Alex had cast his bread upon the waters and it was returning after many days.

The other legacy Alex has left in his adopted area is that of the Summerhill Eventide Home. In the late fifties he, more than any other, had the vision to see a home established which would provide a high standard of care and comfort for elderly believers from in and around the city. A working group of interested brethren began to meet but the reception given to Alex's exercise was cool at that time. Alex would not allow anything to cloud his vision of a home for the elderly and the proposed venture was out in the open again in 1962, when the scope was widened to include brethren from Montrose to Lossiemouth, as well as from Aberdeen. In November 1965 the purpose built Summerhill Eventide Home was opened. Alex served as chairman of the management committee for more than twenty years, expressing his continuing interest in what was primarily his own exercise. He ensured that as high a standard of care and comfort as was possible in those early days was maintained and also that the spiritual needs of the residents were met. Many were the occasions when either on his own or with a visiting missionary or preacher a short service would be conducted in the morning.

It was fitting therefore that when the burden of years became too heavy for Alex and his wife to look after themselves in their own home, they themselves should benefit from the care and comfort which his original exercise could now provide for them. It was from there that he passed to be with the Lord in June 1997.

This brief biography of Alex Ross shows that while he had a sense of tradition, he was by no means a person who was trapped in the past; he was constantly looking to the future. He had the eagle's eye to look into the future and the lion's heart to go forward. The richly coloured tapestry of his life is a clear demonstration of the workings of divine providence in the life of a devoted and committed Christian.

Eddie Taylor, Aberdeen

Other Recollections

A characteristic of Alex Ross's Christian life was his deep love for the Scriptures. It was said that, as a young man, he and some of his contemporaries used to meet regularly in order to study the Word and to memorise it. Even in later years, when many less his age might have taken a more relaxed attitude to study, Alex was obviously still engrossed in the Scriptures. The culmination of his researches was the publication in 1972 of his book, "Fifty Years in Christ".

As the title suggests, it marks half a century of sustained study of many sources and is a remarkable anthology of his uncounted hours of reading, researching, collecting, classifying and arranging outlines, prose passages, poems, meditations, messages and ministry. This work was undertaken before recent technological advances removed much of the labour and tedium out of it. It is also a tribute to his tenacity of purpose, particularly on the part of one who had but a basic education and who continued in business beyond the normal work-span. His years of study brought further reward in commendable fluency of expression both orally and in writing.

The writer well remembers Alex being asked to address a week-night children's meeting in the days when 200-300 boisterous youngsters would assemble. Alex was introduced as an author! A respectful hush descended upon the gathering and they listened intently. Alex was always keen to present the gospel as a preacher and as a writer by means of pamphlet and tract.

To Alex Ross the Scriptures were bread to the eater and also seed to the sower. His delight was in the law of the Lord and in his law he meditated day and night.

A poem he used to quote crystallises how he enthused about the Scriptures:

"Oh, wonderful, wonderful Word of the Lord!
True wisdom its pages unfold!
And, though we may read them a thousand times o'er,
They never, no never, grow old.
Each line hath a treasure, each promise a pearl
That all, if they will, may secure;
And we know that, when time and the world pass away,
God's Word shall for ever endure."

Matthew Brown, Aberdeen

Alex had an active interest in the gospel being preached in other countries, and in 1958 visited north west Spain with some brethren from Aberdeen. During his visit, Alex was asked to preach one Sunday afternoon in Corunna Gospel Hall. Having completed his scripture reading he announced he would use an acrostic to help the audience understand his message. His interpreter, Frank Haggerty (Bolivia) gave a big smile and said, "You can't translate English acrostics into Spanish." Undaunted Alex pressed on with his message. As he concluded he quoted Hebrews 13.5, "I will never leave thee nor forsake thee." Now said Alex, "If you read this text backward it will greatly help you to understand its meaning." "Backwards?!" exclaimed Frank, doing his best not to laugh, "it has been a big enough struggle going forwards!"

Alex applied the same undaunted approach when in 1962 the need arose for a home for elderly believers. He spearheaded an attempt to get assemblies in the area to fund and open a home. While the interest of those invited to consider the project faltered and too many difficulties were perceived, Alex's vision never waned. The minutes of early meetings record how he continued to seek the help of those who were interested. He opened a fund, gave personally, and decided it should be a completely new structure - "No good patching up an old garment," he said. A site was procured, he arranged for a Christian architect to draw up plans, and in the Autumn of 1965 the Summerhill Eventide Home was opened, which today cares for 24 residents. His vision was realised.

Peter Keith, Aberdeen

Alex Ross loved God's assembly and God's people. Always exercised to take part in assembly gatherings, ever ready to participate in the Bible Readings and never short of a word of exhortation from the Scriptures, he was an example to us younger (often silent) men. While his contributions did not always follow an orthodox line, he always encouraged us to get back to the Book and do our own homework.

Alex was involved in all aspects of assembly work, and I have rarely met anyone his equal at open-air meetings. His voice carried the gospel message above the sound of traffic and the opposition of hecklers; passers-by showing fresh interest gave him renewed vigour.

He was a faithful visitor to those unable to attend meetings, and his hospitality was legendary. He opened his home to others, gave of his substance, and often used his car for the benefit of those who did not have their own transport – a common feature in those earlier days.

Alex was a man who could truthfully say, "I have set my affection to the house of my God" (1 Chr 29.3), and who exemplified the injunction to "do good unto all men, especially unto them who are of the household of faith" (Gal 6.10).

Iain Wilkie, Aberdeen

Willie Scott
1906 - 1993
"And even to your old age I am He;
and even to hoar hairs I will carry you."
(Isaiah 46.4)

Willie Scott was born at West Calder in Scotland on 28th of March 1906, the youngest in a family of three. He was not brought up in a Christian home and had no Christian influence in his life until in his teens he moved to Fife for employment in the mining industry. He found himself working beside the late George (Dod) Dryburgh and Willie often recalled that he realized this young man had something that he did not have. At Dod's invitation he attended a gospel meeting in Buller Street, Lochgelly where Mr Abe Moffat was preaching, and was saved that night when he was almost twenty. Back home in West Calder he became an active member of the little assembly.

In 1931, five years after his conversion, he was commended by the assembly to the work of the Lord, together with his companion Mr Bob Thomson, and they moved to Galloway in the south west of Scotland to preach the gospel. The pattern of activity in those early days was to have at least one effort in each of the assemblies, and in the summer months to have meetings in the Wigtownshire Gospel Tent, a wooden sided structure with a canvas roof. Other meetings were held in public halls, farms and kitchens and also in the open-air. Willie was very fond of open-air preaching and many times when on his own driving around Galloway he would stop the car if he saw a potential audience, set up his loud-speaker and preach the gospel. He laboured faithfully in this way for eight years until the outbreak of the Second World War when a different avenue of service was presented to him.

The Stranraer area become a strategic place for the war effort

257

with a seaport at Cairnryan and a seaplane base at Wig Bay, and subsequently many military camps were established. The sight of thousands of young men and women thronging the district aroused a concern in his heart for their spiritual welfare, and he decided to visit the camps with a supply of New Testaments and gospel tracts. He was greatly encouraged by the response and found that numerous opportunities were presented for personal discussion. When he saw so many of these young people crowding into local public and picture houses he felt that it would be good if he could provide a place to give them a cup of tea and tell them the gospel message. He obtained the use of the village hall in Leswalt and with the help of local believers commenced a work that proved to be tremendously fruitful. Every Sunday evening hundreds of young men were coming, the numbers continually increasing until in 1942 he was informed that due to the war effort, the hall would no longer be available. However undaunted he set his sights on an old unused hall in the village, "Aldouran Hall", which was in need of repair, and having obtained permission from the owner was given free use of the hall for as long as he needed it.

With the help of local believers and a number of RAF lads from the Camps, he set about putting the hall in order and making all the tables and chairs that would be needed to seat all the men who would attend. His vision now was to open what he described as a "Canteen and Christian Rest Room for HM Forces" every evening during the week from five till ten o'clock, where facilities were provided for reading, writing and a cup of tea with a half-hour gospel message. So great was the response that there were between two and three hundred men coming every night and waiting on to hear the gospel being preached. There were no rules and regulations, all he asked was respect for the Word of God and never failed to receive it. Willie had been going round all the local bakers each day with two suitcases trying to buy as many cakes and buns as possible, but with problems of rationing could not obtain enough supplies. His answer was to get an old stove and griddle and bake pancakes himself! His day then commenced at 7.30 am until between

2 or 3 o'clock the following morning. Asked how he did it he would humbly reply, "As thy days, so shall thy strength be." Space would not permit the many stories of those saved through this work, some that soon were to lose their lives on the battlefield. Heaven will reveal the true extent of the fruit borne through the labours of this great man of faith. Willie reckoned that during this time he distributed free of charge twenty-five thousand New Testaments plus thousands of tracts and booklets. The cost of material provision was over three thousand pounds, a substantial sum in those days, and characteristically he would say, "God has graciously met all our needs."

After the war Willie continued to evangelize and in 1949 placed an advert in the "Believer's Magazine" inviting young men to spend their holidays in "Bonnie Galloway" preaching the gospel. This would become a feature that would mark the work for many years to come. His solution then for accommodation was to pitch the Wigtownshire Tent in a village for the gospel meetings and let the young men sleep in the Gospel Hall. His opinion then was that an independent venue for the meetings often produced better attendance at the meetings.

In 1947 Willie married Marjory Henry from Kirkcowan, setting up home in Park Terrace, Creetown, and for Willie it was the first time he had a home of his own. Their marriage was unique in that Willie had arranged that the ceremony would take place at the conclusion of the assembly's annual conference, so those attending the conference were guests at their wedding! Characteristically, as he never sought to draw attention to himself, he had kept it a well-guarded secret.

The Lord was soon to reveal another avenue of service for Willie. Both he and Marjory had been aware that many aged saints at the eventide of their life had to spend their last days in institutions, separated from Christian companions. They had both been praying that the Lord would exercise someone to provide a place for elderly saints to be cared for, and on the same day some time later, unknown to each other, both had arrived at the conclusion that the Lord desired them to do this work. Around this time Machermore Castle at Newton Stewart came on the market for sale and by a remarkable step of faith Willie and Marjory's offer of three thousand pounds was accepted in March 1953, despite being told by those responsible for selling the property that an offer of such a low price would not considered. They took possession of the property at the end of October that year and commenced the considerable task of renovating and altering the building to provide the first assemblies eventide home in the UK. Again without asking anyone for support the Lord touched the hearts of many saints and practical and financial support was wonderfully provided for this new venture of faith.

Sadly grief was to enter Willie's life. Earlier both he and Marjory had grieved together at the loss of their only child, and on 1st January 1954, after a serious illness, it pleased the Lord to call Marjory home. She had seen Machermore bought but did not see it occupied. Undaunted this noble servant of Christ carried on with the work and in May 1954 Machermore opened its doors to receive its first resident, Miss Bartlett who had served the Lord for many years in China. It had twenty-six single rooms, as Willie believed that everyone should have a place they could call their own without sharing with others. This principle remains to this day.

Despite having the burden of the day to day running of Machermore, Willie's zeal in the gospel never waned. He now had a final answer to the problem of accommodation for the young men, or "his boys" as he called them, who were still encouraged to come and help in the gospel work during the summer. The outbuildings at Machermore became sleeping quarters. The facilities were not "five star", especially the washing outside every morning at a tap with only cold water! However the writer looks back with happy memories to the fellowship we enjoyed with Willie tracting and having open air meetings in the villages in Galloway. He would stop the mini bus in a village, set up the loud-speaker, and if you had never preached in the open air before he would say, "Now lads have a text ready to shout to the folks." That was all, only a text of scripture with no comment, but for many of us that was what was needed to give us the confidence to progress further. He was unstinting in his praise and encouragement, and looking back it is a joy to remember those who have served the Lord at home and abroad who were one of Willie's "boys".

To celebrate Willie's eightieth birthday our late brother Jim Anderson from Annbank, with the help of Robert Revie and others, arranged a surprise birthday celebration in the town hall in Newton Stewart. Somehow or other Willie found out what was intended and arranged to provide the purvey for the occasion to avoid anyone being burdened with the cost! Right up to when he was eighty he was still acting as relief cook at Machermore every week-end and during holidays (he had progressed a lot since his first attempt at pancakes at Leswalt!), but not long after this his health began to fail. During this period he was lovingly cared for by our dear brother Sander Oxenham. Sander was one of the local young men who was first contacted by Willie in 1958 and was subsequently saved and added to the assembly at Newton Stewart. He has worked at Machermore for many years, the last twelve as Superintendent.

On 26th August 1993 the Lord called Willie peacefully into His presence from his beloved Machermore. Machermore still stands today as a testimony not only to the goodness of God, but to the vision and faithfulness of a noble servant of Christ. Galloway too has been privileged to have had such a zealous soul-winner labouring in the district. There is not one village or town that he did not reach with the gospel; truly a servant who is worthy to "rest from his labours; and their works do follow them" (Rev 14.13).

Robert Miller, Mayfield

Other Recollections

My first meeting with Mr Scott was in 1958. A friend and I were walking down the street when Mr Scott came along in his minibus with the loudspeaker on the top inviting people to tent meetings. He stopped and asked my friend and me to the meeting, and we said we would come. He replied, "Now lads if you say you will come, remember and keep your promise." We both went to the meeting and I learned that night that I was a sinner and needed salvation. From then I continued to attend gospel meetings and was saved in 1959. Little did I realise then that the sincere invitation from this kindly man to meetings would lead in the goodness of God to the start of a long, happy and close friendship with him.

At Mr Scott's invitation in March 1964 I left my employment and worked with him at Machermore, sharing in his exercise to care for the Lord's elderly saints. During all the years we were together I valued him as a true spiritual father, someone that I could always feel free to confide in. His confidence and dependence on the Lord to provide in all the circumstances of life, whether material or spiritual, were qualities in him that I will never forget.

He was a very happy person, and enjoyed having a laugh with the young lads who frequently helped him in gospel work. One incident stands out in my memory. We were all in the mini bus making our way to an open-air meeting in Newton Stewart, when suddenly smoke started coming from the loud speaker system. He stopped the mini bus and every one quickly jumped out. Unperturbed he sat still, pulled the plug out of the amplifier, and with a big smile on his face said, "Well you are a fine lot of lads, going to tell folks how to get to heaven, and when you get the chance to go yourselves, you all run away." I treasure the memories of him and thank God for the day that the Lord used him to bring me under the preaching of the gospel.

Alexander (Sander) Oxenham, Newton Stewart

The first time that I met our dear brother was as a result of an advert in the Believer's Magazine in the early 1950s advertising a preaching holiday for young men. I travelled down to Newton Stewart and when I was introduced to Willie Scott I became aware almost immediately of a man who had a great concern for the lost.

Willie would organise a variety of outreach activities in the gospel. Because he loved children, meetings would be arranged in the afternoons when we would go off in his car to one or two of the villages in Wigtownshire. I remember being asked to speak one evening in a village where midges were very active! I hadn't been speaking too long when all the rest of the young men and brother Scott disappeared into the car. After a short time I had to stop preaching because of the midges and as I entered the car he said with a twinkle in his eye, "When you preach in the open air always remember to be brief!" Many of the young men who went to Machermore to help him at that time are now serving the Lord either at home or abroad. We had met a true servant of the Lord whose great burden was to strive for spiritual balance and evangelistic zeal.

Robert Revie, Tarbolton

I visited Machermore 35 years ago with my wife and daughter and met Willie Scott for the first time. He was a big man with a big heart and big ideals. Although he never took a "ministerial" attitude he taught me a lot. When I last saw him about six weeks before he was called home, I had sent him a card that said I was indebted to him and that I hoped to see him again, but wanted him to know he had taught me a lot. He was completely amazed that I should say that - that's the kind of man he was!

The stories of his unofficial chaplaincy to the Americans and all the troops in the west of Scotland would fill a number of volumes. As a "sassenach" I was often amused at some of the figures of speech he used, for instance, once when he was opening a gospel session at Jubilee Hall he spoke of God "looking over the battlements of heaven and seeing the human dilemma". Even although that may appear strange, we knew the man and that he "lived near to Christ".

Paul Foot, Manchester

Fred Stallan
1921 - 1998
"Fervent in spirit; serving the Lord."
(Romans 12.11)

In Fred Stallan's study, a quotation from scripture stood framed on his desk for many years : "I press toward the mark" (Phil 3.14). These words inspired him throughout his life as a believer and were often referred to in his public ministry. A favourite illustration he gave was that of the fifteenth century navigator Christopher Columbus who, when lost in the vastness of the Atlantic Ocean, exhorted his discouraged crew with the cry: "Sail on!"

Fred Stallan was born into a humble Glasgow family on 1st August 1921, his father and mother being from Church of England and Roman Catholic backgrounds respectively. He was the fifth of seven children. Due to the early death of his father in 1929, he had to leave school at fourteen to ease the plight of his widowed mother and found work as a telegram boy for the Post Office. Some five years later, and in the providence of God, a colleague invited him to Knightswood Gospel Hall, Glasgow, where one evening listening to the preaching of an elderly brother, he trusted Christ as his Saviour. Fred also had the joy in future years of knowing that at least three other members of his immediate family circle had obtained "like precious faith".

It was as a member of Knightswood assembly and by now in his early twenties that Fred developed what was to become a lifelong love of study of the Scriptures and of theological books. In the early 1940s, his Saturdays were spent with other young men of similar zeal in Glasgow's second-hand bookshops laying the foundation of a comprehensive library. As money was scarce, books purchased were read, exchanged within the group and reread in a constant cycle. Such was his thirst for knowledge, he used to recount with a smile that during the years of World War II, and eager to study in every spare moment, he occasionally even carried books around in his (otherwise empty) gas mask container!

On 27th November 1947, Fred married Wilma Brough of the Knightswood assembly. Although allocated a tenement flat in a rundown area of Glasgow city centre, they both, undaunted, joined themselves to the small local assembly known as Townhead and threw their energies into expanding the work. Endowed with a strong voice and clarity of diction, Fred often preached in the notorious backcourts of the nearby tenements where he and his fellow workers were regularly assailed with household debris. Reflecting on experiences of this nature in later years, his wife would simply remark : "It was an education." Popular Saturday evening Bible Readings and ministry meetings were commenced, together with series of consecutive Bible teaching from esteemed brethren such as Fred Cundick and William Trew. Throughout the 1950s, the assembly enjoyed some numerical growth and valued times of Christian fellowship.

In the late 1950s, Fred commenced what was to become a long association with the Believer's Magazine. Conscious of a lack of experience in writing, he somewhat tentatively submitted an article on "Prayer" to the editor, Andrew Borland, and felt honoured not only to see its publication but also to be encouraged to make further contributions to the magazine. Articles on "David's Mighty Men" followed, and many others; his gift with the pen had been identified.

Residing by 1959 in the west end of Glasgow and a member of the assembly at Summerfield Hall, 1960-70 were landmark years in Fred's life for a variety of reasons. Following a decade of being increasingly sought after for his own public ministry and yet aware of the danger of approaching Scripture with the primary aim of producing sermons, he adopted a system of in-depth Bible study which would provide him with a solid reference base for the future. It would also gradually channel him towards assuming a more expository style in his Bible teaching. The system, which afforded one friend who subsequently used it "hours of pleasure with the Word", is now briefly outlined for the particular interest of young Bible students.

Fred purchased several large, leather-bound, loose-leaf notebooks and, concentrating on the NT epistles, began painstaking verse by verse annotation, one page of a notebook devoted to one verse. In the first instance, the verse was typed in the AV, noting the RV rendering above any word as appropriate. Alternative translations of the verse by JN Darby and Kenneth Wuest followed underneath the AV, the former writer being considered a sound textual scholar, the latter a source of helpful word pictures to illuminate the text. Thereafter, selective quotations from AT Robertson's Word Pictures, Vincent's Word Studies, the Expositor's Greek NT and Dean Alford's Greek Testament were inserted, along with Fred's own comments to round off the page. Vine's Expository Dictionary and Strong's Concordance were also referred to in conjunction with Wigram's and Thayer's Lexicons to assist with the interpretation of Greek words. The completed notebooks were outstanding examples of systematic and meticulous word study and are prized by his family.

As a related aside, Fred developed an early fondness for Newberry's Englishman's Bible and was reluctant to use any other Bible for public reading – even when family members drew his attention to its loose pages and to the print which seemed to diminish with the passage of time!

It was in the early 1960s when conducting occasional series of Bible teaching that Fred had the inclination to distribute printed handouts summarising the Scripture references, headings and points he alluded to throughout the ministry. To put this idea into practice, he acquired a second-hand duplicator and enlisted his wife, a shorthand typist, to assist him. The venture, fairly novel for its day, was so warmly received that an Irish brother who had seen a set of the printed notes arranged for Fred to minister in Northern Ireland – a journey he regularly undertook with great pleasure over the next thirty years.

Mid 1962 was a time of testing for the family. Due to a

cost-cutting exercise within the company where he was employed, Fred received three months notice of redundancy. With two young daughters, Linda and Moira, to provide for, he and his wife were driven to their knees in earnest prayer and the Lord answered in a remarkable way. Within the three month period, Fred not only obtained a preferable administrative post in the Health Service, he was also able to use the redundancy payment to purchase his first car – a second-hand VW Beetle! He now rejoiced that in a totally unforeseen manner his days of travelling the country by public transport were over. But he never forgot those weeks of anxiety and in the future would empathise with many fellow believers who faced a similar trial.

Notwithstanding a very busy preaching schedule, in 1970 Fred fulfilled a long-held ambition. Approaching fifty years of age, he enrolled at Strathclyde University, and successfully completed a four year, part-time course in managerial studies. Throughout his life, he proved the truth of Matthew 6.33 on several occasions. In another instance, as a candidate at an internal job interview within the Health Service, he was asked the question : "What is your greatest strength and your greatest weakness?" He replied : "My greatest strength is also my greatest weakness – I am a Christian." He told the panel of his faith, that it was the motivating factor in his life and therefore he would require to act with integrity at all times – a perceived weakness by some in the professional world. He got the job.

In 1971, the family relocated to Linwood, Renfrewshire and there was born in Fred a special love for that local assembly which remained undimmed until his homecall. The Gospel Hall was in need of renovation. Putting some DIY skills into practice, he mobilised a small group of local believers, enthusiastic volunteers who over a three year period and on most week nights semi-demolished, rebuilt and refurbished the premises. The building stands as a tribute to the expertise and commitment of that worthy team of labourers.

During the mid-1970's, Fred was invited to become secretary of the Renfrewshire Gospel Campaign Committee which for years had been dedicated to gospel outreach in the county, both by assisting established assemblies in the convening of campaigns and by organising pioneer evangelism in areas where no testimony existed. Having had a deep personal interest in outreach since his conversion, and with a burden for the spread of the gospel in Renfrewshire, he liaised diligently with the shire assemblies regarding the twice yearly campaigns and fully participated in the tracting teams throughout his tenure of approximately sixteen years as secretary.

Fred enjoyed a ready affinity with young people – not unrelated to being a good conversationalist with a lively sense of humour! Ever-conscious of the import of 2 Timothy 2.2, he convened at Linwood Friday evening Bible Readings for youth during the years 1980-84. His aim was not only to nurture younger generations in spiritual things but also to encourage young men to speak in public without embarrassment or trepidation. The meetings were well attended, with the first winter session being devoted to the study of 1 Timothy, helpfully outlined in printed handouts to stimulate discussion. In later years he was greatly heartened to see fruit from his labours on hearing several younger preachers identify these gatherings as a stepping stone to their public ministry.

With retirement from the Health Service pending in 1986 and still with undiminished zest, Fred felt privileged to receive an invitation to become secretary of the Lord's Work Trust in Kilmarnock, a position he held for twelve years and, in his view, the most fulfilling years of his life. One of his greatest joys was composing a monthly letter of encouragement to missionaries based on a text of scripture, adding personal footnotes, in copperplate handwriting, relevant to the recipients' circumstances. These letters, almost 150 in number, were published individually in the North American magazine "Counsel" and, after his homecall, as a collection in the attractively presented book, "A Treasury of Inspirational Readings". He was also delighted in 1986 to join the editorial panel of the Believer's Magazine as coordinator of material, exchanging his blue pen for red, and found yet another role with which to occupy himself profitably throughout retirement years. Any remaining spare moments were spent entertaining his young grandson, Justin, born in 1984!

Restricting his public preaching to a local radius due to age, Fred achieved another long-held objective in 1990 by seeing the publication of his first book, "Things Written Aforetime". The book's counterpart "Written for our Learning" followed in 1994. His last work, a Commentary on Romans to complete the Ritchie New Testament series "What the Bible Teaches", was penned in fifteen months against a background of terminal illness, such was his desire to leave behind a written legacy which would endure long after his public ministry had ceased.

On 27th November 1997, the day of his golden wedding anniversary and a day of deep sadness for his beloved wife and family, Fred entered a hospice. He was called home on 1st January 1998.

It would be fitting to conclude by returning to Fred's notebooks and, in particular, to his comments on Phil 3.14: "The prize of the high calling must be the resurrection state. Till he (Paul) reached that point he was content to run: this was his occupation, his business, his sole concern in the world. In the pursuit of the prize Paul suffered, but his heart was still filled with joy." Surely Fred Stallan has left on record an apt commendation of his own life of consistent christian service.

Gordon Dunbar, Ayr

Other Recollections

One of my earliest memories of Fred was of him speaking at a packed Saltcoats conference in the late 50s. One of my last was at Bridge of Weir at a small weeknight ministry meeting not so very long before he was called home. Over that period he gave of his best to both small and large companies with his characteristic attention to careful exposition of the text yet laced with illustration and a touch of humour such that he never bored.

Again I recall in the early 60s Fred at Abingdon Hall

speaking at a weeknight meeting at a time when I was a student. After the meeting I was invited back to his home for supper where he and Wilma were kindness itself. That the conference preacher took time to have fellowship with and encourage us younger saints was good especially so while having the pressures of daily work and family life in addition to all his preaching engagements.

Bill Stevely, Aberdeen

It was in the late 70s that I first met Mr Stallan in Larne, Northern Ireland. Listening to his ministry from the platform, our brother's precise manner, appearance and demeanour led me to expect him to be reserved, if not somewhat austere. However on Sunday at supper he returned from preaching elsewhere and proceeded to light up the evening with amusing stories.

It was these initial impressions, both on the platform and in the home, which encouraged many of us to attend the "Conversational Bible Readings for Young Christians" he organised during the early 80s. I still have the notes he prepared for us on 1 Timothy and Philippians. He not only gave us an outline on each passage, but also thorough, yet very readable notes on the key words.

Alistair Sinclair, Crosshouse

We lived near to each other for a good number of years and worked together in the Renfrewshire Gospel Work in that area. Fred always put his all into whatever work he did. When the Gospel Hall in Linwood was being rebuilt he was there every spare moment he had and did every type of task cheerfully.

In addition to becoming Secretary of the Lord's Work Trust he joined Tom Wilson, Keith Stapley and myself on the editorial panel of the Believer's Magazine after his retirement in 1985 from a busy life in the National Health Service. His contribution soon became invaluable and his early passing to be with the Lord was great blow to his fellow editors. He was always cheerful and helpful and above all spiritual in all the work he did.

Jim Baker, Hamilton

My memories of Fred Stallan span the years when he lived in Renfrewshire, in fellowship in the assembly in Linwood. He was above all things a careful and detailed student of the Scriptures. As a young man I learned from him the value of word by word study and the beauty which was revealed by hard painstaking labour.

It was as a friend, however, that I remember him best. On more than one occasion I turned to him and found sane, balanced and perceptive advice. He was worth listening to. On one occasion in the early 1970s accompanied by another brother I went to seek guidance on a problem which I considered needed urgent and drastic attention. Fred sat and listened and I was a little perturbed that his indignation did not appear to be roused as I told the story. What then do you advise that we should do? After a pause of some moment he said, "Nothing." How disappointed I was. How right he was, and later events proved how sound was his advice.

John Grant, Bridge of Weir

While waiting upon the Lord for further confirmation as to full-time service, my wife and I attended a conference weekend in Lossiemouth in April 1973, where Mr Stallan was one of the speakers. His message on the Lord's Day was based on three commands in the Word of God: Genesis 12.1, Abram "get...out", Joshua 1.2, Joshua "go over", Colossians 4.17, Archippus "take heed". As he delivered his powerful message and emphasised each command it was obvious God was speaking to us through His servant.

In a subsequent letter from him, he stressed the fact that time was short, the need to be up and doing, and he felt the challenge in his own meditation.

Sam Matthews, Forres

Those who remember him will recall his immaculate appearance which matched his precise handling of the Word. Well do I recall one lovely summer's afternoon walking with him from our home to the hall via the pier. How he enjoyed the fresh air and the lovely outlook, but his joy turned to alarm when we discovered that the bridge over the railway was closed that day for repairs. Too late to retrace our steps we had to climb over the barricade and sprint over the bridge, hoping that we wouldn't be spotted! Breathless we arrived at the hall and still he was able to open the Scriptures and expound them to us in his inimitable way.

Our closest bond was probably our mutual love of good books for he freely acknowledged that he was a true bookworm unable to pass a bookshop, especially one specialising in 'second hand theology'.

A W Foster, Gourock

Although I had known him before he came to the Lord's Work Trust, having appreciated his ministry and particularly his gift of leading Bible Readings, it was during his time in Kilmarnock that we became good friends. He telephoned twice a week, and always announced himself as "Kilmarnock calling"!

He had a great knowledge of the Scriptures, and there seemed to be no scriptural subject on which he had not expended a great amount of time. While holding the Secretaryship of the Trust and being an Editor of the Magazine, he wrote two reference works of exceptional value to the Bible student of today – "Things Written Aforetime" and "Written for our Learning". He wrote the commentary on Romans for the Ritchie New Testament Series in fifteen months, completing it shortly before he died. To be able to write such a valuable work when suffering pain and discomfort, truly manifested his great grasp of the Word of God.

Denis Gilpin, Jersey

Robert R. Walker

1919 - 1990

"Not slothful in business;
fervent in spirit; serving the Lord."
(Romans 14.11)

Robert Walker was a pharmacist by profession. When he left his secular employment to launch into the Lord's work full-time, the owner of the pharmacy in which he had been employed for several years, was very disappointed at losing his services. As a token of his esteem and gratitude he presented Robert with a gold watch. Talking about the matter, to a doctor friend at the time, the owner of the pharmacy summed up his feelings by stating: "In due course, I'll no doubt find another pharmacist but I'll never find another Robert Walker!" Throughout his life, even from early years, Robert was a Christian beyond the ordinary ranks of those who profess the name of Christ.

Robert Russell Walker, was born in Aberdeen in October 1919. He was the eldest child and only son of Mr & Mrs David Walker who after their marriage in April 1917, set up their home in Aberdeen. His father was a well-known and highly regarded evangelist who had embarked as a full-time worker in 1910 from Bellshill, Glasgow.

Robert's conversion he traced back to 2nd January 1931 after he had attended the Aberdeen New Year Conference. He was afterwards baptised and received into fellowship in the Fountain Hall Assembly, in the Woodside district in the north of Aberdeen. There he spent his formative years. He would often tell us that he was only a few weeks old when his mother first took him to the meetings at Fountain Hall.

Robert's secondary education was at the well known Aberdeen school, Robert Gordon's College; from which he moved but a short distance across the campus to the School of Pharmacy.

After qualifying, Robert spent several years at Lossiemouth where he was keenly involved in the work and witness of the assembly. During that period he married Miss Jeannie Walker and the first part of their married life was spent at Lossiemouth which had an abiding place in his affections. Often, during steamy, hot days of summer, when campaigning in industrial areas of the south, he used to say that he frequently longed for the fresh breezes of the Moray Firth.

Towards the end of the 1940s, they returned to Aberdeen when Robert took up an appointment in the Torry district of the city. He resided in Torry and he was in fellowship in the Victoria Hall, Torry. This is an area in the south of Aberdeen which is cut off geographically by the river to the north, the sea to the east and the Grampian Mountains to the west. For many years the district was largely populated by people connected with the fishing industry.

Robert fitted into this community very well and became a well known and well liked figure as he walked to and from his home and his place of work. He also met a large cross-section of locals across the counter of the chemist's shop and through his association with the Victoria Hall and its activities.

He was very approachable and had a kind, cheerful word for everyone. As a result, in course of time, people would seek him out with their problems, and his advice was sought on personal, domestic, moral and, of course, spiritual matters. He was able to empathise with people in a way that few can. A local academic (whom Robert and the writer knew) used to counsel his students: "If you have a problem then seek advice from a spiritual man because a spiritual man is a person of vision." Although most members of the community could not have articulated their feelings in so many words, this was doubtless how they reacted to Robert Walker.

It was, therefore, no great surprise to those who knew him when he advised the local assembly that, subject to their blessing, he intended to devote much more of his time and effort to the Lord's service. He proceeded to give up his secular employment and supported himself by undertaking locum work. What is perhaps not well known is that in this new sphere he began by engaging in door-bell evangelism and he started by ringing the bells of his nearest neighbours and speaking to them about spiritual affairs. He was fulfilling the commission given to the disciples: "Ye shall be witnesses unto me in Jerusalem, Judea and Samaria and to the uttermost parts of the earth."

Eventually, he sought and was readily accorded full commendation to the Lord's work in April 1957. Over the next quarter of a century – and more – his work as an evangelist took him to many parts of mainland Britain as well as to Ireland frequently; also to Denmark, the Faroe Islands and United States.

Robert was what is often called colloquially, "a good all-rounder". He could speak equally well to children or young people. He was very acceptable in preaching the gospel to adults, ministering the Word to believers or visiting the sick, the bereaved, the aged and the lonely. He was a good listener and folks found a therapy in telling him of their difficulties. Invariably, he understood and had a little word that would brighten their way and show that the dark cloud also had a silver lining. He had a natural talent for personal work and this was sanctified by a keen spiritual sensitivity. He could so readily speak a word in season to those who were weary, making the sick-room become a sanctuary.

In public speaking, his deep, rich, resonant voice gave his preaching, which was always well backed up by references to Scripture, the ring of sincerity and the stamp of certainty. His delight was in simple things and he could make simplicities become superlatives. He built up an excellent rapport with his hearers, whether addressing large or small audiences or in personal contacts. He was something of a word-smith and he had the rare gift of employing simple but meaningful and memorable expressions. Never long-winded, he was able to pack the maximum of meaning into the minimum of words. Thus, in a neatly turned phrase which is readily remembered, he would say, "We don't know what the future holds but we know the One who holds the future."

Sometimes he would resort to poetic vein; for example, in warning of the dangers of speaking unkindly and without thinking, he would say:

> *"If you your lips would keep from slips,*
> *Five things observe with care:*
> *Of whom you speak, to whom you speak*
> *And how, and when, and where."*

Robert's ministry was very much of the nature of exhortation, together with what is practical and devotional. It always bore the hallmark of the two vital criteria: it was always glorifying to God and edifying to the hearers.

One has often known preachers use alliterations but only once has the writer ever heard an acrostic used in ministry. The occasion was an address given by Robert Walker at the opening of Fernielea Gospel Hall, Aberdeen, in April 1968. Thus 'F' brought to mind the Foundations of the work, Fellowship, Freedom of the Spirit and Fruitfulness; 'E' stood for Evangelism, Example, Education and Exhortation; 'R' for Reverence, Rectitude and so on it went, highlighting features which should be seen in an ideal assembly, using the other letters of Fernielea. A unique approach indeed!

Robert's presentation of the gospel was invariably searing and solemn. He did not try to pander to the intellect but to appeal to the heart and conscience. Soon after he embarked on full-time evangelism, he told the writer that he felt it a little disconcerting one evening when he went on to the platform to see the late Mr J M Shaw (of London and, later, of Leven) in the audience. Mr Shaw was a well-known preacher and teacher. However Robert delivered his message, just as he would otherwise have done. At the end of the service when he went to the door to bid the folks goodnight, Mr Shaw shook him warmly by the hand and said, much to Robert's gratification, "Tonight Christ was preached and I therein do rejoice, yea and will rejoice." No finer endorsement could be desired on the part of any preacher.

It has to be said, however, that Robert had a keen sense of humour which frequently surfaced, both in private and in public. On one occasion, a lady was explaining to a few friends over a cup of tea that she had been able to secure the services of a

Christian girl to give help in the house. She continued, "I think she is quite pleased to be coming here as her present employers are publicans..." "...And sinners!" added Robert, to a ripple of laughter.

On another occasion, he was focussing on the issue of appropriate messages, couched in language that the audience would understand. His remarks were based on Ecclesiastes 12.9-11. He laid emphasis on the fact that the Preacher, we are told, was persistent – "he still taught"; he was careful in his matter – "he gave good heed"; he was methodical – "he sought out and set in order many proverbs"; he was careful over his presentation – "the Preacher sought to find out acceptable words...even words of truth." This last point led him to comment on the tendency to use jargon and clichés which most people, outside the assemblies, would not readily understand and he went on to tell of a boy (from an assembly background) who called on his chum one evening. The chum's mother answered the door whereupon he asked: "Is Billy coming out to play?" "No", answered mother, "he's having his tea just now." "All right", ventured the boy, "could you ask him if he would be exercised about a game of football later?"

As the years rolled on, failing health on the part of Robert and his wife meant that during his later years his activities were centred more in the north-east of Scotland. He was a very good visitor of the sick, the bereaved and those with problems. His visits were brief but uplifting; he was never in danger of out-staying his welcome. On several afternoons most weeks, he was to be found visiting in the various Aberdeen hospitals. Nor were the older folks forgotten. Every week, he would call at the assemblies' Eventide Home at Summerhill in Aberdeen, where his visits brought comfort and cheer and were much appreciated by the residents over the years.

Often he would volunteer to undertake practical tasks such as providing or arranging transport for elderly folks; or simple jobs such as changing a light bulb which can be daunting for an older person. In the list of gifts which God has given to the church (1 Corinthians 12.28) one which is seldom mentioned is "helps". In addition to many other talents, Robert was very willing to carry out the functions of a "help". No task was ever too menial or too much trouble. Nor was his natural desire to help others curtailed in spite of his own dwindling strength.

During the last decade of his life he was much concerned about "strengthening the things which remain that are ready to die". One aspect of this which weighed heavily upon him was the need to buttress the efforts of small assemblies which were struggling to survive. Thus he regularly gave help at Insch, at Elgin as well as elsewhere. Also during his last years, Robert was responsible sometimes for some forty funeral services in the course of a year in the Aberdeen district and its hinterland.

Eventually, the state of his health necessitated hospitalisation and he passed to be with the Lord on Sunday 16th September 1990. On the very last day of his life on earth, he said to his wife and to other friends who were present that he thought he would be going Home that day. Thinking, at first, that he was referring to his discharge from hospital, they suggested that they thought it unlikely he would be allowed home that day. "No, no," he remonstrated, "You don't understand. I don't mean home to our house, I mean Home to be with the Lord."

His words were prophetic for within a few hours the Lord had granted him his heart's desire and he no longer viewed the land; he had entered in.

Speaking after the manner of men, one might well consider it a waste – even a pity – that one who gave so much and had so much to give should be called from the midst of his labours in this needy world. But such are the decrees of love we believe. He finished his course well: unswerving in his devotion, unstinting in his commitment and untiring in his efforts to further the cause of Christ's kingdom on earth.

Matthew Brown, Aberdeen

Other Recollections

I have been a personal friend of Robert Walker for over fifty years. At the close of the second World War he qualified as a pharmacist, and worked as a chemist in my brother John's shop. That was our first contact with Robert. He had a keen interest in gospel work, so we hired a hall in Old Lossie and had gospel meetings with thirty to forty children nightly.

After that he was commended to full-time service for the Lord, and friendliness with people became his objective. His father was a good help, and encouraged him, introducing him to many places and people in Ireland where he worked faithfully for a while.

Peter Murray, Lossiemouth

Memories of Robert Walker are always pleasant to recall. My first contact with him was as my Sunday School teacher, and later on, just prior to his call to full-time service I was in his Bible Class. Upon repeating the "I ams" of John's Gospel when in his class, I was rewarded with the Traveller's Guide - a book which, some years later, was a strong link in the chain which brought me to the Lord.

Robert was a real encourager of young men making their first acquaintance with the platform. He would sit bolt upright, drinking in every word, smiling and nodding his approval.

Twenty years ago my cousin died suddenly in Liverpool. When Robert offered us his condolences he enquired of our travel plans in view of the funeral, which were to be by train. The next day he phoned and began by quoting the words of Ahasuerus in Esther 6 "On that night could not the king sleep". The thought came to him at bed-time that he could have offered us the use of his car, and not having thought about it sooner had disturbed his sleep. His kind offer, typical of his gentlemanly character, was gratefully accepted and on our return he left the car with us for several weeks, an action which was much appreciated by us and our young family.

John Michie, Aberdeen

At a conference in Perth in the 1970s, Robert was the first speaker, when half way through his message a bus load of visitors from the south east of Fife arrived. Their bus had broken down twenty miles away, but had got going again. To allow them to find seats and not be embarrassed, he announced a short interruption to his message, welcomed the latecomers, and led the singing of an appropriate, short hymn. He then continued where he left off, briefly summarising what had already been covered, for the benefit of all. He was most adaptable to any situation, and always considerate for all.

Bert Cargill, St Monans

On the last occasion I visited Robert in hospital, he asked me to tell him the readings on the heart machine because it was facing away from him. I thought he knew too much, so I said it was fluctuating a little. He seemed satisfied and did not pursue the matter. He then asked me to give him a shave with his electric razor. He said, "That's much better. It makes a difference when a man does it!"

Before I left I read Psalm 145 to him. When I had finished he said, "That is what your father read to Jeannie's (Robert's wife) mother and father when they were dying. Also it was the number of your grandfather's boat, the Crysoprasus, which was sunk by the Germans in the first World War." He had a remarkable memory for detail.

Andrew Philip, Aberdeen

Robert R. Walker

T. Ernest Wilson

1902 – 1996

"A good man, and full of the Holy Spirit and faith"

(Acts 11.24)

Ernest Wilson was of solid working class Ulster stock. The family lived in a simple 'row house' in Belfast where his father was a postman, and the son's first employment was that of Telegram Boy. He often spoke of the grief and anguish he witnessed in those days during the First World War when most of the messages were from the War Office announcing the death, wounding or imprisonment of loved ones. How happy he was later to be the bearer of good news of eternal life for 'those who sit in darkness and in the shadow of death'.

He was reared in a godly home and brought up in the assembly which met at Donegall Road Hall in Belfast, where he was early involved in all kinds of Christian work. To this assembly came FT Lane, a missionary home on furlough from Angola and telling of the needs of that land, especially in the unevangelised areas of Chokwe and Songo tribes. The youth's heart was touched and he gradually became conscious that God was speaking to him. He was then working as a carpenter in the Belfast shipyards, a useful craft in primitive Angola.

In 1923 the elders commended him to the Lord for the work to which he was so evidently called, and sailed for Portugal, to learn its language. After almost a year there in study and also doing gospel work among the roughest parts of Lisbon, he proceeded to Angola. He had little baggage and no guarantee or 'understanding' of financial support from his own or any other assembly. He did not find this in the Scriptures. He trusted God, and that covered everything.

On arrival in Angola he worked first in and around Capango where the Lanes and others lived, and here he learned

Umbundu, the tribal language. He also visited other stations at Chilonda, Hualondo, and Chitau, though his burden was still for those who had never heard the gospel. So he and Lance Adcock, also at Capango, made plans for a long trek to the North and Northeast where the gospel had never penetrated. With a few Umbundu men to carry their scanty belongings – bed-bags, some non-perishable foods, and personal clothing – they covered hundreds of miles among the Bangala, Shinji, Chokwe and Songo tribes, looking for a suitable place for a permanent gospel outreach site, preaching by interpretation as they went. They chose Chitutu, between the Chokwe and Songo tribes, being well populated and relatively healthy. They got permission from the local administrative officer to build about 5 km from his post. Shortly afterwards brother Adcock felt obliged to return permanently to Capango owing to the death of Mr Lane, so Wilson had to carry on alone. With the help of local labour, he cleared a site in that lonely spot, built a clay and wattle shack with a grass roof and earthen floor, and while he built he preached, one of his Umbundu workmen translating.

He then tramped eight or ten days east, through virgin forest and plain, to Luma on the Cassai River, which was the nearest station in the Chokwe tribe. Here he enjoyed Christian fellowship, had some lessons in Chokwe from brethren Olford and Gammon, bought some supplies for his new home, as well as for the trip back to it. He also found time to propose to a godly lassie called Elizabeth Smythe, born in Scotland of Ulster parents, who later moved to the USA from where she was in due time commended to the Lord's work. She had caught his eye while studying in Lisbon at the same time, and he was now convinced, that 'it was not good for man to be alone,' especially in the isolation of Chitutu! She accepted and he began the long tramp back with lots to do.

He enlarged the original shack to three rooms and built a shed for meetings. He also started a small garden with corn (maize), cabbages, lettuce, and tomatoes with seed brought back from Luma. All the rest would have to come from the railhead at Malange about seven days away on foot. He was also making contacts with the local people, explaining why he had come, and always preaching the gospel. Meanwhile, letters had been going and coming by native runners, making plans at Elizabeth's end for their wedding. He walked back to Luma and they went on with the other missionaries to Boma, the first Chokwe mission, which was a further two days away and their nearest neighbours. This was closer to the Provincial capital, where they were married by the Portuguese Commissioner, because a 'Protestant' wedding had no validity in Angola. At the Boma mission station they had a Christian ceremony with all the Chokwe missionaries and a large crowd of local believers present. Then back at Luma they spent a few days sorting and packing their belongings into 60 lb. loads for native porters to carry. On their thirteen day honeymoon trek to Chitutu, as he says in *Angola Beloved*, they lived in a tent for almost six months while he made doors and windows to "improve" their three roomed shack.

In 1929 three men were baptised and these with four missionaries (Mr and Mrs McJannet were visiting them) sat down to remember the Lord for the first time in that whole dark area. There I joined them in late 1933 or first days of 1934 and by that time there were twenty four Africans in the fellowship, though few of them could read with much comprehension. Ernest believed in quality before quantity. Shortly after my arrival there was another baptism and another dozen or so were added.

By this time Ernest had built a larger and better house with four main rooms and a small 'den' where he could study in quiet. All furniture was simple and hand-made by himself and two 'learners' and everything was simple and cosy even if primitive. The floor was still of hard earth and the roof was of grass, but it had windows with glass. The 'station' consisted of this house, a small 'guest house' of the same structure, with two rooms, one of which was Miss Murphy's home. She ate with the Wilsons, as did I for the first year. There was also the 'meeting room' of the same materials, which seated about fifty, with seats of rough planks nailed to upright posts stuck into the ground, and of course, no backs. It was also used for school. Next was the 'clinic' or 'medicine house,' a tiny place with a table, some shelves for the basics; bandages, medicines (mostly for malaria), eye drops, carbolic acid for tropical ulcers that ate away large holes in legs and for large wounds by flying arrows in hunting or axe-heads used in the forests, as well as wounds from leopards, crocodiles, snakes etc. We had no radios, no newspapers, and got little news except from the Portuguese officer up the road and from letters that came very slowly by boat. At most this was every two weeks, and occasionally as long as two months. Later, kind friends sent us magazines, but of course, always out of date when they reached us.

All this was very primitive, and the only others around us were a growing number of houses built by Africans who upon conversion were driven from their villages and wished to be among Christians. There was also the remains of an old house built by Lance Adcock before he returned to Bie (pronounced Bee'aye). It had been abandoned to termites and rot, but before I arrived Ernest and Elizabeth had reclaimed and cleaned up two rooms for me, patched the grass roof, putting in a home-made bed with bedding, frame for mosquito net, and a reed mat beside it. Elizabeth dug out of her trunks some print material for my two windows. That was Chitutu. All of it! This site was slightly north of the centre of Angola, and there was one dirt track into it from the NW, because of the Government Post, but no road out of it, north, east, or south. It was the end of civilisation or the outside world. The nearest mission, or indeed any civilisation to the east was Luma, some eight to twelve days away on foot. South of the nearest station was five to seven days, while north or north east there was no gospel work of any kind to the Congo border until much later an assembly work was started at Saurimo.

So what kind of man was this, who chose such a path and such a place? He was basically a pioneer. The Chokwes were indeed rather harsh, tough, and proud, even by African standards. A warrior people, they had raided and slaughtered neighbouring tribes for ages, carrying away slaves. Livingston and Arnot, both of whom passed through their territory, had trouble with them, the first on their way to the coast, almost being murdered. Arnot, however, when he met Maitland and Taylor in Lisbon said, "They are tough and harsh, but once won they will be warriors for Christ, do go to them." He was right. Maitland, an Ulsterman commended from the USA started the work at Boma on the south side of the Cassai River, and after a few years accompanied Cuthbert Taylor north of the river to start work at Luma. The latter, a true pioneer and a saintly man, worked there and in the surrounding country for about six years and never saw one conversion as far as is known, dying at 29 years of age of chronic malaria, exhaustion, and maybe a broken heart, leaving a young wife and two children. Later on other workers saw rich fruit at Luma where hundreds found eternal life, and for twenty-two years my wife and I lived and laboured there.

Ernest Wilson was just as tough a man, but God spared him to see a large assembly at Chitutu, but perhaps even better, when he visited years later, he saw over twenty indigenous assemblies in the area, started by African brethren, and carrying on for God into the period of brutal pre-independence savagery in which at least twelve African full time evangelists and leaders were callously shot to death.

He was an unspectacular but very courageous pioneer, soft spoken, polite, and self-effacing who could be startlingly outspoken, and on occasion quick to puncture a social balloon. Once down country a rather pompous missionary wife reminded a social gathering that her sister was married to an Anglican Bishop. TEW's quiet remark was, "One of the best bishops I ever knew sold coal by the bag from a horse-drawn cart in Belfast." He was referring to one of the elders who signed his commendation, and who indeed was still an elder when ten years later that assembly joined in my own commendation. Ernest had little time for any sort of conceit.

When I first arrived in Chitutu he told me that he and Elizabeth with Lyla Murphy had a Bible study in their home each Sunday evening while the African Christians had a singing meeting at the hall. This was 'to feed their own souls while they were kept busy feeding the African Christians, often on a rather kindergarten level.' He now insisted that I, only a beginner, lead this study on my own subjects on alternate Sundays. The thought frightened me and I tried to escape the responsibility, but he would have none of it. We did this all the years we were together. He pointed out that because of constantly giving out on a lower lever some stunted their own growth and failed to develop their expositional ability in the mother tongue. How often I thanked God in later years for the gracious advice and humble attitude to a beginner.

This man, to who I deferred as a senior worker with more experience than I, never took a superior attitude. With a core of steel and the courage of a lion, who never yielded an inch in matters of principle, he was one of the kindest, and gentlest men I ever knew. Recently, while hunting for some of my own notes of those days I stumbled across a few lines in a tiny pocket diary, which brought back warm memories. After only four months at Chitutu, largely because of my own carelessness, I was laid low with a bad spell of malaria plus sunstroke, during which I drifted in and out of consciousness for days with soaring temperatures. I found this brief note written in the diary: 'Ernest sat by my bedside day and night from first to last.' We trekked together on bush paths throughout the Chokwe and Songo countries. We studied together, prayed, rejoiced, and wept together, without an angry or heated word between us through all the years.

When we were forced out of Chitutu by the authorities, he and Elizabeth returned to his old centre at Capango, while my wife and I went inland to Luma where we spent the remaining twenty two years of our African service. Later still, when the pre-independence savagery reached its peak those of us remaining were finally forced out. The Wilsons had had already gone to the USA while my wife and I went to Canada where our sons were finishing their education. Through the remaining years when in our ministry in these two countries our paths often crossed. We frequently shared the platform at conferences, continuing our warm and easy partnership to within a short few months of his home-going to glory.

He had been 'best man' at our Portuguese wedding back in Chitutu days, and when my wife was unexpectedly called home in Canada while I was in Ireland in ministry, my sons met me at Toronto airport, and after greetings my first word was, "If Ernest can be contacted anywhere in North America I would like him to take the funeral." The answer was, "He is upstairs in the airport waiting for you." When the Lord took him home I had just left hospital and could not be at funeral, but my eldest son, in full time work for the Lord, read my tribute. He shared in the funeral with Ernest's son who is also in the Lord's service. That, I felt, was just as it should have been.

David Boyd Long, Ballygowan

Other Recollections

From my early childhood, the name 'Ernest Wilson' has been familiar to me. As a boy, I attended Cregagh Street assembly, Belfast, where Victor Wilson, brother of Ernest, was a valued member. This family link ensured that the Cregagh Street assembly was kept in touch with Ernest and Elizabeth's missionary endeavours in Angola.

In the summer of 1945, the Wilson family arrived in Belfast. They came to live in a home right next door to ours! This resulted in a deepening of our friendship, and in a growing appreciation of the spiritual stature of a much-loved brother. At that time, when wartime shortages were so keenly felt, he passed on to me a suit of clothes which had become too small for him!

George Hall, Dundonald

Many years ago I was invited as a young preacher to speak at the assembly where the Wilsons fellowshipped. At the last minute in came Mr. Wilson and slipped into a back seat. As I looked down and saw this beloved servant of the Lord, I confess I trembled. I need not have feared, since brother Wilson was not a critic and always ready to encourage.

Mr. Wilson invited me back to the house for a cup of tea. As we walked together, I longed for some word of counsel. I said, "What advice would you give a young man on Bible Study?" In his humble way, he replied, "When I was a young man, I asked an old Irish brother the very same question, and he told me, 'There are three rules of Bible study, the first is - Accuracy, and the second is - Accuracy, and the third is - Accuracy'." It was obvious in His reverent handling of Scripture that he had followed that advice these many years. I never did forget his answer.

J B Nicholson Snr, Ontario

For me, it was always his face. I was drawn to it; and tried to memorize every expression, each nuance, and the kindness and graciousness it held. I had reason to do this - for somehow I instinctively knew that this might be the closest manifestation of the face of our Lord Jesus that I'd see before Heaven. I remember, as a child, wondering if this was what angels looked like! If eyes are "mirrors of the soul", the face of Mr. Wilson was a reflection of Christ. He radiated Him.

Perhaps the greatest honour I've had was to labour with him. It can be intimidating to work with a hero, but the notion of that would have horrified Mr. Wilson. He often asked me to call him Ernest. I would have found it easier to call Queen Elizabeth by her first name! When you were with Mr. Wilson, you were in the presence of heaven's royalty. But I will always treasure his human side; warm, wonderfully humorous, unfailingly encouraging, and profoundly humble. In his every facet, he was true greatness.

Alan Parks, USA

It was with warm feeling I heard him minister God's Word to comfort the hearts of sorrowing and bereaved saints. He illustrated the meaning of sympathy with an African story - The African mother had lost her son, was visited by a mother who had also lost her son too. He observed some who came had much to say, but this mother was different, she put her arms around the grieving mother and quietly said, "I just know how you feel."

Albert Aitken, Lisburn

T. Ernest Wilson and his wife were forced to leave Angola in 1961. There was no thought of retirement, but it was the commencement of a fruitful written and itinerant ministry. However, he never lost touch with or interest in the mission field and missionaries. In fact just five months before his "homecall" he attended our annual conference for missionaries and revelled in the company of eight former colleagues from Angola. Angola was his first love, but his interest spanned the globe.

Often at the local assembly or when visiting in his home or

mine, he would ask questions about various missionaries around the world. I was amazed at the scope of his interest and the details he knew about so many missionaries and their work. On occasions he would drop by the office to share some concerns or news he had received. Although busy, he always had the time to talk over problems and situations. We miss his valued advice and counsel.

Sam Robinson, New Jersey

Brother Wilson never tried to make the audience laugh and yet he had a good sense of humor. In speaking at a conference in Pawtucket, R.I. he told about a woman who asked him if when he was walking in the bush country of Angola, he came face to face with another missionary and his wife whom he didn't know, would he embrace and kiss them? He answered, "Not only would I kiss them, I would even kiss their dog."

On another occasion in taking Mr. Wilson to the train station, it was after midnight and he was exhausted after a busy day. I asked him if he would be able to sleep on the train, and he said, "I could sleep on a clothes line."

When I was a teenager, I visited T. Ernest Wilson at his home in Hartford, Connecticut. When I arrived there, Ernest was in the yard taking the old Chevrolet car engine apart. I was very impressed with the way he worked and the knowledge he seemed to have in making repairs. He told me he enjoyed doing things like that. Ernest was a man of God and knew the Scriptures. He was also a very capable man at many jobs.

Tom Serpliss, USA